The Culture of the Body

D1500842

THE BODY, IN THEORY   Histories of Cultural Materialism

The Culture of the Body
Genealogies of Modernity

Dalia Judovitz

Ann Arbor

The University of Michigan Press

2004   2003   2002   2001   4   3   2   1

A CIP catalog record for this book is available
from the British Library.

Library of Congress Cataloging-in-Publication Data

Judovitz, Dalia.
    The culture of the body : genealogies of modernity / Dalia
Judovitz.
        p. cm. — (The body, in theory)
    Includes bibliographical references and index.
    ISBN 0-472-09742-3 (acid-free paper) — ISBN 0-472-06742-7 (pbk. :
acid-free paper)
    1. Body, Human (Philosophy)—France—History.   2. Philosophy,
Modern.   3. Body, Human in literature.   4. French literature—
History and criticism.   I. Title.   II. Series.
B1809.B62 J83   2000
128'.6'0944—dc21   00-009179
                                                          CIP

To Erna Judovits
In Memoriam

What is most surprising is rather the body;
one never ceases to be amazed at the idea that
the human body has become possible.

—FRIEDRICH NIETZSCHE

Acknowledgments

This project was inspired by the writings of Maurice Merleau-Ponty and Michel Foucault. This volume also marks the untimely passing of Jean-François Lyotard, my former teacher, colleague, and dear friend, whose extraordinary intellect, generosity, and vitality has decisively informed and enriched my own work. My special thanks go to James Porter, Tom Conley, and Michael Schwartz for their generous and insightful comments, suggestions, and support. Thanks are also due to my former colleague Martin Jay, whose intellectual contributions I admire, and to my friends and colleagues from the International Association for Philosophy and Literature, whose responsiveness as audience for portions of this book was a major source of motivation. I am also grateful for the research opportunities offered by a sabbatical year fellowship and grant awarded by Emory University that enabled me to bring this manuscript to completion. Special appreciation is owed to LeAnn Fields, executive editor at the University of Michigan Press, for her encouragement and support, to Jennifer Wisinski, who supervised the production of the manuscript, and to Richard Isomaki, for his talented copyediting. Last but not least, the production of this volume is indebted to the invaluable assistance of Patrick Wheeler, my former maverick research assistant, translator, and copyeditor, and to Leonard Hinds, Madeline Pampel, Louise Barry, Michael Kazanjian, and Sebastian Dubreil, who helped out with further bibliographic materials and translations. Inscribed in the margins of this volume and permeating its very substance is the unflagging love and support of my husband, Hamish M. Caldwell.

Contents

Introduction

The critical literature of the past decades bears witness to a renewed interest in the body, in its literary, philosophical, social, and historical construction.[1] The confluence of these discourses that shape the destiny of the body is grounded in specific historical conditions that determine its particular modes of existence. Rather than treating the body as a given, these studies compel us to question and explore its conditions of possibility. However, this effort to inquire into the construction of the body must take into account the obstacle presented by its conceptual consolidations, which attain over time a factual authority and stability that are very difficult to overcome. As Maurice Merleau-Ponty points out regarding the advent of subjectivity in philosophy: "There are some ideas which make it impossible for us to return to a time prior to their existence, even and especially if we have moved beyond them."[2] The fate of the body as an idea, like that of subjectivity to whose emergence it is linked, is haunted by the foreclosure of its past meanings and history. Once consolidated in the modern period, the idea of the body takes on the character of a given that renders its prior forms and modalities of existence difficult to perceive and understand. This dilemma becomes even more pronounced today, since contemporary formulations of the body appear to have done away with the body as we conventionally understand it, by displacing and replacing it with various artificial and virtual analogues, whose simulational logic erases the boundaries between the human and the machine. The predominance of virtual bodies and notions of virtual reality today attests to the persistent legacy of the Cartesian mind-body duality that continues to obscure and even elide prior formulations of the body. In so doing, this legacy forecloses the conceptual import of earlier paradigms to new ways of thinking about cultural constructions of the body and notions of embodiment.

What does it mean to speak of the body in terms of culture, understood both as the medium for the articulation, cultivation, and elaboration of the body and as a defining tradition? This project is inspired by Michel de Montaigne (1533–1592) and his comment in the testamentary essay "Of Experience," from the *Essays* (1588): "I, who operate only close to the ground, hate that inhuman wisdom that would make us disdainful enemies of the cultivation of the body *(culture du corps)*" (III, 13: 849).[3] The inhuman wisdom that Montaigne decries denies the pivotal role of the body and of experience and seeks to exceed or even overcome the embodied and mixed nature of the human condition. His insistence on the cultivation of the body implies a revalorizing of its culture, along with that of the mind. Montaigne suggests that it is through physical and mental cultivation that the body attains worldly being in its various embodiments.[4] And for the reader today, this notion of cultivation finds its determining horizon in the modern notion of culture, within whose traditions the body's condition and potential for transformation are inscribed.[5]

Montaigne's essay concludes with a warning against efforts to dissociate the mind from the body in order to transcend the human predicament as a hybrid or immixed condition:

> They [philosophers] want to get out of themselves and escape from the man. That is madness: instead of changing themselves into angels, they change into beasts; instead of raising themselves, they lower themselves. These transcendental humors frighten me, like lofty and inaccessible heights. (III, 13: 856)

Written approximately fifty years before René Descartes's interpretation of the body as a machine and his elaboration of the mind-body dualism, Montaigne's visionary comments anticipate the fate of the body and its elaboration in Western metaphysical discourse. If Montaigne admits to fright when faced with "transcendental humors," which he regards as lofty and inaccessible heights, his reluctance and resistance to accede to them constitutes a premonitory warning of the danger inherent in the efforts to transcend the human as an embodied condition. The Cartesian account of body represents precisely what Montaigne most feared, for the efforts to elevate rational subjectivity to a universal and thus transcendental position entail its disembodiment, the disengagement of consciousness from the body understood as an organic and experiential entity. Montaigne's extensive discussions of the cultivation of the body in its philosophical, literary, social, and sexual modalities reflect his understanding of the body not as a given but as a changing horizon of multiple becomings. This notion of cultivation implicates culture in the modern sense, understood as a defining tradition and as a generative medium for embodiment.

Rather than presupposing a knowledge of the body as a term defined since Descartes in opposition to the mind, this study explores the construction of the body as an entity whose historical character emerges as a function of specific conceptual and cultural frameworks. For it is within particular discursive frames and practices that bodies "materialize," attaining their specific embodiments, be they literary, philosophical, social, anatomical, or technological. The notion of discursive practices evoked here, by reference to Michel Foucault, is not reducible simply to ways of producing discourse. Rather, Foucault suggests that discursive practices are "embodied in technical processes, in institutions, in patterns for general behavior, in forms for transmission and diffusion, and in pedagogical forms which, at once, impose and maintain them."[6] Hence, they do not restrict the meaning of the body to its linguistic elaborations, but rather expand it to include technical, social, institutional, and pedagogical processes through which it attains embodiment and that assure its transmission and perpetuation. The question of the body and its modalities of cultural becoming are thus embedded in the larger social, institutional, and technical practices that sustain the horizon of embodiment. In this study, the question of the body is framed by notions of embodiment, understood as defining traditions and paradigms through which the body achieves its conceptual and material realization.

This volume traces the cultural transformations of the body and the notions of embodiment that underlie its representations from the late sixteenth century through the eighteenth century in French literary and philosophical works. The literary and philosophical focus of this study enables a specific examination of the various modalities of representation that inform the body and its embodiments in terms of the interplay of their conceptual and material elaborations. At issue is an understanding of the body as an always provisional construction, grounded in changing worldviews that entail different understandings of representation, subjectivity, and identity. The works chosen, by such authors as Montaigne, Honoré d'Urfé, Descartes, Pierre Corneille, Julien Offray de La Mettrie, and the marquis de Sade, are emblematic of their time, since they magnify and clarify shifts in cultural sensibility, understood as modes of apprehension and representation. These works are products of a period marked by great social, political, religious, and artistic upheavals, a period that stretches from the emergence in France of the new print culture during the final years of the Wars of Religion through the French Revolution of 1789. This period spans conflicting interpretations of bodies, ranging from an understanding of the body in terms of issues of legibility that script its complexion into the fabric of the world, to its abstraction and subsumption within a new order based on the mathematization of knowledge and the world, and culminating in the catastrophic efforts to retrieve its material character, albeit as a social and institutional abstraction. These cultural shifts reflect a turning point in the West-ern literary and philosophical traditions, the emergence of a new concept of the body whose dissociation from both the mind and experiential reality dis-engages it from the sphere of embodiment. The advent of Cartesian subjec-tivity leads to the exclusion of the body from the purview of metaphysics, and to its reduction to a notion of materiality, whose logic is governed by the regime of the machine.

It is important to note that this study is less historical than "genealogi-cal," in the Nietzschean sense, to the extent that it seeks to establish the var-ied and often conflictual traditions and lineages that mark the emergence of modern notions of the body.[7] These genealogies of the representations of the body are neither linear nor progressive, insofar as they reference a his-tory of struggles, contradictory impulses, and infringements that emerges out of a series of discontinuous, overlapping, and episodic moments. They trace the struggles in the assertion of meanings attached to the body, mean-ings that engage with past traditions in order to rewrite and thus reissue their future embodiments. Rather than equating modernity with develop-ments in nineteenth-century industrial culture, this study demonstrates how these competing early modern cultural discourses inform, suppress, or acti-vate the meanings attached to the body in the modern period. If the post-modern functions according to the logic of the future anterior, as Jean-François Lyotard suggests, then it is precisely that which has become unpresentable and postponed in the representations of modernity that needs further consideration, so that we may begin to understand why an early modern author such as Montaigne may be deemed postmodern, rather than modern.[8]

The book is divided into three parts that roughly coincide with the baroque, classical, and postclassical periods, each part outlining specific conceptual frameworks and discursive practices for staging the body and its horizon of embodiment.[9] The first, "Baroque Embodiments," outlines in the works of Montaigne and d'Urfé (1567–1625) a way of thinking about the body that is grounded in a notion of representation understood as shifting semblance. As examples of early print culture, these works present the body's engagement in the fabric of the world through reflections on repre-sentation and its legibility. The presentation of the body occurs in the modality of a script, as a transitional imprint that bears the traces of social and cultural practices. The body is staged; its complexion is not given, but rather constructed like a scenario that derives its meaning from its context and finds new meanings through its transpositions into other contexts. The logic of the body thus emerges in the order of translation, understood not as an originary given, but as a script that attains specific meanings through its transpositions. In both Montaigne and d'Urfé, this scriptorial account of the body proves to be nonessentialist, to the extent that it defines the body as a process of embodiment whose provisional instances mark moments in the history of its becoming. This emphasis on embodiment rather than being provides insight into the particular freedom and instability of baroque bodies, their capacity to sustain multiple identities that challenge philosophical, social, and sexual expectations.

Entitled "Cartesian Bodies, Virtual Bodies," the second part examines the emergence of a new concept of the body whose purely mechanical and material definition breaks radically with previous philosophical and literary accounts based on the experiential or lived body. Descartes's elaboration of a rational subjectivity founded on the primacy of reason entails the redefinition of the body as a machine whose objective reality is sundered from its subjective existence. This disembodiment of subjectivity, accompanied by the mechanical reduction of the body, has important consequences, since embodiment will cease to define the condition of the lived, experiential body and will refer instead to its submission, manipulation, and incorporation within the framework of knowledge and disciplines that legislates and governs its existence. The problems entailed in the Cartesian virtualization of the body are echoed in the early plays of Corneille (1606–1684). Given their social, political, and artistic focus, these works provide a worldly, public frame to Descartes's scientific and philosophical explorations of the body. In Corneille's works, the dismemberment of the lived experiential body coincides with its virtual reconfiguration in terms of political and economic paradigms that sublate its organic logic into the organization of the body politic.

The third part of this study, "Materialist Machines," elaborates the influence of Cartesian ideas on the development of French materialism in the eighteenth century. The import and legacy of Cartesianism finds both its realization and destruction in the works of such thinkers as La Mettrie (1709–1751) and Sade (1740–1814), the philosophical critic and parodist of the Enlightenment. Following La Mettrie's mechanization of man, Sade's works document the reification of the experiential body through social and cultural practices that displace its materiality onto the codes governing its philosophical foundation and social administration. Sade's radical philosophical critique coincides with literary experimentation, with a parodic expenditure of the body that tests the capacity of the human as a sustainable category. In Sade the technological destiny implicit in the Cartesian formulation of the body is brought into explicit conflict with the transcendental foundations of metaphysical discourse, raising the specter of the inhuman as Descartes's major legacy to modernism.

Before proceeding to a more detailed account of the contents of specific chapters, a brief discussion of the critical background and premises of this study becomes necessary in order to elucidate the particular nature of its philosophical and literary contributions. Friedrich Nietzsche (1844–1900) was the first modern philosopher to call explicit attention to the body, particularly in relation to representation, by locating culture within the purview of the body rather than the soul. It was Maurice Merleau-Ponty (1908–1961), however, who made the body a central topic of investigation throughout his philosophical works. In his groundbreaking study *The Phenomenology of Perception* (1945), he sought to recover the body from both its Cartesian reduction to an ordinary object and its isolation from consciousness by considering the body as a necessary condition of the knowing subject. It is the embodiment of the subject of knowledge that determines the subject's capacity to take a position and attain a point of view on the world, a knowledge that by virtue of this inherent positionality will be contingent, fragmentary, and incomplete. Noted primarily for its insistence on the "primacy of perception," the claim that all consciousness, including self-consciousness, is perceptual, this work sought to conceptualize perception as the phenomenal horizon of an embodied subjectivity. Although Merleau-Ponty touched on the question of embodiment in terms of issues that exceed perception, through his discussion of the sexual body as speech and gesture, these analyses remain conceptually undeveloped. It is in his later works that Merleau-Ponty attempts to find a new philosophical language that moves beyond the perceiving body by assimilating linguistic and psychoanalytic concerns into the notion of embodiment. His growing fascination with language as intersubjective communication, and with its constitutive role in the formation of experience, attests to his efforts to decenter the notion of the subject by endowing it with a posthumanist inflection, that re-enfolds its logic into the fabric of the world.[10]

It is within the purview of Merleau-Ponty's double legacy that this volume situates its own critical agenda, insofar as it seeks on the one hand to recover experiential accounts of the body, and on the other hand to reconceptualize bodily experience in a scriptorial modality that generates a new understanding of embodiment as a material process of folding and unfolding that involves inscription, transcription, and interpretation. This latter model of embodiment has the advantage of decentering the subjective presence of the body by inscribing the logic of experience within an intersubjective modality based on communication. The capacity of the body to attain signification through embodiment reflects its provisional assumption of a position within representation, as well as its potential transpositions made available by the material substrates of representation. This focus on embodiment as a function of representation expands the philosophical scope of this study to include literary considerations regarding language, interpretation, and style. It is within the conceptual horizon of these literary concerns that the meanings attached to representation find both their expression and articulation.

In addressing the relation of embodiment to representation, it is important to consider the philosophical differences and ultimate incompatibility in Montaigne's and Descartes's positions as regards the definition of knowledge.[11] The question of epistemology, as a theory of what constitutes the basis and essence of knowledge, is crucial to the shift witnessed in the meaning of representation, and thus in modes of presentation of bodies and embodiment. In Montaigne's writings, knowledge is not yet defined according to foundational principles. This is less a reflection of his putative skepticism than a recognition that doubt is a condition inherent in the representational or embodied nature of knowledge. In Montaigne's *Essays* knowledge is embodied, not only because it takes as its horizon the lived, experiential body, but also because its terminology and meanings are situated within representation. The body is not independent of the ways of knowing, but attains embodiment through them. Its materiality is not a given, since it is constituted provisionally through representation, understood as a material signifying process.

With Descartes, however, begins a new way of thinking, since as Martin Heidegger has noted, a theory of knowledge now becomes a requirement for all understanding of the world.[12] Descartes's demand that philosophical knowledge conform to the objectivity of mathematical discourse displaces the priority of the body as locus of knowledge and reduces representation to the attainment of certitude. This delimitation of representation to certitude, by restricting its meaning to forms of adequation and conformity patterned on mathematical schematism, elides its material character and eliminates embodiment altogether from its purview. The foundational disembodiment of the subject of knowledge, entailed in its definition as a thinking subject, reduces the body to a pure object of knowledge, defined as matter and extension. With Descartes, the body ceases to function as the expression of embodiment, since its materiality no longer references the subject of knowledge, nor its modalities of existence as a representational entity. Devoid of any formal or conceptual potential, the objective materiality of the body attests to its submission to reason, to a system of rational criteria and mechanical laws that governs its projection.

But, as I suggested earlier, the consideration of embodiment as a function of representation cannot be addressed uniquely from a philosophical vantage point. The notion of embodiment references representation and consequently also implies particular understandings of language and interpretation. In Montaigne's *Essays,* language is presented as a material medium that in the process of representing things gives them body and endows them with physical effects. Representation bears in its materiality as a signifying practice the trace of alterity, of an excess that modifies and expands any intended meaning. This is why interpretation in Montaigne proliferates and proves to be inexhaustible, because representation as material embodiment opens itself up to multiple interpretations that undermine efforts of subjective closure. It is precisely this proliferation of meanings within representation that Descartes seeks to contain by modeling philosophical discourse on the objective ideality and certitude of mathematics. His effort to redefine philosophical discourse as the discourse of certitude and truth leads him to conceive thought as a transparent and immaterial entity that exceeds the confines of both language and representation, to the extent that this entity is posited as their condition of possibility. Even as thought is ascribed a priority that appears to supersede the material substrate of speech, still the subject of consciousness, in claiming its existence, finds itself speaking, unable to escape the materiality of representation. The disembodiment of the subject that underlies its definition as "I think, therefore I am" marks its virtual existence, its hypostatic position within a new representational order that has elided its own signifying and material functions.

The notion of embodiment is central to sexuality insofar as the subject signifies its assumption of a gender identity through the negotiation of cultural signs. At issue is less the anatomical identity of the body than the subject's assumption of gender positions through the appropriation of cultural and social representations that define its construction as an embodied entity. To think sexuality in the mode of embodiment is to resituate the logic of the body by positing its materiality as a result of its engagement with cultural norms and representations. In this respect, Foucault's works on sexuality and ethics in *The History of Sexuality* (1976–84), and Judith Butler's more recent *Bodies That Matter: On the Discursive Limits of "Sex"* (1993) are important insofar as they locate sexual difference within discursive practices whose normative force is derived from their reiterative character.[13] Foucault and Butler suggest that the materiality of the body is constructed as a function of regulatory norms, whose forcible and reiterative character implicates the body in a dynamics of power.[14]

While recognizing the socially compelling and regulative function of sexual norms, this study argues that the freedom and fluidity of the representation of sexuality in the baroque texts of Montaigne and d'Urfé reflects an understanding of embodiment where sexual difference is not foundational, but merely an expression of the play of resemblances that define representation. This is not to suggest that social and cultural roles are not at play, but rather that their normative and regulative function becomes enforceable only upon the formal emergence of the discourse of sexuality.[15] While they exercise a certain force, their contingent character opens them up to forms of deployment that can challenge their conventional meanings and associations. In Montaigne's *Essays,* the referential character of sexuality is dislodged from physical reality and transposed into representation, so that its meaning is contextually defined as an intertextual gesture marked by intersexual overtones. In d'Urfé's *Astrea,* the undecidability of representation as scriptorial or figurative embodiment leads to the surprising presentation of heterosexual love through the bias of a lesbian register, where sexual difference, and ultimately identity, is erased through the play of travestied resemblances.

At first glance, the radical disembodiment of the subject implied in the Cartesian definition of subjectivity appears to render the question of sexuality moot, if not altogether inappropriate. However, this study argues that it is precisely the exclusion of embodiment from the framework of Cartesian subjectivity that leads to its "sexless" and impersonal appearance as the universal subject of truth. This perception is reinforced by the reduction of the body to a machine, apparently excluding sexuality altogether from its purview. Yet this denial of embodiment, which underlies the foundation of the subject of truth, also corresponds to the emergence of the notion of ontological difference. The disembodied subject of truth is the abstract being that stands as the condition of possibility for all other ordinary beings. Thus the question arises whether this ontological difference, which distinguishes the metaphysical subject of truth from its phenomenal and empirical incarnations, does not become paradigmatic of the emergence of sexual difference as a foundational and regulative concept. The denial of embodiment and its representational character does not mean that the body ceases to exist, but simply that its materiality is translated into institutionalized relations of power; for the solidity of the Cartesian body resides not only in its ostensible material and mechanical nature, but also in its passive submission to the discourses that govern and discipline its administration. Along these lines, ontological difference is seen as paradigmatic of sexual difference, to the extent that it redefines the question of embodiment as a function of power differences. It is this Cartesian legacy that Sade violently challenges by attempting to eradicate not only sexual difference, but the ontological difference that underlines its metaphysically transcendent foundations.

A rapid summary of the chapters in this volume will provide the reader with a more precise road map of its contents. Chapter 1 takes as its point of departure Montaigne's warning to the reader, "Verses have fingers," as a reflection on the power of embodiment implicit in representation. The text points its figurative finger at reality and, in so doing, risks physically grabbing hold of the reader. Locating the material and physical effects of the *Essays* within the materiality of representation, Montaigne opens up the question of the experiential body to a broader inquiry that dislocates its phenomenal solidity by resituating it within the reiterative logic of such cultural practices as custom and habit, forms of gestural or discursive expression. If style emerges as a major concern, this is because representation itself is understood as a kind of pattern already available in culture, but one that can be transferred, transformed, and redeployed. Style for Montaigne is not merely the expression of eloquence, but a model for understanding the generative logic of representation. In the *Essays,* style functions according to a logic of transplantation in which words and quotes are transposed, so that their meaning derives its force from their circulation and context, rather than from an intrinsic essence. The notions of body and embodiment in Montaigne thus gain new meaning from the way representation functions figuratively and stylistically both as a culture and as medium for cultivation.

In chapter 2, the question of the baroque body receives further elaboration, in its relation to both the perceptual and the sexual realm. The representational instability of the body in Honoré d'Urfé's *Astrea* (1607–27) is examined as a function of allegory whose figurative principles provide a description of the body as a composite rebus of image and language. The unstable referential relation between body and name (the freedom to change name, identity, and gender) is equated with its emblematic character, that is, with its freedom to signify both literally and figuratively. The impossible closure of both identity and the body reflects the recognition that knowledge is mediated through representation, which, as embodiment, can neither be contained nor reduced to a formal schema.

In chapter 3, I examine Descartes's redefinition of the organic character of the body as a system for the circulation of blood and the extensive technological analogies of the body to a machine in his earlier writings, including such works as the *Discourse on Method* (1637) and *Treatise on Man* (1629–33, but not published until 1664). Unlike the Renaissance and baroque body governed by humors, each of which determines the physical complexion of an individual, the Cartesian description reifies the corporeal body in order to resituate its meaning within the mechanical order and the solidity of the discourse of science. In chapter 4, this initial attempt to "decorporealize" the body finds its metaphysical expression as all aspects of the experiential lived body come into question. In Descartes's metaphysical opus, *Meditations on First Philosophy* (1641), the denunciation and ultimate exclusion of the body, as a site for error, from the metaphysical elaboration of subjectivity leads to its virtualization, its disappearance as body, and its reappearance as an errant specter haunting the margins of metaphysical discourse. The triumph of this virtualized image of the body that negates all experiential and historical reality summarizes Descartes's legacy to both classicism and modernity, a "history" of the body that has ceased to be a "culture."

Chapter 5 examines the representation of blood and the body in Corneille's theater—concomitant with Descartes's description of the anatomical body in terms of the circulatory system—in order to explore its symbolic, social, and political connotations. The transfer of notions of organicity from the physical body to the body of the state is at issue, as evidenced in the metaphorical fragmentation of body and the social exchange and circulation of body parts. As developed explicitly in *The Cid* (1636), but also present implicitly in such later plays as *Horace* (1640) and *Cinna* (1641), the body is presented as an object of contention between competing systems of social exchange and obligation. At issue is the reduction of the physical body to its social functions, fostering its administrative incorporation into the body politic of the nascent absolutist state. The expenditure and economy of the social body challenges the body's identity as physical organism, thereby marking a shift in the way it is conceived both as private and as public entity.

In chapters 6 and 7, the Cartesian legacy to the development of eighteenth-century French materialism comes into question, both the apparent realization of the Cartesian technological dream, La Mettrie's *Man-Machine* (1748), and its phantasmagorical, explosive, and perverse destruction in the marquis de Sade's *Misfortunes of Virtue* (1787) and *Philosophy in the Bedroom* (1795). Working out of Descartes, La Mettrie emphasizes the body's material and mechanical reality, not in opposition to the mind, but as a way of usurping through materialism its Cartesian ascendancy. Sade carries this materialism to its hyperbolic and parodic limit through a strategy that violates not only the body, but the philosophical, legal, and social laws that legislate its existence. The body is presented as a parody of the Cartesian logic of the machine, since it is saturated with forms of activity whose violent nature it cannot sustain without destroying the very meaning of sexuality as embodied expression. The Sadean equation of sexuality with extraordinary violence and violation, where pleasure is purely an expression of power, parodically restages the violence inherent in the philosophical disembodiment of the body and its social and institutional reembodiment in terms of a dynamics of power.

While this study takes as its focus pivotal literary and philosophical texts that mark historical shifts and transformations in the way the body is defined and conceptually understood, the questions that it opens up are by no means restricted to its past history. Insofar as it is the Cartesian legacy that has proved decisive to a modernist understanding of the body, the effort to recover Montaigne's and d'Urfé's positions does not merely enable an insight into historic change, but opens up new horizons for thinking about the body. It is precisely their discursive and conceptual incompatibility with the Cartesian paradigm and its legacy, that can prove to be conceptually productive for the contemporary context. For the paradox that confronts modernity is that its historical development has elided previous worldviews, such as those of the Renaissance and the baroque, and in that sense postponed access to their discursive and conceptual frameworks. It is this very postponement, however, that constitutes the cultural resource of postmodernism as it redeploys and reappropriates the semblance of the past in order to reconfigure the promise of a future already nascent in its margins. Rather than functioning as the insignia of historical archaism, these earlier conceptual frameworks can be redeployed in contemporary critical discourse, in order to provide new ways for conceiving and representing the body as a plural entity whose multiple embodiments attest to its embeddedness in the fabric of the world.

Part 1
Baroque Embodiments

Chapter 1

Montaigne's Scriptorial Bodies: Experience, Sexuality, Style

Since the publication of Michel de Montaigne's *Essays* (1588), commentators and critics alike have continued to argue about both the philosophical and the stylistic merits of the work. The advent of Carrtesianism and classicism in the latter half of the seventeenth century had an impact on the critical reception of Montaigne's works, since new criteria emerged for judging the adequacy of its philosophical and discursive representations. In *The Search after Truth* (1674–75), Nicolas Malebranche criticizes Montaigne's lack of philosophical reasoning and argumentation in terms that recall his own adherence to Cartesian standards:

> It is not at all his arguments that persuade us; he hardly ever uses any in support of the things he advances, or at least he hardly ever puts forth arguments with any foundation. Indeed, he does not have principles on the basis of which he founds his reasoning, and he has no order for making deductions from his principles.[1]

Noting the lack of foundational principles, of an ordered development of arguments based on the preeminence of reason, Malebranche judges Montaigne's work in terms of its retroactive failure to conform to Cartesian notions. Neglecting the tentative and reflective nature of the essay as a genre, Malebranche dismisses the irregular character of the *Essays,* their perceived lack of reasoning and orderly disquisition, by relegating them to philosophical insignificance, to an unruly collection of anecdotes and apothegms.[2] It is interesting to note, however, that earlier commentators, such as Guez de Balzac, commented on the digressive logic and style of the *Essays,* only to argue that these very features may in fact explain their ultimate success.[3]

Not content to question the philosophical and discursive logic of the *Essays,* Malebranche also condemns the nefarious influence of this work upon the reader. At issue is the physical impact of the *Essays,* since the text is accused of producing physical effects, of affectively "touching" the reader, thereby engendering "concupiscent" or criminal pleasures:

> It is not only dangerous to read Montaigne for diversion, because the pleasure we take in him insensibly engages us in his views, it is also dangerous because this pleasure is more criminal that we might think. For this pleasure surely arises principally from concupiscence, and supports and strengthens only our passions, since the author's style is agreeable only because it affects us *(nous touche)* and imperceptibly arouses our passions.[4]

Malebranche's warning against the dangers of reading Montaigne captures the physical impact of the *Essays,* insofar as their writing style generates pleasure by awakening imperceptibly the reader's passions. It is precisely this capacity to engage the reader physically, to address the body not merely as topic, but as a mode of presentation, that constitutes the text's perceived material threat. Malebranche's reaction pinpoints one of the most notable aspects of the *Essays,* the fact that Montaigne's presentation valorizes experience and the body, as well as the physical and material nature of the text. The consideration of the body as topic is reflected in its representation, its embodiment as material and physical fact. Montaigne alerts the reader to the embodied nature of his writings by quoting Juvenal: "And verses have their fingers to excite" (III, 5: 645). Verses not only point their fingers at reality, but may in fact come to embody a particular reality so powerfully as to literally grab hold of the reader. Thus Montaigne's concern with the body doubly inflects the *Essays,* both on the level of content and in the manner or style of its presentation.

Why Montaigne's engagement with the body should become the subject of such discomfort for Malebranche is a question that can only be answered by briefly considering the rise of Cartesianism and its influence on the emergent classical aesthetic ideology. The elaboration of a Cartesian epistemology whose model for certitude is founded on mathematical principles entails the valorization of the mind at the expense of the body. Designated as the defining horizon for Cartesian subjectivity, reason undermines the authority of the lived body, of experience as a governing paradigm.[5] Descartes's usurpation of the body, which functions as the insignia of doubt and error, impacts on the philosophical elaboration of subjectivity and its discursive representation insofar as they involve notions of embodiment. The question of embodiment in Descartes's writings is framed by his is search for certitude. Defined in terms of clear and distinct ideas, certitude implies a particular understanding of representation in terms of transparency and self-evidence. The development of the aesthetic ideology of classicism implements this demand for clarity and transparency by fostering a notion of representation that attempts to elide its own embodied character as material and physical fact. Thus the difference between classical style and Montaigne's mannerist/baroque style is not simply a superficial matter, but a matter of substance.[6] Montaigne's stylistic complexity cannot be reduced to mere ornamentation or decoration.[7] Montaigne's style reflects his philosophical understanding of the embodied nature of the self and its representation as material framework and texture.[8]

Recent critical studies on Montaigne have focused on the body as a function of the material aspects of textuality in the *Essays,* thereby attempting to reinscribe the body within the text.[9] While invaluable in terms of expanding the notion of the body through an elaboration of its textual representations, they do not explicitly examine the question of the body as a function of philosophical and stylistic concerns. The revalorization of the body as material text and texture also involves its philosophical and stylistic redefinition in terms of embodiment. This study will demonstrate that Montaigne's account of the interplay of reason, experience, and language in his last essay, "Of Experience," enables a new understanding of the body as a scriptorial entity. As the site of inscription and transcription, the modality of the body emerges in the mode of communication or speech, that is, a transitional figure constituted through dialogue or exchange. Lacking definition as a stable entity, the transitive logic of the body reflects its shifting complexions in a process of perpetual becoming. Its multiple embodiments trace the outline of its encounters with alterity, the discovery of the otherness of the self as script and representation. Since the body is a figure whose materiality and composition are also marked by stylistic concerns, this study will also examine Montaigne's essay "On Some Verses of Virgil."[10] In this essay, the representation of sexuality as a mode of embodiment is tied to the question of style as mode of expression. Associated with commerce, with forms of social and discursive exchange, sexuality will be at issue, not as an essential difference, but as a transitive mark negotiated by the quotational structure of Montaigne's text. The inscription of the mark of gender as a provisional trace will be elaborated as a function of stylistic concerns, since the material body of the essay bears the imprint of the changing autograph of sexuality. The generic instability of the body of the essay, suspended transitively between text and intertext, inflects the provisional status of gender as an intersexual relay that sets into motion conventional gender positions.

The Limits of Experience

In his essay "Of Experience" (III, 13), Montaigne explains that he seeks to portray himself according to experience, that is to say, in a manner commensurate with the exigencies and limits of his body. If traditional self-portraits are misleading, this is because Montaigne seeks to present himself as a being whose life and activity involve movement and change. This valorization of movement, of the self as a "being in passage" (III, 2: 611), emerges from his recognition that our natural thirst for knowledge is delimited by the diversity of forms of both reason and experience. "Of Experience" begins with an affirmation of our natural desire for knowledge, echoing Aristotle's inaugural statement in the *Metaphysics*.[11] However, unlike Aristotle, Montaigne emphasizes the diversity of both reason and experience as embodied forms:

> Reason has so many shapes *(formes)* that we know not which to lay hold of; experience has no fewer. The inference that we try to draw from the resemblance of things is uncertain, because they are always dissimilar: there is no quality so universal in this aspect of things as diversity and variety. (III, 13: 815)

By associating reason with its multiple embodied forms, Montaigne goes against the Platonic and Aristotelian traditions that define reason in terms of its universality and ideality, as an organizing formal principle.[12] Unlike Aristotle, who privileges the universality of reason over the contingency of experience, Montaigne affirms the variety and diversity of both reason and experience.

According to Montaigne, the multiplicity of experience can only be tangentially retrieved through the bias of its already mediated representations:

> As no event and no shape is entirely like another, so none is entirely different from another. An ingenious mixture on the part of nature. . . . All things hold together by some similarity; every example is lame, and the comparison that is drawn from experience is always faulty and imperfect; however, we fasten together our comparisons by some corner. Thus the laws serve, and thus adapt themselves to each of our affairs, by some roundabout, forced and biased interpretation. (III, 13: 819)

This double movement of resemblance and difference qualifies the Janus-like face of experience, and functions as an index of its impossible reduction to a fixed schema and predetermined laws.[13] If experience is irreducible, it is not simply because it exceeds the limits of reason by virtue of its material and contingent character, but rather because it informs and shapes reason and its laws as diversely embodied representations.

The effort to contain the mutability of experience can be no more successful than the effort to contain interpretation. Montaigne represents the dilemma of the reader as interpreter by referring to an anecdote by Aesop. In this anecdote, Aesop's dogs discover something like a dead body floating in the sea. Unable to approach the body, they attempt to drink up the water in order to dry up the passage, and choke in process. The point of this anecdote is that the reader must become a "good swimmer" (III, 13: 817), which, according to Montaigne, is what Crates said of the writings of Heraclitus.[14] Otherwise, as Montaigne warns, the text may stifle the reader through the density of its suffocating materiality, like silkworms entangled in their own work. This warning to the reader against sinking or drowning serves as a reminder both of Heraclitus's depth and weight of learning and of the threat of the material density of the fabric of the *Essays*. Thus, the story of this dead body at sea outlines from the beginning of the essay the dilemma of the corporeal nature of the text. The threat of its materiality and physical character is figured through the bias of a double register. The text's material existence may be perceived to be solid like a dead body, but this effect of "thinghood" or material existence is mediated through the fluidity of the sea, which, like the medium of the representational language of the essay, threatens to overwhelm and thus drown the reader.

Montaigne's analysis of the relation of interpretation to representation leads him to an examination of language, particularly in its attempts to represent materiality in the most elementary and brute sense, by tackling the definition of a stone:

> Our disputes are purely verbal. . . . A stone is a body. But if you pressed on: "And what is a body!—'Substance.'—And what is substance?" and so on, you would finally drive the respondent to the end of his lexicon. We exchange one word for another word, often more unknown. (III, 13: 818–19)

The effort to name things leads to a proliferation of words: the stone is defined as body, the body is defined in turn as substance, and so forth. The question of representing materiality leads back to an economy of language, to the endless proliferation and exchange of words that equate representation to the marketplace: "The question is one of words, and is answered in the same way" (III, 13: 818). The indexical relation between words and things is reduced to the metaphorical or metonymical displacement of one word for another, an exchange in kind. This deferral of materiality through representation relocates the question of the body into language by demonstrating that the body's relation to language is as oblique as the general relation of representation to experiential reality. However, it is precisely this notion of representation as detour and deferral through diverse embodiments that for Montaigne constitutes its force, that is, its physical impact and corporeal character. As he explains later in "Of Experience," even truth cannot enjoy universality, since its meaning is dependent on its representation, its usage and particular forms: "For truth itself does not have the privilege to be employed at any time and in any way; its use noble as it is, has its circumscriptions and limits" (III, 13: 826). Thus the notion of truth itself is delimited by Montaigne, since its meaning is circumscribed by its particular context and usage. Truth's universality is purely provisional, subject to the particular conditions of its representability.

Montaigne inquires into the nature of both law and medicine as the two institutional systems that legislate the representation of experience. If these two institutions are found to be lacking in terms of the appropriateness of the representations they provide, this is not for want of power and authority. Rather, it is because their description and management of experience is so general in its formal and prescriptive character as to deny both the diversity and the specificity of experience.[15] More often than not, the rights of a specific legal case are overwhelmed by the technicalities and conventions of the judicial system. As Montaigne explains: "On one side were the rights of the case, on the other side the rights of judicial forms" (III, 5: 820). Insofar as the law aims at the preservation of its own conventions, which it defines as universal, its perpetuation of judicial forms gives precedence over the circumstantial evidence of experience.

In this regard, the behavior of the law is no different from any other system or institution that seeks to perpetuate its own rules at the expense of contingent experience. Thus even reason is subject to rules whose formal character demands an adjustment of experience to fit a predetermined, greater paradigm. As Montaigne observes:

> All this reminds me of these ancient notions: that a man is forced to do wrong in detail if he wants to do right in gross, and injustice in little things if he wants to achieve justice in great ones; that human justice is formed on the model of medicine, according to which all that is useful is also just and honest. (III, 13: 820)

The detail is often sacrificed for the sake of the greater idea, just as in law or medicine a particular fact only gains evidentiary status insofar as it fits, proves useful to, a preordained order. Thus the authority of the law derives less from its encounter with contingent experience than from the experience of its conventions as a universal given, leading Montaigne to conclude: "Now laws remain in credit not because they are just, but because they are laws. This is the mystic foundation of their authority; they have no other" (III, 13: 821). The justice of laws is based on their statutory nature, not on their intrinsic or essentially just character. Laws, like currency, are based on the authority of credit; they are legitimized not by the fact of being just, but because they are laws. The legitimacy of the law is virtual, based on conventions whose authors, according to Montaigne, are "vain and irresolute men"—when they are not outright "fools." Thus the script of the law, its universal and formal character, is tainted by the faulty complexion of its authors, who seek to perpetuate its authority by drawing upon its virtual credit.

Following this stinging account of law, medicine fares no better.[16] Montaigne describes the limits of medicine as an institution that legislates in kind the experiences of the body. While medicine "professes always to have experience as the touchstone of its workings" (III, 13: 827), its relation to experience is circumstantial and indirect, since, as Montaigne points out, doctors have no direct experiences of the diseases they are treating. Rather, their experience of disease is through its manifest signs, representations that are often tangential and not always on the mark.[17] Medicine's descriptive and prescriptive character often fails in the face of the contingent particulars of disease:

> For the others guide us like the man who paints seas, reefs and ports while sitting at his table, and sails a model of his ship there in complete safety. Throw him the real thing, and he does not know how to go at it. They make a description of our diseases like that of the town crier proclaiming a lost horse and a dog: such-and-such a coat, such-and-such a height, such-and-such ears; but present it to him, and he does not know it for all that. (III, 13: 827)

The doctor is like an artist or model-maker, who though distant from a certain experience must understand it through a simulated model that re-creates and reproduces the workings of nature. The risk is that medicine relies on such general forms of description that it may be no easier to identify an illness than to name the particulars of a lost dog or horse. The animal in question is rendered almost unrecognizable by its schematic and notational representation. Thus medicine is revealed to be more art than science, for its mission is to make legible the experiential body in order to achieve through a simulated model an understanding of actual illness.[18]

Consequently, whether one attempts to describe or to legislate the body, either through jurisprudence or medicine, the conventional and contractual nature of these institutions (whose laws are on credit) reduces the body to a set of principles whose arbitrary and often irrelevant character denies the body's complex modalities of existence. This is why Montaigne keeps on coming back to a study of himself, to his self as a "university" wherein his effort to understand himself as subject, as object, and as representation will lead to the congruence of metaphysics and physics. Alluding once again to Aristotle, he explains: "I study myself more than any other subject. That is my metaphysics, that is my physics" (III, 13: 821). If Montaigne returns back to the self, it is not out of personal indulgence. Rather, this return to the self functions as the mark of the necessary detour that all representation of knowledge in general must make in attempting to inscribe within representation the position of the observer. This effort to "conform" to oneself implies less the affirmation of a stable entity than a faithfulness to the diversity and multiplicity of experiences that define it. For what Montaigne discovers through writing is precisely his lack of a stable identity. The effort to represent the self by bringing it into nomination entails its actual propagation into multiple entities. Montaigne's designation of the self as "me" *(moi)* is echoed in his self-reflexive double "myself" *(moi-mesme),* but also in his reference to himself as "another-myself" *(un autre moy-mesme).* This reference to oneself as if in the third person captures the alterity of the self as representation. The gesture of coming back to oneself in order to represent the self as the ground of experience leads to the impossibility of "conforming" to the self as a predetermined schema. Thus, Montaigne's appeal to conformity is deceptive insofar as it involves an adherence not to a given schema, but to the multiple forms or embodiments of experience.

If the body, like experience, resists categorization, are we simply to suppose that no rules govern it? Quite the contrary, for we find that Montaigne circumscribes and designates the limits of the body. Rather than merely writing about it, Montaigne urges us to listen to and read the body, in order to understand the worldly limitations that define it through habits, customs, sickness, and pleasure. The body, as the object of our observation that we consider to be most private, personal, and intimate, is also that part of ourselves which bears extensively the imprint of our society and culture. By valorizing custom and habit, Montaigne emphasizes the social construction of the body: "It is for habit *(coustume)* to give form to our life, just as it pleases; it is all powerful in that; it is Circé's drink, which varies our nature as it sees fit" (III, 13: 827).[19] This emphasis on habit as reiterative experience brings into view the body's receptive and constructed character. This receptive submission of the body to a social imaginary embeds within it the very practices that come to define its daily complexion. Rather than affirming the mastery of reason over the body, Montaigne inscribes the body within the social fabric that comes to constitute its very texture: "habit *(coustume),* imperceptibly, has already so imprinted its character *(caractères)* upon me in certain things that I call it excess to depart from it" (III, 13: 830).[20] The body bears the marks or characters of habits and customs, inscribing upon it the traces of the social and cultural symbolic. At the very moment when one attempts to experience the body in its most "proper" sense, through its personal and private habits and gestures, Montaigne finds that the body has already been written and marked by its social and cultural context. Like an inherited illness passed on through genealogical reproduction, customs and habits reinscribe the self in the domain of social and cultural reproduction. Montaigne's kidney stones, an illness inherited from his father (Pierre de Montaigne), function like the mark of the alterity of culture that infuses the proprietary domain of the self, immixing and contextualizing its nature. Just as death is constantly confusing and mixing with life, inscribing within the passage of life the decomposition of bodily forms, so does Montaigne discover within himself the radical infusion of an otherness that is indissociable from his own representation.

Even when he attempts to experience his own body directly, Montaigne finds that his desires and appetites are often regulated by external agents. The discourse of the body is mediated through a system of medical, legal, and cultural interdictions that devalue its authority. His stoical reiteration of the authority of desire, his affirmation that the body is governed by principles founded on pleasure, rather than discomfort or pain, makes explicit his effort to rehabilitate the experiential aspects of the lived body:

> Both in sickness and in health I have readily let myself follow my urgent appetites. I give great authority to my desire and inclinations. I do not like to cure trouble by trouble; I hate remedies that are more nuisance than the disease. . . . The disease pinches us on one side, the rule on the other. Since there is a risk of making a mistake, let us risk it in pursuit of pleasure. (III, 13: 832)

But the body in question here is more expansive than the physical body. For to speak about desire and pleasure means to speak about the body both as experienced and as imagined. Desire does not issue simply from the body, but involves mediation through the intervention of the imagination, a faculty that though proper to the individual is mediated and constructed through others.

Montaigne underlines the significance of imagination *(fantaisie)* and its relation to desire: "And then how much it is to satisfy the imagination *(fan-*

taisie)! In my opinion that faculty is all-important, at least more important than any other. The most grievous and ordinary troubles are those that fancy loads upon us" (III, 13: 833).[21] If Montaigne valorizes the imagination above all other faculties, including reason, it is because the imagination is the faculty that mediates desire in terms of its tangible, physical forms. Like Thomas Aquinas, who defines imagination *(fantasia)* as the faculty that mediates the relation of the body to the soul, so does Montaigne privilege the imagination as the faculty of embodiment.[22] Fantasy, the imagination, makes desire tangible as embodied form, thereby bringing representation within the purview of the body. Thus the body in Montaigne emerges as more than a pure physical and material entity, as also an imagined and represented one; for the logic of desire is representational, and the body that incarnates it becomes its modality of expression.

To give authority to desire is to learn to address the body, both as experienced and as imagined. In Montaigne, the body "speaks," even as its complexion has already been written, scripted through custom and habit. But what does the body "say" when it "speaks"? Does it have a voice, a particular tone or tenor? Montaigne focuses on the relation of body to speech, by first observing that when he is wounded or sick, talking excites him and hurts him as much as any other irregularity he may commit (III, 13: 834). By emphasizing the physical impact of speech, Montaigne brings the voice within the realm of physical expression, at the same time as he brings the body into the realm of speech. But speech is by nature dialogical; it is issued as an address and it involves an addressee.

> Speech belongs half to the speaker, half to the listener. The latter must be prepared to receive it according to the motion it takes. As among tennis players, the receiver moves and makes ready according to the motion of the striker and the nature of the stroke. (III, 13: 834)

The dialogical character of speech brings into relief an understanding of the body as a representational and experiential entity that is constituted as both process and mediation. Rather than conceiving the body as a fixed, inert, and voiceless entity, Montaigne suggests that the experiential body communicates; its configuration and complexion "speak" not as a single voice or tone, but as a mediated exercise, a dialogue of multiple voices that must be attuned to each other.

By equating the body with speech and the gesture of communication, Montaigne focuses on the body as a site for mediated representation, where the body itself is conceived as a medium of, and for, exchange.[23] The physical reality of the body thus becomes inscribed in communication, as part and parcel of representation. This is why Montaigne can describe his essays as "consubstantial" with both his written, represented self and his physical body. For if the body has been scripted by custom, habit, illness and pleasure, its legibility emerges in the order of exchange and dialogue, as a process of a mediated understanding. As the body "speaks," its speech emerges in the mode of an address whose destination and whose destiny coincide in the gesture of communication. Thus the body never "speaks" directly, since it is merely the trace of a communicative exchange, mediated by both experience and imagination.

The principles of pleasure that govern the body as a physical and as an imaginary identity are adumbrated by the very limits of its embodiment as a material and mortal entity. The physical decomposition of the body, marked through falling teeth and extruded kidney stones, is echoed by a mental rigidity and the gravity of the aging body. Both become the living emblems of the reality of death, the anamorphic inscription of the corpse onto the living body. If the writing of the *Essays* corresponds to a process of both incorporation and elimination, this process is one that confirms the congruence of composition and decomposition in the essay. Commenting on his kidney stones, Montaigne expresses his interior perception of otherness, of an indigestible, inassimilable difference, as a kind of death experienced by the body: "It is some big stone that is crushing and consuming the substance of my kidneys, and my life that I am letting out little by little *(vuide)* or voiding, not without some natural pleasure, as an excrement that is henceforth superfluous and a nuisance" (III, 13: 840). Underlying the coincidence of life and excrement, Montaigne stages the drama of his own existence as an event where he is no longer an active agent.[24] Here the body is consumed and destroyed by a stone *(pierre* or *gravelle)* that, although an extension of his own body, threatens to empty out and void the substance of his own life. The kidney stone becomes the inassimilable difference, the memento mori of the *Essays*, of an autobiography that takes the form of a thanatography.

The inscription of death upon the body and the complexion of the self is made explicit in a passage from "Of Experience" where Montaigne describes his painful efforts to pass a kidney stone. The kidney stone is both a product of the body and the mark of an inassimilable difference, which the self must eliminate in order to protect its bodily integrity. The stone *(pierre)* doubly alludes to the author, both to his father's first name (Pierre) and implicitly to his surname (Montaigne, which also means "mountain" in French). Thus it would appear that Montaigne's affliction is both physical and nominal, since as he explains, it bears the mark of the paternal imprint *(faveur paternelle)*. When Montaigne describes the passing of the kidney stone, he does so in the context of a complex citational structure, where he is at once agent, spectator, and commentator of the experience of bodily pain:

> There is pleasure in hearing people say about you: There indeed is strength, there indeed is fortitude! They see you sweat in agony, turn pale, turn red, tremble, vomit your very blood, suffer strange contractions and convulsions, sometimes shed great tears from your eyes, discharge thick, black and fright-ful urine, or have it stopped up by some sharp rough stone that cruelly pricks and flays the neck of your penis; meanwhile keeping up conversation with your company with a normal countenance, jesting in the intervals with your servants, holding up your end in a sustained discussion, making excuses for your pain and minimizing your suffering. (III, 13: 836–37)

Montaigne's painful description coincides with a dramatic spectacle, where Montaigne self-reflectively and in conversation with others experiences the body's convulsive efforts to expel the kidney stone. The effort to pass the stone coincides with the effort to speak. All the while, the effluvium of the two is experienced at the limits of pain and the ensuing pleasure of relief. The complex citational structure of this scene serves to emphasize, accord-ing to Jean Starobinski, the inability to articulate the body any way but indi-rectly, since the appeal to the internal reality of the body renders inevitable the recourse to external witness:

> Even as the individual suffers in the depth of his flesh, meaning can be artic-ulated only when the experience of suffering makes contact with others: for us, Montaigne's readers, sweating, turning pale, flushing and trembling are *events* that we experience by identifying ourselves first with the man racked by his stone and then with the spectators that his text gathers around him to *watch* his suffering. It is because he shows himself as he is looked upon from the outside that we have a sense of participating in what he feels within.[25]

This conjunction of speech and the experience of eliminating the kidney stone captures the liminal nature of the body, experienced as self and other, as the site of sexuality and excretion, of pleasure and pain. The attempt to delimit the proper character of the body through the expulsion of the for-eign body of the kidney stone leads to violent disruption, since neither the body nor the self can be reappropriated exclusively. The alterity of the paternal imprint and the alterity of other authors will continue to immix and redefine the physical and discursive complexion of the author.

The process of writing the essays by registering his thoughts (*mettre en rolle* or *enroller*) involves organic and bodily principles based both on pleasure and on loss. As Montaigne explains, he composes and reconciles himself to the loss of his own life, without regret, as something that by its nature must be lost (III, 13: 853). If Montaigne composes and proposes himself in the *Essays,* he does so in a "thousand forms" that—rather than merely "passing time," letting it flow away or sidestepping it—mark his taking charge of his life, owning up to it and embodying it to the fullest. By defining writing as a process governed by the principles of composition and decomposition, which correspond to the movement of resemblance and difference in the essay, Montaigne successfully depicts himself as a being in passage, that is, as a figure of multiple embodiments engendered by the movement of style.

Sexuality: Gendered Styles

Unlike the titles of many of Montaigne's essays, which name his topic explicitly, the title "On Some Verses of Virgil" suggests that this work is but a literary commentary on Virgil's verses. And yet this is the essay that addresses the question of sexuality, thereby inviting the reader to ask why sexuality may be situated in the realm of literary commentary, instead of being named and discussed directly as a topic. At the beginning of the essay, Montaigne, burdened by the exigencies of his aged body, revisits retrospectively the sensual pleasures of his youth.[26] A closer look at the opening passage reveals that the burdens of the aged body, its being "too sedate, too heavy and too mature," are but the reflections of thoughts, which though "fuller and more solid, . . . are also more absorbing *(empechans)* and more burdensome *(onereux)."*[27] He then clarifies the nature of these weighty thoughts: "Vice, death, poverty, disease, are grave *(graves)* subjects and grieve us *(grèvent)"* (III, 5: 638). The French words *graves* and *grèvent* suggest not only the ponderous materiality of thought, but also the capacity of thoughts to figuratively engrave and mark the body.[28] This incisive engraving and marking of the body is underlined subsequently by Montaigne's avowed sensitivity to the slightest pains: those that previously only "scratched" him, now "pierce him through and through" (III, 5: 640). Montaigne's text thus introduces itself in terms of its figural force, since it outlines a process of inscription that scrambles the distinction between body and thought.[29] Mediating between body and thought, material text and its formal organization, the issue of style is obliquely scripted into the fabric of the essay. Style is alluded to figuratively as the capacity to form and inform, and literally, since the meaning of *stylus* is that of an instrument for both writing and engraving. Montaigne's allusion to style at the beginning of the essay suggests an alternative manner for conceiving the body, as a process of inscription and as a figurative movement. It also serves to alert the reader that the question of sexuality, raised later in the essay, may be inflected by style.

When after many deferrals, Montaigne begins to speak about sexuality, the topic of sex is raised through a complex web of citations from Latin, which serve both to dissimulate and also to emphasize the topical nature of the subject matter.[30] As Terence Cave points out, "It might seem, indeed that Latin is used as a kind of veil to hide the ultimate *pudenda:* when the writer wants to speak disparagingly of his own genitals, he does so by quoting the *Priapeia.*"[31] While Cave astutely observes that quotations, and in particular Latin quotations, are used to carry the weight of Montaigne's most explicit sexual references, the question lingers as to why Montaigne, who according to Cave "claims the right to uninhibited self-portrayal," chooses to represent sexuality through such an indirect and complex citational structure. Why is the topic of sexuality embedded in what the reader experiences as a set of deliberate deferrals? What is more, do the style and the figurative structure of this essay provide us with information about the nature of sex as a topic?

A preliminary clue to these questions can be found in Montaigne's comment in an earlier essay, "Of the Education of Children," that Latin, not French, was his mother tongue (I, 26: 128–30). According to Montaigne, his father's wishes were that while he was still nursing, he be put under the charge of a German tutor who taught him Latin.[32] The rest of the family complied with this unusual educational experiment. And it was not until after the age of six that he came to master the use of French, his native tongue. Thus it was that his first taste for books came from the pleasures he experienced in reading Latin authors such as Ovid and Virgil. This reversal of the maternal and paternal tongue, of the language of institutions and the language of affect, may help explain Montaigne's preference for Latin as a language of affective expression. But this gendered reversal of tongues or languages, this crossover and hybridization of the maternal and the paternal, the affective and the institutional, also suggests that Montaigne's understanding of sexuality and gender may be inflected by his particular linguistic experience. Given this nonessentialist account of language, mediated as a set of transitions from one language to another and as the translation from one text to another, would the representation of sexuality in language also take on this provisional and conditional cast?

When Montaigne, after lengthy digressions, finally gives us a representation of the sexual act, he does so by quoting Virgil; hence, the title of the essay. As Montaigne explains, this representation of Venus in poetry is more alive than life itself: "Poetry reproduces an indefinable mood that is more amorous than love itself. Venus is not so beautiful all naked, alive, and panting as she is here in Virgil" (III, 5: 645). The depictive powers of poetry are such as to animate things in an imaginative manner that exceeds their ordinary reality.[33] A reproduction of life carries greater power than life itself, thereby displacing the sexual referent with a textual one.[34] The process of reproduction, of generating copies, enhances as it were the original, suggesting that sexuality itself is indelibly tied to its transposition and displacement into a poetic representation.

However, Montaigne is not content with Virgil's poetic representation of eroticism between Venus and Vulcan, which takes place in a marital context. He supplements Virgil's erotic scene with Lucretius's description of Venus's adulterous enjoyments with Mars.[35] He thus substitutes the description of one erotic scene with another, which he finds more appropriate because of its illicit character. In both of these cited passages, the sexual act is suspended between speech and silence, as a transition bridging the gap between the two sexes.[36] Montaigne then proceeds to expand his discussion of eroticism to a more general reflection on Lucretius's and Virgil's styles and their capacity for portraying the erotic:

> When I ruminate that *rejicit* (flings), *pascit* (devours), *inhians* (widemouthed), *molli* (soft), *fovet* (fondles), *medullas* (marrow), *labefacta* (trembling), *pendet* (suspended), *percurrit* (runs through), and that noble *circunfusa* (blended), the mother of the pretty *infusus* (out-poured), I despise those petty conceits and verbal tricks that have sprung up since. These good people needed no sharp and subtle play on words; their language is all full and copious with a natural and constant vigour. They are all epigram, not only the tail but the head, stomach and feet. There is nothing forced, nothing dragging; the whole thing moves at the same pace. "Their whole contexture is manly; they are not concerned with pretty little flowers." [Seneca] This is not a soft and merely inoffensive eloquence; it is sinewy and solid, and does not as much please as fill and ravish; and it ravishes the strongest minds the most. (III, 5: 664–65)

Montaigne literally welds and weaves together Lucretius's and Virgil's erotic vocabulary, since *rejicit, pascit, inhians, pendet,* and *circunfusa* come from Lucretius, while *molli, fovet, medullas, labefacta, percurrit,* and *infusus* come from the earlier quoted Virgil text.[37] He even implies a filiational, generative, even reproductive relation between the two texts, since the Lucretian *circunfusa* (blended) is described as the "mother of the pretty *infusus* (out-poured)."[38] This sense of borrowing, of immixture, contexture, and engenderment between these two texts is further emphasized by the sexualized vocabulary that brings together male and female activities and attributes. Speaking about sexual intercourse, Montaigne resorts to forms of verbal exchange or intercourse that issue out of his verbal coupling with the two Roman poets. The generative dialogue instituted between the two Roman texts produces Montaigne's own text, as an interstitial entity.[39] It thus becomes paradigmatic for the representation of sexuality itself as interstice and as quotation, that is, of sexuality not constituted nominally, in an essentialist mode, but dialogically, as performance.[40]

Montaigne's admiration for Virgil's and Lucretius's styles is expressed in a language that, at first sight, has an explicit, virile character: "their language is all full and copious with a natural and constant vigor."[41] But the virility in question is not localized. It is not a phallic extension of the text, but, rather, intrinsic to its general texture.[42] When Montaigne quotes Seneca, one of the classical proponents of a virile style ("Their whole contexture [*contextus*] is manly"), this ostensible affirmation of a virile style, as opposed to a soft and inoffensive eloquence, constitutes an affirmation of the tensile solidity of texture.[43] But in French, the language of Montaigne's essay, the word for texture *(contexture)* also has feminine connotations *(con-texture)*, thus infusing female sexuality into the notion of texture.[44] Moreover, it is important to note that Montaigne chooses to uproot Seneca's pronouncement about virile texture, by recontextualizing and reweaving it within the fabric of his own essay, written in French. As opposed to Latin, French "succumbs under a powerful conception," "growing limp and giving way under you" (III, 5: 666), thus suggesting an inherent weakness, and even the threat of impotence.[45] This insufficiency of French language, which is less "pliable and vigorous" than its ancient counterparts, is supplemented by its rhetorical manipulation and transposition into the language of the essay.[46]

While expressing his admiration for the Latin authors, Montaigne reauthors and thus reissues their pronouncements by transplanting and transposing them into the textured web of his own essay, written in French. As he explains: "And forms of speech, like plants improve and grow stronger by being transplanted" (III, 3: 665). Montaigne thus defers the virile eloquence of the Latin authors through an intertextual operation that has intersexual overtones, since it mixes allusions to both sexes. The analogy between sexual activity and the relation between the reader and the text becomes less the insignia of male virility than the allegorical emblem of a mold where masculinity and femininity are cast as reversible forms. As

Montaigne concludes his essay, "I say that males and females are cast in the same mold; except for education and custom, the difference is not great" (III, 5: 685).[47] The reversibility that Montaigne ascribes to the two sexes is not to be understood as a denial of sexual difference. Rather, it indicates difference's reconceptualization as a transitive, rhetorical gesture whose meaning is derived from its transpositional or translational character. Just as the referential character of sex is dislodged from physical reality and transposed into representation, so does the meaning of sexuality emerge here as an intertextual gesture marked by intersexual overtones.

Montaigne's use of borrowed Latin texts to represent the reality of sex conflates the horizon of sexuality with that of poetry. The intertextual conjunction of Latin and French texts opens up the horizon of sexuality transitively, as the space of translation. Just as Montaigne revalues "language by means of its displacement," so does sexuality gain meaning from its transposition.[48] Gender in this context emerges in the mode of quotation, not as an essential characteristic, but as a rhetorical relation where meaning is generated through position and juxtaposition. If poetry "reproduces an indefinable mood that is more amorous than love itself" (III, 5: 645), then Montaigne's essay conjures up the sexual referent in its dialogical and intertextual structure more effectively than any nominal or purely descriptive efforts. Understood in the register of human commerce or exchange, sexuality derives its meaning from its transitional, intersubjective character. Its reality is located in the order of the dialogue, the quotation, or the intertext, that is, as contextually generated meaning.

The facticity of sex does not rely upon the enforced polarity between the sexes, but on their potential reversibility. This can be seen most clearly in the descriptions of the two sexes, which are defined less by their specific anatomical nature than by their virtual status as projections of personal imagination and cultural myth. Quoting Plato, Montaigne describes the male sex as "tyrannical member" and a "furious animal," and the female sex as a "gluttonous and voracious animal." While he ascribes violence to the male sex in its desire "to subject everything to itself," this violence is also present in the female sex in its "rage" to satisfy its hunger (III, 5: 654). However, this initial affirmation of what appear to be conventional sexual roles (insofar as the male is presented as active and the female as passive or receptive) is undermined by a series of anecdotes demonstrating the incalculable nature of female sexual activity and pleasure.[49] Even in the case of female chastity, this lack of sexuality or inaction is defined as more active than actual sexual expression: "There is no action more thorny, or more active than this inaction" (III, 5: 655). Not only is the virginity of women revealed as a function of social strictures, but this sexual inactivity is described as more active and arduous than forms of male virtue and valor.

Montaigne describes the sexes in terms of excess, less as a function of their anatomical reference than as a function of the human imagination. Anecdotes describing the immeasurable nature of female sexuality are juxtaposed with anecdotes that grotesquely magnify male sexuality.[50] These excessive representations of sexuality serve to demystify its mythic character. In both instances, sexuality functions in the order of simulation and myth, since its reality reflects the doubled projection of the personal and cultural imaginary. In the case of male sexuality, the anatomical reality of the male body is sublated by its excessive aggrandizement: "In the place of real parts, through desire and hope, they substitute others three times life-size" (III, 5: 654). And in the case of female sexuality, the queen of Aragon's efforts to measure and legislate female pleasure in conjugal relations ends up with the compromise formula of six times a day, "relinquishing and giving up much of the need and desire of her sex" (III, 5: 650).[51] This "easy and consequently permanent and immutable formula" leads the doctors to cry out: "What must the feminine appetite and concupiscence be when their reason, their reformation, and their virtue are set at this rate?" (III, 5: 650). Montaigne's playful comments place both male and female sexuality under the sign of simulation and myth. This excess that he ascribes to female sexuality revalorizes its activity, correcting as it were through myth the mythic projection of male sexual activity.

While Montaigne clearly understands the relationship between sexuality and the imagination, hence its mythic character, he does not shy away from what appears to be a more physically direct, almost anatomical, account of both love and sex. Claiming to be leaving books aside, and speaking more "materially and simply," he concludes that "love is nothing else but the thirst for sexual enjoyment in a desired object, and Venus nothing else but the pleasure of discharging our vessels" (III, 5: 668).[52] But this discharge of vessels that equates man, woman, and animal is no simple business, since according to Montaigne it is the most common and yet the "most confused of our actions" (III, 5: 668). Sexual pleasure is complicated and confused in Montaigne's text because such pleasure, as subjective experience and expression, is understood in an intersubjective mode. Sexual pleasure must be both consensual and shared. Despite its individuated character, as an experience proper to the expression of the body, the experience of sexual pleasure, like other experiences, is governed through social categories of convention and contract. It is a transaction, an exchange or commerce, that Montaigne defines in the context of marriage as "mutual obligations" (III,

5: 647).[53] But the reciprocity that Montaigne ascribes to sexual pleasure in marriage turns out to be also present in the case of love. Speaking of love, Montaigne comments: "Now this is a relationship that needs mutuality and reciprocity. The other pleasures we receive may be acknowledged by recompenses of a different nature, but this one can be paid for only in the same kind of coin" (III, 5: 682). While marriage may involve a variety of recompenses, the currency of sexual pleasure in love is solely in exchange, in payment in kind.

Montaigne critiques the idea of privileging sexual pleasure for its own sake, of extracting it from the logic of exchange in order to hoard it for personal gain: "He who has no enjoyment except in enjoyment, who must win all or nothing, who loves the chase only in the capture, has no business mixing with our school" (III, 5: 671). As he explains, such an attitude is analogous to forms of defilement, and even necrophilia: "I abhor the idea of a body void of affection being mine" (III, 5: 672). Pleasure derived simply out of possession, rather than reciprocity, is an act of defilement that reduces the body to an inanimate object: "I say likewise that we love a body without soul and sentiment, when we love a body without its consent and desire" (III, 5: 673). Although Montaigne earlier affirmed the difference between marriage and passion, since the first is ostensibly based on contract and has posterity as its aim (III, 5: 645–46), while passion is founded "on pleasure alone" (III, 5: 649), he is forced to admit that even in love pleasure is mediated through an unspoken commitment: "I have kept my word in things in which I might have easily have been excused" (III, 5: 679). Consequently, sexual pleasure, whether sanctioned through official ceremony or purely as reciprocal exchange, retains its transactional and transitive character. Whether understood as commerce, exchange, or negotiation, the affirmation of sexual pleasure functions under the sign of reciprocity, inscribing the presence of another, and by extension the social, into the most intimate representation and expression of the self. Even desire in Montaigne's text cannot escape the logic of exchange; its meaning is dialogically defined as transaction, thereby scrambling the dichotomies of nature and culture.

Just as the representation of truth in Montaigne is defined not as universal, but as positional and context-bound (III, 13: 826), so does the representation of sexuality emerge as the mark of a productive rather than essentialist principle. To represent sexuality in the mode of quotation is to posit the fluidity of its meaning as a product of its positional character.[54] Defined by its context and articulation, the fluidity of sexual difference and its intersexual overtones reflect the intertextual movements and productive character of the essay as a genre. Neither essentially feminine nor masculine, the mark of gender and the mark of genre coincide in the transitional movement of the essay that offers itself both as text and as intertext. The productive interplay between text and quotation becomes the shifting terrain for the deployment of gender and genre as transitive categories.

The Autograph of Style

Montaigne's earlier reflections on Lucretius's and Virgil's styles also constitute an implicit reflection on his own style. His examination of the material and physical impact of words, and of their rhetorical and stylistic manipulation, suggests that language does not simply bear meaning, but rather embodies and generates it. As Montaigne observes: "Plutarch says that he saw the Latin language through things. It is the same here: the sense illuminates and brings out the words, which are no longer wind, but flesh and bone. The words mean more than they say" (III, 5: 665). Noting Plutarch's experience of the Latin language in the encounter with material things, Montaigne extends this notion of materiality to the realm of language, insofar as words incarnate meaning, not as wind, but as flesh and bone. Rather than considering the word as a "transparent sign of a world of substance outside itself," Montaigne locates substance in the representational medium of language.[55] The world of language and the world of things are here enmeshed; their consubstantiality attests to their shared capacities for embodiment. Instead of treating language merely as an instrument of expression, Montaigne inscribes its logic in the order of things. If "words mean more than they say" (III, 5: 665), this is because speech generates material and physical effects in excess of any intended meaning. Given this incarnate and physical interpretation of language, the question of style acquires new meanings as well. Style emerges, not as the artificial expression of eloquence, but as the organic expression of a language that has been fashioned and shaped, thereby inscribing the author's signature in its manner. However, Montaigne's essays are not reducible to stylistic mannerisms, to a set repertoire of stock figures and rhetorical conceits. Just as the essay becomes, through its shifting texture and shape, the bearer of physical and erotic eloquence, so does style emerge as a movement derived from the deployment of the changing patterns of the figurative and rhetorical structures of the text.

Rather than separating form and content, Montaigne's style incorporates thought and expression by emphasizing their material embodiment. Expressing his admiration for Latin authors, Montaigne exclaims: "When I see these brave forms of expression, so alive, so profound, I do not say 'this is well said,' I say 'This is well thought.' It is the sprightliness of the imagination that elevates and swells the words" (III, 5: 665). Breaking down the oppositions between thought and language and between form and content, Montaigne brings them together under the aegis of the imagination as the generative mechanism of embodied meaning. To say or express things well is not a superficial matter of eloquence, but a matter of combining thought and imagination. Thought attains its physical impact through its imaginative embodiments, thereby achieving form through expression. At issue is not style understood in its literal sense of "manual dexterity," as artistic conceit and ornament, but rather as a manner of impression that materially influences the soul: "The painting is the result not so much of manual dexterity as of having the object more vividly imprinted in the soul" (III, 5: 665).[56]

Just as the meaning of content may shift in terms of its stylistic disposition and composition in the essay, so may the use of language and particular forms of speech be renewed through their transposition into new contexts. Reflecting on both the material nature of the French language and the manner of its usage, Montaigne emphasizes the seminal role of style as it transposes certain forms of speech:

> In our language I find plenty of stuff *(etoffe)* but a little lack of fashioning *(façon)*. For there is nothing that might not be done with our jargon of hunting and war, which is a generous soil to borrow from. And forms of speech, like plants, improve and grow stronger by being transplanted. (III, 5: 665)

His emphasis on fashioning *(façon)*, rather than just material *(etoffe)*, reveals Montaigne's insistence that the material fabric of his essay also presents formal and stylistic concerns. The question of style is not purely about the choice of certain forms of speech, but also about their particular deployment in the essay. Montaigne's use of the metaphor of transplantation expresses his metaphoric translation of conventional speech forms into the particular idioms of his own essay.[57] The meaning of language and its forms of speech is not an essential given. Like value, it is generated through use and circulation. Montaigne valorizes his own appropriation and manipulation of language in physical terms: "Handling and use by able minds give value to language . . . by stretching and bending it" (III, 5: 665). The issue is not innovating in language by bringing new words into it, so much as enriching it by teaching "language unaccustomed movements" (III, 5: 665). By wresting language from its accustomed usage, Montaigne redeploys language by transposing and transplanting it, so that its meaning can be renewed each time with its new position and disposition. This capacity for fashioning language as plastic material becomes the imprimatur of style understood as physical engagement with language in order to renew and reactivate its representational potential.

Not only does Montaigne transpose forms of speech by revalorizing them in new contexts, but he also transforms the speech of others when he embeds their quotations in the fabric of his own text. However, Montaigne's essay is fraught with the anxiety of borrowing from other authors; he admits that "they may interfere with my style" (III, 5: 666). Admitting to his own aping and imitative nature, Montaigne is conscious of the imprint of others upon his own text: "Anyone I regard with attention easily imprints on me something of himself" (III, 5: 667). While recognizing other authors' presence in, and influence on, his text, Montaigne's emphasis on style or fashioning, on his own manner of transposing and disposing the speech of others, suggests a new way of understanding value and artistic originality. Just as Montaigne appropriates forms of conventional language by refashioning it as the bearer of "unaccustomed movements," so are his quotational borrowings from others renegotiated through their inscription into the fabric and formal movement of his essay. Functioning in the mode of appropriation, the style and quotational structure of the essay script an encounter with alterity in the transpositional logic of the text. Insofar as this appropriation is strategic and is redeployed in a particular manner, it becomes the signature of a new way of defining the value of writing as reembodiment, and of authorship as intersubjective embodiment.

Speaking of other forms of writing, such as those encountered in the sciences or philosophy, Montaigne notes their specialized, artificial, and thus alienating mode of address. He takes as an example his own attendant, his page: "My page makes love and understands it" (III, 5: 666). However, this page will be unable to recognize his actions in the philosophical writings that are read to him. This example is particularly telling, since the word for page *(page)* is identical to the word for a page of a book (or "attendant"). Conflating in the same breath his own page and the pages of the *Essays,* Montaigne affirms the uniqueness of his own text in terms that refuse its assimilation to more technical and specialized philosophical writings. The problem is that such language fails to capture, because of its general character, the particular and contingent nature of experience. Hence his refusal to travesty the content of his actions by dressing them up in the philosophical language of the schools: "I do not recognize in Aristotle most of my ordinary actions: they have been covered up and dressed up in another robe for the use of the school" (III, 5: 666). The language of the essay does not hide or dress up its author by disguising or generalizing ordinary actions beyond any common recognition.

Montaigne's resistance to representing experience, according to the philosophical and writerly conventions of his time, is apparent in his musing afterthought: "If I were of the trade, I would naturalize art as much as they artify nature" (III, 5: 666). His claim to naturalize art reflects his particular position as a writer who seeks a new manner for representing ideas. The claim to "naturalize art," rather than "artify nature," alludes both to his conceptual emphasis on experience and to its physical and material embodiment in the essay. Montaigne's reference to his page's making love and understanding it, captures in effect the physical and material interplay of the pages of the essay. The allusion to sexuality, physically figured in the very pages of the essay, reveals its pervasive presence throughout not merely as topic but as matter and manner of representation. Sexuality and physicality thus emerge here no longer as exterior forces that shape the text of experience and that of the essay, but as intrinsic forces that govern the movement of style. "On Some Verses of Virgil" thus stages a reflection on the experience and representation of sexuality as a form of erotic expression, a stylistic movement engendered by the interplay of material content and its changing forms.

Montaigne's interest in style understood as movement, rather than a static representation, is also visible in other essays. Speaking of his portraits in his essay "Of Experience," he observes their obsolescence and alterity in regard to the present: "I have portraits of myself at twenty-five and at thirty-five; I compare them with one of the present: how irrevocably it is no longer myself!" (III, 13: 846). The problem of self-portraiture is not about simply temporal differences, or the fact that such portraits are imbued with the taint of mortality. Montaigne's discursive portraits raise more fundamental questions about the relationship of being and identity to representation. When Montaigne represents himself in writing, his self-reflective stance generates effects of alterity, the discovery of the self as an "another myself" (autre moy mesme). This difference that the process of writing inscribes in the representation of the self leads to its proliferation as multiple embodiments.[58] This is why it becomes impossible to capture the self, to seize it other than as representations whose multiple, partial, and fragmented character figure its existence as a provisional entity.

In "Of Repentance," Montaigne explains that his ambition is not to portray being, but its passing: "I do not portray being: I portray passing. Not the passing from one age to another, or, as the people say, from seven years to seven years, but from day to day, from minute to minute" (III, 2: 611).

But how does one portray passage? If being is elusive, then its imperceptible passages are all the more so. In "Of Vanity," Montaigne hints that his desire for change finds expression in the concurrence of style and thought: "I seek out change indiscriminately and tumultuously. My style and my mind alike go roaming" (III, 9: 761). Reflecting on the flux and mobility of nature, Montaigne's essays locate in the movement of style the conflation of thought and its changing forms.[59] In the essay "Of Experience," the pursuits of the mind are described as "boundless and without form": "It is an irregular, perpetual motion, without model and without aim. Its inventions excite, pursue, and produce one another (s'entreproduisent)" (III, 13: 818). The stylistic discontinuities of the material text of the Essays reflect the changes and rapid movements of the mind, setting both the subject matter and the reader into motion.

Commenting on his own style, Montaigne in "On Some Verses of Virgil" stages a kind of internal dialogue with the reader and his own text, documenting the stylistic particularities of his own work:

> When I have been told, or have told myself: "You are too thick in figures of speech. Here is a word of Gascon vintage. Here is a dangerous phrase." (I do not avoid any of those that are used in the streets of France; those who would combat usage with grammar make fools of themselves.) "This is ignorant reasoning. This is paradoxical reasoning. This one is too mad. You are often playful: people will think you are speaking in earnest when you are making believe." "Yes," I say, "but I correct the faults of inadvertence, not those of habit. Isn't this the way I speak everywhere? Don't I represent myself true to life? Enough, then. I have done what I wanted. Everyone recognizes me in my book, and my book in me." (III, 5: 667)

Montaigne's dialogue with the reader and with himself, his answers to the reader's objections concerning his peculiar choice of words and paradoxical, even maddening, reasoning, constitutes his affirmation of his style of writing, which bears the authentic signature of the author as he attempts to represent himself true to life (vivement), as being alive. Quoting itself, the text of the essay establishes an internal conversation that mimics through its own address both the presence of the author and that of the reader, thereby creating the illusion of life. As Richard Regosin notes: "Montaigne claims his real, physical presence in the work, both by saying he is there and by giving the reader the sense that he is there."[60] This live representation of the author thus emerges not merely as a textual conceit of the author, but rather as a stylistic inscription of presence generated through quotational and interstitial movements.

This quotational and self-generative aspect of Montaigne's essays allows the text to reproduce its author with the utmost sincerity and fidelity, suggesting through its physical immediacy its capacity to intercept and directly address the reader.[61] It is not surprising, therefore, to hear Montaigne say, "If there are any persons, any good company, in country or city, in France or elsewhere, residing or traveling, who like my humor and whose humors I like, they have only to whistle in their palm and I will go furnish them with essays in flesh and in bone" (III, 5: 640). Readers only have to whistle in their palms to be provided with Montaigne's presence, furnished through the essay, not merely as writing matter, but as flesh and bone. The illusion of presence that the *Essays* foster is provisional upon a performance enacted by the written text, which effectuates the corporeal incarnation of its author. Montaigne's embodiment in his encounter with the reader reflects the movement that the text initiates and then perpetuates as a literary performance.[62] Reaching out its fingers to the reader, the fabric of Montaigne's essay grabs hold of us, all the while enfolding and unfolding its author before our very eyes.[63]

While borrowing from many other authors and decrying his imitative nature, Montaigne inscribes through his style the trace of an irretrievable difference, that of having lived and having represented his experience in the most original manner possible. Montaigne's stylistic originality demarcates the *Essays* from the works of the past and differentiates them from any common or traditional use of language, allowing the author to rightfully claim: "In Paris I speak a language somewhat different than at Montaigne" (III, 5: 667).[64] The language of the *Essays* is particular to its author, like a regional dialect. It reflects the position of an author whose provisional embodiment is constituted through the particular handling and redeployment of language as contextualized performance. The incorporation of other voices and other authors into the fabric of the text defines the alterity of its complexion. Thus the quotational structure of the *Essays* attests to embodiment, not merely as topic, but as the very mechanism that subtends the production and proliferation of the essays. The manual dexterity of the author inscribes within the language of the *Essays* the autograph of style, which redefines representation in the very process of attempting to reproduce itself.

If Montaigne in "Of Experience" speaks about a "culture of the body," this is because he seeks a new kind of human wisdom, one that takes into account the self's "mixed condition" or constitution (III, 13: 850). Operating "close to the ground," Montaigne chooses not only to speak about experience and the body, but to rethink the nature of wisdom as a knowledge that is commensurate to, and reflective of, the exigencies of the body. Montaigne's admission that "transcendental humors" frighten him like lofty and inaccessible heights represents his rejection of conventional forms of wisdom or knowledge, of forms that seek to exceed the human condition. Whether it involves forms of idealization or devaluation, such wisdom is prosthetic, to the extent that it relies on the body even as it seeks to overcome its limits. As Montaigne trenchantly concludes: "Yet there is no use our mounting on stilts, for on stilts we must still walk on our own legs. And on the loftiest throne in the world we are still sitting only on our own rump" (III, 13: 857). The wisdom of the *Essays* and their legacy to posterity will be that of a hybrid knowledge that is "intellectually sensual" and "sensually intellectual" (III, 13: 850). Rather than separating the body from the soul, and ideas from their representation, this wisdom will take the body both as a point of departure and as destination, while recognizing embodiment as the horizon of possibility of its always provisional condition.

Chapter 2
Emblematic Legacies: Regendering the Hieroglyphs of Desire

To hear with eyes belongs to love's fine wit.
  —Shakespeare

Although widely read and broadly disseminated throughout the first half of the seventeenth century, Honoré d'Urfé's monumental pastoral novel *Astrea* (*L'Astrée*, 1607–27) soon lost its appeal to the general public.[1] This decline in interest reflected a shift in taste of the readerly public, who, guided by the emergent classical aesthetics in the second half of the seventeenth century, demonstrated a preference for the leaner and more tightly structured novella *(nouvelle)*, as evidenced by the success of Mme de Lafayette's *The Princess of Clèves* (1678).[2] Such a development is not altogether surprising, since the novel's deliberate manipulation of figurative and literal language, as well as its narrative conventions involving multiplying story lines, no longer corresponded to the highly restrictive aesthetic criteria of verisimilitude and plausibility that define classical norms and mores.[3] The novel's linguistic excesses and its perceived preciosity are compounded by discontinuities in time and space that fail to locate subjectivity as a unified agency. The emphasis on illusion, deception, doubling, metamorphosis, and transvestism further destabilizes the representation of both subjectivity and the body. A veritable encyclopedia of love, documenting in over five thousand pages its every possible permutation, *Astrea* shocks the reader by its unusual conceit of representing the love interest of the two central characters, Celadon and Astrea, through the foil of a love story between women. While appealing to Neoplatonist ideals, the novel audaciously operates through transvestism the material transformation of a male character into a female protagonist, only to progressively unhinge gender positions and ultimately the subjective agency of the protagonists. If this novel became illegible, first for the classical readers who were no longer able to appreciate its allegorical devices and representational structure, and then later for the modern readers who were unable to overcome its perceived archaisms, this resistance to legibility began to give way once it was understood that the novel's representational structure is not merely the insignia of baroque style, but perhaps a worldview founded on altogether different subjective and representational premises. A brief overview of the critical approaches to baroque style and its epistemological underpinnings will enable us to elaborate the historical legacy of emblematic traditions that inform the novel's linguistic and representational strategies.

The analogy of painting to literature, embodied in Horace's phrase *ut pictura poesis* ("as in painting, so in poetry"), has been the implicit premise that informs and guides baroque literary studies.[4] Once we consider the preeminence of visual metaphors in baroque literature, the dominance of illusion, and the trompe l'oeil character of both protagonists and narrative, the impetus to apply pictorial categories to poetry is not surprising. In France, the major approaches to baroque literary style are art-historical, based on Heinrich Wölfflin's concepts of architectural and pictorial style elaborated in *Renaissance and Baroque* (1888) and *Principles of Art History* (1915).[5] Wölfflin associates the baroque with the painterly style, as opposed to the linear style of the Renaissance, and defines it by its focus on open form, on movement—as the expression of form in function, that is, on the thing in its relations, rather than the thing in itself.[6] These features are the signatory conventions of baroque representation: the "apprehension of the world as shifting semblance."[7] The baroque thus represents a new way of conceiving plastic form, reflecting technical and artistic transformations in the way vision is conceived and the manner in which it organizes the space of representation.[8]

Recent attempts to reassess the baroque have been marked by an effort to move beyond stylistic considerations, in order to come to terms with its specific historical character.[9] Concomitant to these approaches is the emergence of philosophical studies that examine the baroque, not merely as the expression of a style, but as a particular manner of apprehending and representing the world, a worldview.[10] In this study, Wölfflin's observations are recontextualized by considering Walter Benjamin's seminal contribution to baroque aesthetics. In *The Origin of German Tragic Drama* (1928), Benjamin observes that in baroque works, the "written word tends towards the visual."[11] This appeal to the visual establishes the plastic dimension of baroque allegory as a "crossing of the borders of a different mode."[12] The figurative character of the baroque represents for Benjamin the crossover of poetic and pictorial conventions that baroque allegory enacts as it seeks to go beyond expression in the self-conscious invocation of convention.[13]

Instead of considering allegory as an illustrative technique, Benjamin examines it as a mode of thought, whose historical character is grounded in the legacy of literary and visual emblem books of the late Renaissance and the baroque.[14]

Recent scholarship has provided us with a clearer understanding of the historical and conceptual scope of this emblematic tradition.[15] Although the earliest examples of emblem books have no illustrations, using epigrams instead to suggest mental images, by the 1540s the emblem emerges as a device in which a picture is framed by a title above and a motto below that acts as a commentary on the image.[16] By the late sixteenth century, the emblem becomes primarily a literary device whose function is to give figurative reality to abstract concepts.[17] The emblematic tradition thus represents a particular way of communicating, compiling, and storing knowledge, one in which intellectual conceits are translated into sensible images.

The emblem is a ternary representation, in which the visual content is supplemented by a title, telling us what we are intended to see and by the motto that tells us from what perspective—moral or otherwise—the image and its title must be understood. The interplay of the visual and discursive aspects of the emblem, between representation and interpretation, is allegorical since "that which is depicted means more than it portrays."[18] If allegory as a symbolic mode represents a process of encoding knowledge, as Angus Fletcher suggests, the question is how to think historically the specific nature of seventeenth-century baroque allegory.[19] As this study will show, baroque allegory represents a particular manner of encoding literal meaning by exploring its figurative character. The baroque takes as its subject matter the very conventions that were used from antiquity to the Renaissance to distinguish painting from poetry (defined respectively as "mute poetry" and "speaking picture").[20] As the embodiment of plastic and rhetorical arts, the double nature of the emblem as mute poetry and as a speaking picture provides a conceptual nexus for rethinking the literal and figurative character of baroque allegory.

Instead of thematizing such stylistic features as the obsession with illusion, deception, doubling, metamorphosis, and transvestism, this study demonstrates that these elements are an expression of *Astrea*'s emblematic worldview. Rather than documenting the presence of actual emblems in the text, this study elucidates how representation is conceived and structured emblematically, as a composite of speech and sight: the interplay of literal and figurative elements. In *Astrea,* neither speech nor image functions as the exclusive purveyor of meaning. By problematizing the relation between representation and interpretation, between literal and figurative elements, the novel stages its emblematic heritage through the interplay between word and image. Baroque allegory thus presents us with a concept of representation whose ternary structure, as opposed to the modern binary conception of the sign, enables us to conceive meaning as a convention whose interpretative structure relies upon the mediation of literal and figurative elements.

This study of the legacy of these emblematic traditions in *Astrea* focuses on their impact on the representation of subjectivity and the body. The interplay of word and image informs the peculiar features of the novel's depiction of the characters' apprehension, perception, and understanding of the world in relation to landscape, to language, and to representations of self and other. If the novel's protagonists appear to inhabit a world whose phenomenological premises are different from our own, this is not simply because they inhabit the utopic world of the pastoral. Rather, the emblematic nature of the novel's depictions continues to attest to an "apprehension of the world as shifting semblance," one where representation is not yet grounded by foundational constraints. Within this representational framework, even sexual difference fails to function as a stable referent or essence, since difference is undermined by the play of always changing semblances. This is why presentations of the body, gender, and eroticism in *Astrea* are free of conventional oppositions and restraints, since notions of identity are tied to the logic of appearance. In the pages that follow, the fluidity and freedom of the body, setting, speech, and gender will be read as a function of the novel's implicit reflections on the play of representation.

Emblematic Settings: Narrative as Visual Script

The opening passage of *Astrea* describes the physical setting of the novel. Despite its geographical verisimilitude, the description of this landscape has been linked to pastoral aspirations. Yet the difficulty of orienting oneself within this image is due to an excess, rather than a lack, of deictic markers, and this difficulty suggests that the image is a composite of divergent points of view:

> *In the heart of* the Country is a most beautiful plain girdled by as with strong walls, by hills *close by*, and watered by the River Loire, which originating *not far off,* glides gently *almost through the midst of it.* . . . *Many* other rivulets *in diverse places* go about bathing it . . . one of the most beautiful of which is Lignon, which though *vagabond in its course,* as well as *dubious in its source,* runs *meander-like* through the plain, . . . *where* the Loire *receiving* it,

and *making it lose its proper name,* carries it as tribute unto the Ocean. (1:1, 1:9; emphasis added)[21]

Gérard Genette considers this landscape to be the embodiment of the conventions of pastoral novels, a veritable Eden, whose value is purely symbolic.[22] Stressing the allegorical dimension of this pastoral space, he underlines the fact that this is *not* a "lived-in landscape." If by "lived-in" one means that the landscape should function either as a scenic decor or a space of containment, then this is clearly not the case. Unlike its modern counterparts, this landscape is not a secretion of the psychological or moral state of the characters, as in the realist or naturalist novel.[23] Nor does it function as a coherent frame of reference, since the description is qualified by phrases such as "close by," "not far off," "in diverse places," "vagabond in its course," "dubious in its source," "meander-like," which confuse the ability of the reader to attain a precise focus and totalizing view of the ensemble.

The geographical centrality of the Loire is undermined by the narrative centrality of its tributary Lignon, which despite its physical marginality in the frame of the description, functions as the dramatic locus of narration. In this passage, several landscapes are conjoined, generating a sense of instability through metamorphosis. Already of dubious source ("douteux en sa source"), Lignon is described by its loss of identity as it flows into the Loire and loses its proper name ("luy faisant perdre son nom propre"). Thus, we find ourselves on shaky ground, since the river Loire, or rather its minor tributary Lignon, emerges less as a subject of location than as a "character" in its own right.[24] The fact that the river Lignon emerges as an actual protagonist in the novel should not be altogether surprising, given the aquatic obsession of the baroque. The centrality of water as a theme suggesting fluidity, movement, and metamorphosis is manifest in its proliferation in landscapes, gardens, and architectural elements.[25] However, this obsession should not be mistaken with a fascination with nature, per se, such as we see in the context of romanticism.[26]

The author's formal dedication of his work, "The Author to the River Lignon" [L'Autheur à la riviere de Lignon] at the head of the third part indicates that the centrality of the river is comparable to that of the two main characters, Astrea and Celadon. Lignon is addressed as an interlocutor and accomplice of the author that does not merely witness the narration, but, given the circuitous logic of the text, may be its very source. In his dedication, the author addresses the river directly, as both witness and muse of his affective life. Lignon does not function as a passive source of inspiration. Rather, the river is presented as having an active memory of events:

> If you [Lignon] also have good memory of the agreeable occupations you gave me, since your shores were quite often the *faithful secretaries of my imaginations* and of the sweetness of such a desirable life, I am sure that you will easily recognize that at this time I am neither giving nor offering you anything new which you have not already acquired. (3:5–6; emphasis added)

If the novel is presented as a tribute to the river, this is because the river is the original secretary of his imaginations, oddly recording ("conserveras curieusement"), scrupulously preserving, and publicizing them to the various river nymphs and gods. Lignon is thus posited both as the source of narration and as its authorizing agent. The author's indebtedness to the river is such that the publication of his own work is presented as a repayment to Lignon, as a tribute to its "authorizing agency."[27] Thus the river is designated as the original site for the production of narrative, which corresponds to its reproduction as narrative image and as script. The authority of the author and the landscape become interchangeable, since it is no longer clear which is the true source of the narration. Thus, from what appears to be mere geographical description, we stumble upon allegory: the reduction of the natural world to hieroglyphs whose characters shape the script of the narrative.

In the third part of *Astrea,* the opening description of the novel is reinvoked, not as an element of setting, but as the allegorical embodiment of a state of mind. At this point, for reasons that will be elucidated later in this chapter, Celadon, banished from sight by Astrea, returns to live with her disguised as the druid priestess Alexis. Alexis invites Astrea to look at this landscape, which is now the only living testimony of his former existence as Celadon:

> And upon this word, opening the window and both leaning over the ledge, after looking about this and that way, Astrea began thus: Do you see, Madam, the course of that river . . . that is the fatal and defamed river Lignon, along which you may perceive our hamlet to be seated. . . . If you please to cast your eye a little upon the left hand, you may see the temple of the good Goddess . . . under which runs an arm of the detestable Lignon. . . . Amongst the rest, I observed the picture of the goddess Astrea (for the temple is dedicated unto her) much different from those by which they used to represent her unto us: She is portrayed in the habit of a shepherdess. (2:81, 3:223–24)

Looking through a window, physically leaning on the ledge, or rather the frame of this image, the two characters proceed to point out and discuss various features of the view. This is a wonderful moment in the novel, because as readers we "see" the landscape that the characters inhabit and perceive.

This "fold" in the material structure of the novel provides insights into how representation functions; that is, it provides an outlook on what constitutes "looking" in the novel. In this context, the image of the river Lignon takes on a new meaning. This time the description appears to follow more conventional spatial rules, yet its rationale is less spatial than affective, for Lignon is not just a river, it is a despicable one. Although this landscape is more coherently organized, giving us, in effect, our first true view of the scene, this view is itself a composite of two different perspectives, those of Astrea and Alexis. This mediated perspective reflects the physical and psychological distance that now enables the characters to read their lives in the landscape. This act of reading, which corresponds to visual pointing and interpreting, transforms the landscape into a text whose legibility relies on the affective script of the characters.

At the heart of this description of the landscape lies another image, that of the picture of the goddess Astrea disguised as a shepherdess. Surprisingly, this portrait, as Astrea tells Alexis, resembles her. In true baroque fashion, we have a series of receding representations in trompe l'oeil that enables Astrea to discover and view herself immortalized in the landscape as a goddess within a temple. This discovery is not mediated through vision alone. Rather, Astrea's ability to recognize herself in the image of a goddess is based on her capacity to assume the script of Celadon's love, insofar as it has transformed the landscape into narrative. This portrait of Astrea thus resembles her improperly: its verisimilitude cannot be guaranteed either by her own semblance or by her name. Despite their deictical properties, both image and name emerge as unstable referents, since neither can define itself without inscription into the texture of the other. The reflective mirrors generated by the *mise-en-abyme* structure of this baroque text produce deictical effects, but their referential scope is defined by the narrative fabric of the text.

Thus the protagonists of *Astrea* consider the landscape less a reflective mirror than a scripted surface whose characters must be deciphered. The only apparent exception to this rule, in the novel, is the allegorical "Fountain of Love's Truth," a magic mirror of lovers' sentiments. As its title indicates, this fountain provides the beholder with an image of love's truth, reflecting the lover's innermost thoughts and desires. For Louise Horowitz, the image of the fountain is the concrete symbol of the novel's "metaphysical base," of its Platonic presuppositions. Had access to this fountain not been cut off, there could be no novel, since its absence is equated with the generation of doubt: "doubt so great that it risks destroying the moral foundation of the novel."[28] If the absence of the fountain is to be equated with the generation of doubt, we must examine how love's truth is revealed. Can one even speak of love's truth without inquiring into the representation of love as a source of illusion? In examining the fountain of love's truth, it soon becomes apparent that the fountain reflects not only the desire of the lover, but of the beloved:

> You know what the property of this water is, and how it necessarily reveals the most secret thoughts of lovers; for he who looks into it, shall there see his mistress, and if she loves him he shall see himself by her: but if she loves another, then the figure of that other shall appear . . . as all other waters do represent the body facing them, this one represents the spirits. Now the spirit, which is only the will, the memory, and the judgment, when it loves, is transformed into the thing loved; and this is why when you present yourself here, it receives the figure of your spirit, and not of your body. (1:36, 1:93)

Upon looking into the fountain, the lover perceives the embodiment of his/her desire: the reflected image of the beloved. The transparency of the water yields forth the material shape of desire. This objectification of desire into image, however, depends on the desire of the other, the beloved, whose own desire mediates the visual reference of the beholder. Unless loved, the beholder ceases to exist, or worse, the image of the beloved will be accompanied by that of the rival. The "truth" of this image of love depends not on visual accuracy, but speech: the image can only come into existence as an answer—a response to the image of another desire.

What is peculiar about the "reflective" properties of this fountain is that the images it generates are the embodiment of thought. They are figures of thought, rather than mere reflections of an external reality. The fountain of love's truth is presented as the literal embodiment of Platonism, insofar as it upholds the superiority of ideas over sensible reality. The fact that this fountain does not reflect the lover, but the beloved, is explained by an appeal to the Platonic and Neoplatonic beliefs that love involves the transformation of the soul and its fusion with the love object.[29] This fusion, however, is exaggerated in this passage to the point of caricature. For the beholder is literally erased from the image, as if s/he had no apparent physical existence. Platonic doctrine emphasizes the fact that the sensible merely paves the way for the intelligible. But in the baroque context, the sensible is no longer a vehicle for signifying an idea different from itself. Rather, as the very incarnation and embodiment of the idea, it seems as if "the concept itself has descended into our physical world, and we see it itself directly in the image."[30] The image of love's truth is the literal transcription of desire into visual script. However, this image presents a fundamental problem, to the extent that the physical embodiment of thought implies the potential disembodiment of the beholder. Thus, the script of desire threatens, by its literal character, to negate the potential subjective appropriation of the image. Even when love is reciprocated, the lover's image is subordinate to the beloved; the former stands next to the latter and is defined by it, thereby inscribing one image into another and reducing them both to fragments. Thus, in the baroque novel, the literal embodiment of Platonic and Neoplatonic doctrine represents the ideal as a ruin: an ideology whose decay is scripted in and by representation. It is a poignant reminder that the evocation of this spiritual ideal exists as material fact only insofar as it is embodied in representation.

The fountain of love, which is also the fountain of truth, provides the lover not with a reflection of him- or herself, but with a picture of the beloved. No matter how many times lovers try to lean over the fountain's edge, to add their own image to their beloved's reflection, this effort meets with failure. Thus it seems that the magical quality of the fountain is not merely that of embodying desire, but denying narcissistic self-reflection. This mirror reflects the desire for the other through the actual inscription of the other into the picture. This image is an improper mirror of subjectivity, insofar as the representation of desire appears to disenfranchise the characters of their own reflection.[31] The purloining of the lover's image by the inscription of the rival reflects a linguistic fact: the lover's existence is predicated on a response. The lover's gaze is contextualized by becoming subject to the inscription of another's desire. Thus, neither the lover nor the beloved can be objectified through their reduction to a pure reflection, since desire must "speak" in order to become visible as an image. If the beloved does not "answer" the desire of the lover, then the lover will not be reflected. This interference in the subject's self-reflection, in its ability to see itself as an image, marks the provisional status of subjectivity constituted in the modality of an address.

While the fountain of love's truth may be seen as a restaging of Ovid's story of Narcissus in *Metamorphoses,* the overt rejection of specular self-identification indicates that other narratives might be at play.[32] Pausanias mentions a less well known version of this myth, one in which Narcissus's desire to seek out and contemplate his own reflection is the lamenting answer to the loss of his twin sister.[33] In this version of the myth, the image does not reflect the beholder, since it is the visual substitute for an absent other, mourned through the echoes of resemblance. Visual representation emerges in this instance, not as the insignia of presence, but as a substitute for speech. It replaces an exchange between subjects with an image. However, this image no longer functions as an expression of narcissism—the desire for the self as image—but reveals, rather, an absent other. This version of the myth thus suggests the loss of the self, to the extent that sight redefines the self as an improper site. This is why in the novel, the image is never an object that can exist as a thing in and of itself. Rather, the image is defined contextually through speech. Thus the gaze can no more objectify an image than can names, in this novel of endless disguises, truly designate the protagonists. The referential status of both image and language is in question.

Anagrams: Language in Anamorphosis

If the representation of images in *Astrea* is deceptive, to the extent that their meaning relies on the intervention of speech, this is equally true of the representation of speech. This is not because characters explicitly attempt to disguise what they say, but because speech is revealed to be an uncertain mirror of meaning. Speech echoes with diverse meanings and images. Its figurative character reveals that language is an unstable and mutable bearer of meaning, like the liquid medium of the river. Having examined the scriptorial character of descriptive images in *Astrea*, it is important to understand how language generates figurative effects. This is all the more important because the entire plot of *Astrea* hinges on what some may regard as a mere linguistic ploy. The hero, Celadon, attempts to respect to the letter (*à la lettre*—and what is at issue is the letter, or language) Astrea's injunction not to show himself before her eyes: "I charge thee to never show thyself to me, lest I command it" [garde-toy bien de te faire jamais voir à moy que je ne te le commande] (1:2, 1:13). But he constantly violates the letter of the law by producing anagrams of this injunction so that he can still see her, even if this implies his own loss of identity. While he will appear to respect the literal aspects of Astrea's injunction, he will violate its spirit by disobeying her. In other words, Celadon restructures the terms or letter of the law, in order to produce alternative readings and thus, new figurative meanings that will enable him to see her.

Astrea begins where other novels end, with disaster *(désastre)*. This anagrammatic play on the heroine's name *Astrée* is by no means gratuitous. It is part and parcel of the text's emblematic structure, which does not proceed narratively, but poetically, through a series of linguistic and figurative displacements.[34] In his dedication to the river Lignon, d'Urfé explains that the word "to love" *(Aymer)* used to be pronounced as "bitter" *(Amer)*, thus suggesting that speech is the bearer of deceptive echoes. Like-sounding words may have different and, at times, even opposing meanings. Given the fluidity of language, the word *Aymer* constitutes a material base that can potentially generate different images, some in consonance, and others in total dissonance with each other. It is not surprising that love *(Amour)* is introduced in *Astrea,* as a flatterer who soon changes his "authority into tyranny" [son authorité en tyrannie] (1:1, 1:9). This sudden turn in the plot represents the linguistic ambiguity of love, the fact that its appropriation through speech inscribes in love a double figure: the authority of love's script may also correspond to the bitter anagram of tyranny.

In order to understand how d'Urfé explicitly problematizes speech as the purveyor of figurative meaning in *Astrea,* we turn to an incident in which Silvandre, frustrated by the unresponsiveness of Diana, seeks solace in the echoes of his own voice. While he playfully invokes the mythological nymph Echo, this gesture is framed by the understanding that the "oracular" powers of this nymph, her ability to speak, is nothing more than the physical reflection of the voice as it encounters the obstacle of a material surface. Listening to his own voice, Silvandre experiences it as the expression of another:

> Nymph, who feels in these rocks so hollow
> The painful weight of love's great sorrow,
> Will I ever of its heaviness be relieved?   *I deceived.*
> What! Sacred Echo, isn't it blasphemy
> To charge thee with lying? What calumny!
> Is it thy voice itself I hear above?   *Love.*
> (2:10; my trans.)[35]

While recognizing the fact that this "echo" effect was generated by his own voice, "that he was his own answerer" [que c'estoit luy-mesme qui se respondait], Silvandre cannot help but be pleased by the response, "feeling great consolation from the auspicious answers which he received" [ressentir une grande consolation des bonnes responces qu'il avoit receues] (1:200, 2:11). His pleasure involves hearing his own desire reflected back to him, as if it were the voice of another. But how does speech generate these echoes, and how do they become bearers of the script of desire? Similar sounds resound with different images and may embody different meanings: a fragment of the word for "relieved" *(allegements),* becomes "I deceived," or literally, "I lie" *(je ments),* and "thy voice itself" *(ta voix mesme)* is echoed back as a command in the imperative: you must love ("Ayme"). Echo's responses can be seen as a metareflection on the nature of language. She may not be lying when s/he says "I lie" because speech itself, rather than the speaker, is identified as the site of deception. When Silvandre asks whether the voice he hears is her own *(mesme)*, we witness his experience of the otherness of his own voice, as it literally "speaks" back to him.[36] Echo's response, "Ayme," playfully suggests that the reflexivity of language itself may generate effects of desire, in a personally indiscriminate or generic sense. These echoes are reflections, figurative folds in the material surface of language suggesting that speech rather than the speaker is the site of illusion.

While Silvandre explicitly recognizes the self-reflective character of the echo, this does not prevent him from purloining this reflection as the definitive sign of another subjective presence. Flattering his own desire, Silvandre convinces himself that someone else is speaking through him. This delusion, as the narrator of *Astrea* tells us, is fostered by the desire of lovers to find hope, even when there is no apparent reason to justify it: "since it seemed to him that nothing was governed by chance, but all by an all-wise providence, he believed that those words which the rock returned to his ear, were not pronounced by him with purpose, but were put into his mouth by some good demon, that loved him" (1:200, 2:11). In what appears to be an extraordinary step, Silvandre proceeds to disown his own speech. He is the speaker, but his speech belongs to someone else. He is merely the mouthpiece for a demon who embodies his desire better than himself. Who, then, is this fictitious demon or master ventriloquist who expresses Silvandre's desire better than he can? This demon is speech itself, the alterity of language as a symbolic order that "speaks" before it is spoken. Its arbitrary appropriation by an individual subject reveals speech to be an improper vehicle for communication, but a most propitious medium for generating desire.[37]

If speech is shown to be an unstable medium, its written representation fares no better. Although it would seem that writing stabilizes the inflections of speech, script is itself vulnerable to misrepresentation. In *Astrea*, Celadon's effort to consecrate the laws of love for eternity by engraving them on a set of tablets is perversely undermined. Having dutifully recorded the laws of love (on twelve tablets, as compared to Moses' ten), Celadon's written record is falsified by his novelistic alter ego Hylas, *l'inconstant,* or "the inconstant one" (2:194–201, 1:278–81). With a few erasures and substitutions on the part of Hylas, Celadon's pronouncements begin to express a meaning that is entirely contrary to their former intent. Hylas's subversion of meaning can be seen as inscribing in language a new voice, the figure of another. Silvandre's explanation, that when he read these verses, "they were other than they are now" [ils estoient autres qu'ils ne le sont], marks his belief that the former verses alone expressed his amorous ideal. Silvandre's question regarding this sudden alteration of his verses, "how do you think such a new picture could be made so promptly" [pourroit-on avoir fait si promptement un autre tableau] (1:281, 2:200–201), reveals the mutability of language, the fact that small alterations may inscribe images different from, even contradictory to, an author's intent. Thus it is not surprising that according to Diana they are both right: "for in one and the same place, you may find what you both seek; you, Silvandre, may find it written as you did read, and you, Hylas, as you did correct it" [car en un mesme lieu vous trouvez ce que vous cherchez tous deux. Vous, Silvandre, le lisant comme il estoit escrit, et vous Hylas, comme vous l'avez corrigé] (1:281, 2:201). Diana's comment highlights the instability of represented language in *Astrea:* the fact that, despite its supposedly univocal character, language's scriptorial character can be manipulated so as to open up other figurative interpretations.

In *Astrea,* the fragility of communication is most visible in the case of love. The incessant efforts to communicate love, to ascertain it and assure it, reveal its instability as a representation. This instability is literally captured in the novel by the inaugural catastrophic shift in plot: from happiness to disaster. The disaster that befalls Celadon and Astrea is due to their refusal to recognize the allegorical character of love. Astrea forces Celadon to feign love for other women in order to distract attention from their own love. This ruse, however, quickly turns tragic when Astrea becomes convinced that her lover is actually deceiving her. She stops believing in the illusory character of the feint and mistakes it for reality. This error, the mistaking of the feint for reality, reveals the impossibility of containing the meaning of representation in the novel. The failure to recognize the allegorical character of representation leads to the displacement and anagrammatic restructuring of love *(l'amour)* into death *(la mort).*

Celadon's attempted suicide following the heroine's injunction, accompanied by the near death by drowning of the heroine herself, emblematizes the dangerous anagrammatic displacement of *Astrée* into *désastre* and *l'amour* into *la mort.* The novel thus visualizes to the letter the heroine's injunction. The sudden disappearance of the novel's protagonists into the river Lignon, and allegorically into the fabric of the text, makes visible the strategic analogy of the river and the text:

> She believed him to be dead, for *his feet still did lie in the water,* his right arm slackly stretched above his head, and *the left half turned carelessly hanging behind him and caught under his body.* His neck was awry and *folded* forward by the weight of his head which fell backward, his mouth *half open,* and *almost full of sand, dribbled on all sides;* his face scratched and dirty in

some places, his eyes almost closed; and his hair which he wore very long, so wet, that *water ran like a stream from two springs along his cheeks,* whose effaced countenance was the very picture of death. The middle of his back was so bent as to seem *broken,* and that made his belly seem even *more swollen,* though filled with so much water as he once was full of himself. (1:4, 1:16)

Graphically marked by the force of the river, the body becomes grotesque: it is folded, broken, and discontinuous, to the point that its organic identity is lost.[38] The contortion and fragmentation of the body is the trace of the river's figurative force as it reshapes the body. It reconfigures the body's organic form into a highly artificial shape, one akin to the water-spouting statues of the baroque. This contorted reorganization of the body is an expression of the absence of love; that is, a structuring order whose lack becomes the script of disaster *(désastre).* To emphasize the lack of closure of the body, we are repeatedly told that "the water, which he had swallowed, came out again in such abundance" [l'eau qu'il avoit avalée ressortait en telle abondance] (1:4, 1:16), indicating the extent to which the materiality of the body becomes suffused and confused with that of the river.

This consubstantiality of body and landscape, their shared "liquid" nature, suggests that the materiality of the body is conceived according to a schema that does not make solid distinctions between matter and form. The plasticity of water as a medium, its capacity to generate figurative effects through the movement or "rolling of the wave" [tournoiement de l'onde] is equated with the plasticity of the body, whose disfigurement (torsion and irregularity) simply marks another figurative turn in the script. Rather than presenting the body as an autonomous figure, the baroque text represents it as a material surface that, like water, is capable of bearing different reflections, that is, of embodying different figurative effects. In an earlier passage, the fluidity of the water is also equated with the movement of thoughts, "sundry thoughts . . . which floated like the wave" [divers pensers . . . qui flottants comme l'onde] (1:3, 1:12). The centrality of water in this baroque novel thus emerges less as a stylistic conceit than as the expression of a philosophical and poetic outlook, suggesting a notion of materiality that encompasses figurative effects.[39] If Plato denounces poetry as a form of knowledge because he equates it with writing on water, in *Astrea* it is the material fluidity of water as a medium that becomes the figure of the poetic character of representation as it conflates literal and formal effects.

Saturated and rearticulated by the river, Celadon's body appears as a surface upon which the landscape has left its own marks, its own graffiti. His body is a hieroglyph, inscribed upon and written by nature. In turn, throughout the novel Celadon busily inscribes the landscape with signs of his desire, marking upon nature his own graffiti of love. The landscape thus becomes an extensive hieroglyphic text: it is a surface that purveys the traces of his love for Astrea, its "characters" *(chiffres)* (1:198, 1:486). An emblem in the landscape of this baroque novel, Celadon transforms the entire landscape into allegory: it becomes emblematic. Although he can no longer speak to Astrea, these signs speak for him of his desire. His brother, pointing out Celadon's graffiti on a tree, remarks to Astrea: "You recognize only too well his characters" [Vous reconnaissez trop bien ses caracteres] (1:5, 1:20). These engraved letters are marks that visibly speak Celadon's desire, in his absence, since they become literal emblems of his character as a devoted lover.

The correspondence of Celadon and Astrea is an endless series of exchanges problematizing the representation of love: how can one be sure that one is loved, faithful, et cetera, and that one's feelings signify properly? The doubt expressed in this correspondence, which is also a noncorrespondence of sorts, reflects the impossibility of baroque discourse's guaranteeing itself as a representation, since the absence of the writer opens up the letter to unintended interpretations. The letters are relays attempting to frame, but unable to suture, the absence of the other. The problem is that these letters, like the letters of the alphabet, do not belong to anyone in particular. They circulate, and to that extent they can become the mirror of anyone and everyone's desire. Thus, the letters do not merely represent the metonymic character of desire, by supplementing an absence; they also function as the site of a figurative excess whose hieroglyphic character emerges as the insignia of desire.

Celadon and Astrea's love correspondence is intercepted by the nymph Galathea. Upon reading these letters, Galathea's own affection is awakened and she proceeds to project into the lovers' exchange her own desire. The act of reading, of performing the desire of others, leads to her appropriation of the sentiment expressed by the letters. By adding her own letter to the pack, Galathea adds the image of her own desire to the correspondence, thereby appropriating it as a vehicle for her own love. The correspondence between Astrea and Celadon thus becomes the deceptive mirror of three different desires. Celadon's comment upon getting back his bundle of letters— "Oh secretary of my former, happier life! how did you fall into strange hands?" [O secretaire de ma vie plus heureuse! comment t'es-tu trouvé entre ces mains estrangeres?] (1:65, 1:73)—summarizes the alterity that marks all correspondence. As the novel playfully suggests, all letters come from the hands of strangers, including those one has written oneself. Desire in the novel thus emerges as the literal expression of previous desires, an allegorical circuit into whose conventions it writes itself.

The incident of Silvandre's discovery upon his body of Celadon's letter, intended for Astrea, clarifies how language may serve as a medium for self-expression while generating other subjective effects.[40] Upon finding the letter, Silvandre attempts to identify both the addressee and the letter's signer, but both these identifying marks are missing. Instead, Silvandre finds a hyperbolic formula for both address and signature: "Unto the fairest, and most loved shepherdess in the whole Universe" [à la plus belle et plus aimée bergere de l'univers], signed by "the most unfortunate, yet, the most faithful of your servants" [le plus infortuné comme le plus fidelle de vos serviteurs] (1:230, 2:86). These hyperbolic formulas stand in for the proper name, and appropriate its referential function. Silvandre immediately interprets this exaggerated mode of address as the most proper signature of his own sentiments. Seduced by the correspondence between his own exalted sentiments and those expressed by the letter, Silvandre concludes that he must be the letter's true author:

> When he would find therein something resembling what he had once thought (as when different people quite often come across the same conception when contemplating the same topic), he would pose the tip of his finger on that place, and when he would find another, he marked it in the same manner. But, when he found the conclusion of the letter to be thus subscribed, *The most unfortunate, yet, the most faithful of your servants:* Oh! cried he, there is no doubt that it is me who wrote this letter; and it must be, that my good Demon, who has care of my life, having read the thoughts of my soul, has written them in this paper, that I might show them unto Diana. (1:230–31, 2:86)

Both Celadon (author) and Silvandre (presumed author) consider the letter the truest expression of their sentiments, as well as the signatory mark of their unique identity as suffering lovers. As a figure of speech that expresses more than the truth, the hyperbole creates the illusion of a unique referent through poetic exaggeration.[41] To the extent that it invokes something unique, the hyperbole may be seen as a substitute for the proper name. But the referential status of the hyperbole implies an impossible summation, one in excess of represented truth.

Any individual's effort in *Astrea* to appropriate language exclusively by attempting to produce an excess of determination or meaning runs the risk of complete indeterminacy. This risk is reflected by Silvandre's conviction that he is the true author of the letter. This shift in identity is made possible by Silvandre's mistaking the hyperbolic signature for the actual gesture of communication that is open to anyone. Represented language in *Astrea* thus functions as a relay: it has no meaning in and of itself. Its meaning is constituted through its use, instance, and performance as discourse. Silvandre recognizes the ambiguity of the letter when he admits that perhaps his double, a "demon secretary," wrote it: "I found a better secretary than myself" [j'ay trouvé un meilleur secretaire que je ne suis pas] (1:237, 2:99). Silvandre's double, or demon secretary, is a metaphor for the baroque concept of emblematic language, whose auditory and visual echoes purloin the subjective identity of the speaker. While ostensibly embodying the speaker, these echoes embody the figurative character of speech. This demon is a fictional figure, a "double" whose persona is the embodiment of the alien character of speech. Thus, the hyperbole and the demon thematize the problem of baroque poetic speech, since the interplay of literal and figurative effects is recovered in terms of illusion and deception.

Sexuality: The Materiality of Allegory

The representation of gender and eroticism in *Astrea*, involving elaborate disguises and feats of transvestism, has continued to fascinate readers for centuries. What is most striking for the modern reader is the freedom with which characters shift their gender in order to adopt positions that endanger not only their sexual identity, but also their identity as individuals. Genette interprets this depiction of eroticism in the novel as the affirmation of a spiritual ideal that is systematically violated by the actual conduct of the characters.[42] This distinction between spiritual ideal and physical love, however, is not sustained by either the plot or the metaphorical structure of the novel, which consistently conflate and, ultimately, confuse these terms. While Jacques Ehrmann recognizes eroticism as a generator of illusion, he nonetheless persists in the belief in an essentialist eroticism based on the opposition of the sexes.[43] However, as this study of *Astrea* has shown, the distinction between the spiritual and the sensible is eroded through allegory. In an analogous manner, gender distinctions and the identity of the characters are systematically erased through visual disguise and verbal impersonation. The novel begins with actual transvestism, only to culminate with metaphysical travesty, since the characters impersonate each other so successfully that no one is able to tell them apart. In this novel where everything is reduced to feint and fiction, neither eroticism nor identity escapes the allegorical play of representation.

The turning point of the novel comes when Celadon decides no longer to respect to the letter Astrea's injunction not to show himself before her eyes. The solution that is suggested to him, that of disguising himself as a woman, is offered to him as the only way to prove that he is still a man. As the druid priest Adamas explains: "But now that time is expired, you must return unto your self again, and make it appear that you are not only in love, but a man as well" [il est temps que vous reveniez en vous mesme, et que vous luy fassiez poroistre que vous n'estes pas seulement amoureux, mais homme aussi] (1:329, 2:316–17). Transvestism is presented as the solution to Celadon's failure to recognize that he is not merely a pining lover, but a man. Thus transvestism becomes a way of observing the *dictum* of Astrea's law, while displacing its meaning as *interdiction.* Adamas's suggestion that he pass himself off as his daughter, Alexis, demonstrates his literal interpretation of the law: Astrea has not forbidden Celadon to see her, but merely to be seen by her. Celadon's inability to understand how he will fail to be recognized by Astrea is answered by Adamas's interpretation of what it means to be seen:

> Do you think that she can see you, when she does not know you? And how can she know you, when you are in such a habit? —But replied Celadon, let me be habited as you will, I shall be still Celadon in reality; so that I shall thereby truly disobey her.—That you are still Celadon, there is no doubt, answered Adamas, but still you do not by this disobey her command, for she has not forbidden you to be Celadon, but only to show her this Celadon. When she sees you, she will not see you, but Alexis. (1:361, 2:398)

Rather than considering Adamas's argument as a fine example of casuistry, his interpretation provides a significant insight into the mediated character of vision.[44] Adamas points out that the act of seeing is itself codified: sight is based on recognition, on contextualizing perception on the basis of prior knowledge. Celadon's fears about disobeying the *dictum* of the law are answered by an even more interesting argument. In having assumed the external signs of Alexis, Celadon is not challenging Astrea's law, because he alone and not Alexis has been forbidden to show himself. According to Adamas, Astrea did not command that he cease "being" Celadon, only that he stop "showing" her *this* Celadon.

Thus Celadon's persistence in the belief that "a change of clothes does not change the man," is answered by Adamas's claim that disguise does not merely dissimulate, but also creates a new persona. Visual disguise provides a new frame of reference whose referential status is enhanced in turn by linguistic disguise. Adamas's ability first to establish, and then appropriate, the slippery distinction between Celadon's "being" and his "showing" demonstrates his understanding of the plastic character of identity. Adamas's restaging of Celadon's persona reveals his poetic ability to manipulate visual and linguistic codes. In other words, in assuming the signs and language of another, in assuming another position within representation, Celadon can coexist, as both himself and another, as male and female. However, as the novel continues, Celadon's "being," his identity as a man, will be eroded by his "showing," that is, by his appearance as a woman.

While the prevalence of disguise as a theme in baroque novels has been noted, its significance in *Astrea* clearly exceeds its ostensible function as Romanesque convention.[45] In *Astrea*, disguise is not merely a momentary subterfuge for the characters or a mechanism for advancing the plot. Rather, transvestism is presented as a poetic solution to Astrea's visual ban of Celadon. It is important to recall that Astrea's injunction to Celadon, forbidding him ever to show himself before her eyes, may also be construed as a response to his prior visual transgression of Astrea. Disguised as a woman, Orithie, and playing the role of Paris, Celadon abuses his position as judge of a beauty contest by subjecting Astrea to his voyeuristic gaze and by attempting to extort her consent. Although reduced to a passive object, Astrea refuses to praise her own beauty in order to persuade her judge. By refusing to objectify herself as a spectacle for the eyes of the beholder, Astrea succeeds in maintaining a veil over her nudity. Celadon's efforts to violate allegory, by reducing vision to voyeurism, are punished by his reduction to an allegorical object; for Celadon's very existence is predicated upon the fiction that transvestism engenders. Thus, transvestism emerges as the visual analogue of linguistic anagrams: it implies a restructuring of the visual through the manipulation of its frames of reference.

The novel consequently brings Celadon back into the picture as a travestied self, "an other myself" [un autre moi-mesme]. Starting with part 2, Celadon ceases to exist in the world of the novel, and Alexis, his female persona, takes over. Except for moments of self-reflection, Celadon literally disappears into the fabric of the text. His presence is erased through a double transvestism: the masquerade on the level of plot is reinforced by the supporting structure of the narrative, since both the name and the pronouns used to designate the protagonist are female. Rather than merely disguising Celadon, these linguistic markers inscribe in the novel the pervasive presence of femininity, one whose initial figural character threatens to become literal.[46] A new eroticism emerges in the text, one that uses the figurative conventions of female friendship as a relay for conveying a double sexual script, homosexual and heterosexual, at the same time:

> And while saying these words, she [Alexis-Celadon] was kissing her eyes, sometimes her mouth, and sometimes her breast. And Astrea, thinking her a woman, did freely permit it; on the contrary, she was so extremely contented to be thus caressed by one whose face so much resembled Celadon, that she never remained indebted to Alexis for kisses received, as she immediately paid back kisses unto Alexis with double interest. None can express the fullness of this disguised druid's joy. (2:28, 3:598–99)

Scenes such as this have continued to fascinate readers because they scramble the frames of reference traditionally associated with eroticism. The representation of female friendship receives such avid expression as to suggest lesbianism, yet this lesbianism is also the bearer of heterosexual echoes. Astrea's pleasure at being caressed by her dear friend Alexis is doubled by the fact that Alexis is the living portrait of her dead beloved, Celadon. Thus two different sexual scenarios, homosexual and heterosexual, coincide within the script of the same situation. Their coincidence reveals the profound affinity of sexuality with other terms, such as disguise and illusion, that problematize the status of representation in *Astrea*. Rather than considering the eroticism of the novel in Horowitz's terms, as an "essential sexuality entirely independent of gender," it is more appropriate to regard gender as the figurative expression of sexuality.[47] Considered in these terms, the inscription of these two gender positions is merely an index of the figurative character of eroticism in the novel.

Though thrust from the obscurity of desire into the bedazzlement of its fulfillment, "dazzled with too much light" [ébloui de trop de clarté] (1:334, 2:330), Celadon's daily life with Astrea continues to frustrate his desires. The apparent advantage that he has over the situation by being transvested as Alexis is purloined from him by this very disguise. Although he is able to see and talk to her all day, as well as share the intimate rituals of dressing and undressing, this visual and discursive access leaves him unsatisfied. To behold her properly, he wishes that, like Argus, he could have "a body all covered with eyes" [tout le corps couvert d'yeux] (1:334, 2:330). Unable to totally possess Astrea by visually objectifying her into an image, he desires to hear Astrea confirm her own affection, as object of his love. But Celadon's desire cannot be satisfied, since when Astrea sees him, she sees Alexis, and when she expresses her love, her declarations are made to Alexis, his transvested self and *not* Celadon:

> Oh God, said she, that Alexis would be happy without Celadon and that Celadon would be happy without Alexis! Were I really Alexis, and not Celadon, how happy should I be in Astrea's favors, and how much more happy would I be, if being Celadon, she did not bestow upon me these favors

as being Alexis! Was there ever a lover more happy and unhappy than I? (2:30–31, 3:604–5)

Despite his erotic fulfillment, Celadon is unable to enjoy his pleasure. This pleasure divides him by reminding him that its true referent is not himself, but another: Alexis, his disguised self. If he assumes Astrea's ardent love declarations literally, then his own identity is in question as a man. Celadon thus becomes victim of his own feint, insofar as his assumed persona appears to enjoy pleasures denied to him. Thus the mask attains a "reality" that objectifies its putative author. Having attempted to disrupt the structure of allegory by transgressing its limits, Celadon now finds himself reduced to an object of allegory.

The visual and physical pleasure he derives from being with Astrea only confirms his lack of self-possession. Celadon's identity is fractured by pleasure and purloined from him, thereby reducing his body to an "enigma about the object of its pleasure."[48] Rather than designating Celadon, the experience of pleasure only reaffirms his allegorical status as an object fragmented by love.[49] Although Celadon attempts to sort out whether Astrea's love really applies to Alexis, the name or the person, his efforts meet with failure. While Astrea assures him that she loves not the name, but the person—"what it is that I unchangingly love is your person, your spirit, and your merit" [ce que j'ayme sans changement c'est vostre personne, c'est vostre esprit, et vostre merite] (2:179, 4:263)—her response further perpetuates his confusion. The inability to determine whether he is loved as a man or as a woman leads Celadon to question his identity. Meditating upon his condition, Celadon recognizes his dependence on his fictive persona, leading him to conclude that he is a hybrid: "I am then both Alexis and Celadon mingled together" [Je suis donc et Celadon et Alexis meslez ensemble] (2:174, 4:252). This conclusion highlights the extent to which disguise in the novel leads to the actual transformation of the characters, since by assuming other personae, they come to embody different gender positions at the same time. Scripted upon Celadon's body, these gender roles restage his identity as a composite entity, one whose hybrid essence cannot extricate itself from allegory.

Sexuality in *Astrea* thus emerges as the referent not of some intrinsic essence or reality, but rather as the referent of representation, of one's position within it. If transvestism plays such a crucial role in this novel, this is because it reveals that gender is constructed as the composite of a descriptive image and its frames of reference. As a form of impersonation, transvestism involves the appropriation of someone's image and its fictitious circulation by another name and set of expectations. Transvestism thus emerges as yet another mirror through which the novel reflects its emblematic legacy, since it illuminates how the lover's image may become the bearer of two different names: Alexis and Celadon. The problem is not that the image is marked by difference in some intrinsic fashion, but rather that this image can be framed by different contexts and thus be endowed with different sexual traits. The freedom of this baroque text regarding the question of sexual identity is not an ideological freedom. It is a freedom embedded in the novel's emblematic character, in the fact that representation is acknowledged as a convention, the allegorical character of which is always open to further interpretations.

Disguise in *Astrea* does not stop, however, with the reversal of gender, nor with the usurpation of the concept of identity. Rather, the notion of transvestism is pursued *ad absurdum,* until it becomes the vehicle for an erotic solution otherwise unattainable in the text. Not content to resign himself to be disguised as Alexis, Celadon stumbles accidentally upon the possibility of disguising him/herself in Astrea's clothes:

> Love, who offers his followers extreme pleasures, . . . represented to this feigned Alexis such great delight to be in the gown, which covered the body of her beautiful shepherdess, that failing to undress her quick enough, she began kissing her and pressing her tenderly against her own bosom. . . . Carried away with affection, Alexis then took the rest of Astrea's clothes, kissed them, put them on and adjusted them, so that no one would fail to have taken her for a shepherdess. (2:27, 3:593)[50]

For the modern reader, this scene may be interpreted as a classic instance of fetishism, since it reflects the lover's pleasure in a token or substitute object for the beloved.[51] However, such a reading obscures the fact that clothing in *Astrea* does not function as a mere object, as costume.[52] Rather, clothing defines in crucial ways the identity of the protagonists, since like language it may disguise as well as generate illusion.[53] Celadon's pleasure in being dressed in Astrea's clothes is the literal expression of the erotic proximity that he sought all along, with the exception that his metaphorical fusion with Astrea implies his being further split up or divided from himself. The pleasure of impersonating Astrea to the point of "becoming" her involves his own fragmentation into the three personae of Celadon/Alexis/Astrea. Each of these personae embodies competing desires that redefine the scope of sexuality, as well as its perception, by the reader.[54]

Not content to settle for this new disguise, Alexis and Astrea proceed to exchange their clothes and thus exchange their identities. Henceforth, they reverse not only their roles as lovers, but also their roles as individuals, since they decide to banish any action that may establish a difference between them. Initiated by Alexis, this pact formalizes transvestism as a legitimate expression of love in the novel: "I do ordain therefore that *Astrea shall be Alexis*, and *Alexis shall be Astrea*, and that we banish from amongst us, not only all words, but also all manner of actions that may put any *difference between us*" (2:86, 4:44; emphasis added). Alexis's command literally enacts the spiritual union espoused by Neoplatonism, by presenting the transformation of the lover into the beloved. But this Neoplatonic ideal is transcribed literally, since the mutual exchange of the lovers' names mimics their exchange of identities through transvestism. Their mutual loss of selves in each other, accompanied by the loss of their proper names, can only be sustained through an impossible fiction, that of abolishing all differences. Hence, the spiritual ideology that Neoplatonism espoused through the figurative union of lovers becomes in this passage a travesty of identity. Neoplatonism is undermined by its literal embodiment, since its figurative ideal, that of spiritual union, relies on the actual negation of representation and its material reality.

Consequently, *Astrea* presents us with what initially appears to be a contradictory representation of sexuality. On the one hand, the novel seems to reject the notion of sexual difference as a foundational term, as a given physical and social reality. On the other hand, this work also rejects a spiritual ideal that could be seen as an attempt to overcome the notion of difference. How then is the notion of sexual difference to be thought? The answer to this question lies in the way *Astrea* problematizes representation. As this study has shown, the prevalence of disguise ranging from transvestism to a travesty of the notion of identity demonstrates the power of representation not only to dissimulate, but also to create new situations and identities. The freedom that Adamas and later Celadon display in manipulating representation attests to their understanding of its allegorical character: the fact that neither vision nor language can function as exclusive purveyors of meaning. In a scene where Alexis and Astrea exchange their dresses, their discussion about the way they should be retailored in order to fit properly reveals the plastic nature of the representation of sexual difference in the novel. Alexis explains: "We shall do to mine *the opposite of what I must do to yours*, were I to wear it today, for, said she rising to her feet, you can well see that yours is too short for me, but as soon as I *untuck these puffs and pleats*, it will be to my measure; likewise *one must put a tuck in my hem* for it to suit your height" (2:28, 3:597, emphasis added). The small adjustments to be made in the fabric of these two dresses resituate the notion of sexual difference as a figure generated by the untucking and tucking of material folds.[55] The dress emerges as material surface that can be manipulated to engender different figurative effects. The novel thus suggests an alternative model for representing sexual difference, one in which it is conceived as a figurative construct, rather than as a predetermined entity or essential reality. In a novel where everything partakes in illusion, gender is no more real than the reality of fiction. Like the text, or the river into whose folds the characters appear and disappear, sexual difference emerges as an emblematic mark, inscribed as script but figuratively fluid. If sexual difference is otherwise marked in the text, this is because it does not belong to a fixed symbolic order that would reinforce duality, but to an allegorical order whose figurative freedom marks the rhetorical nature of representation. Sexuality thus emerges as a stance within representation, an allegorical fold produced by the emblematic structure of the text.

The legacy of emblematic traditions in *Astrea* is perceptible in the fact that representation is deliberately structured to highlight the allegorical interplay of word and image, of literal and figurative elements. Despite its ostensible obsession with visual illusion and voyeurism, images in *Astrea* (what is seen and how it is seen) are mediated by the discursive frames of reference (what is said or written). For this reason, baroque representation cannot be reduced to a stable frame of reference, thereby liberating the characters and their setting to continued transformations that prevent them from attaining a fixed or defining semblance. Instead of delimiting and prescribing the protagonists and the settings through an essentializing frame, baroque representation retains its openness by presenting things in their relations, rather than the thing itself. As the expression of form in function, it presents a particular manner for apprehending and representing the world. Whether representing the body, setting, speech, or gender, the fluidity and the freedom that define *Astrea* reflect this emblematic legacy to baroque aesthetics, a mediated apprehension of the world, not as image, but as changing semblance.

Part 2

Cartesian Bodies, Virtual Bodies

Chapter 3

The Automaton as Virtual Model: Anatomy, Technology, and the Inhuman

Although less than fifty years separate the publication of Michel de Montaigne's *Essays* (1588) from René Descartes's *Discourse on Method* (1637; published anonymously), the representation of the body in these works is radically different.[1] Considered from a historical perspective this span of time appears relatively short, yet it marks one of the most significant turning points in the conception of the body in the European tradition. For with Descartes we witness surprising new ways for conceiving the body as an anatomical, technological, and philosophical entity. These include the anatomical redefinition of the body in terms of the circulation of blood, its technological resynthesis as a machine, and its philosophical reduction to a material thing. Descartes's elaboration of the duality of the mind and body will relegate the body to an autonomous entity, the objective and mechanical character of which will mark a fundamental departure from previous traditions. As my analysis of Montaigne demonstrated in part 1, the baroque body is conceived neither as an autonomous object nor as a mere instrument. Fully embedded in the fabric of the world, the body functions as the horizon of subjective being and becoming. Contrary to Montaigne, Descartes advances a conception of the body that not only decontextualizes it from its worldly fabric, but, more significantly, replaces it with various mechanical and virtual analogues. In examining the question of the body in Descartes, we must ask ourselves whether we are still talking about the body, as we ordinarily understand it, or about something so altogether different and new as to render obsolete all our previous conceptions. The experiential, lived body in Montaigne's works is replaced in Descartes's works by an artificial, virtual entity that only summarily mimics certain attributes linked to the body. It is precisely this rupture and radical redefinition of the body by Descartes, so radical as to no longer resemble the experiential body, that will constitute the focus of our discussion.[2]

In order to elucidate more precisely the differences in Montaigne's and

Descartes's accounts of the body, a brief summary is necessary. The latter part of the sixteenth century and the early part of the seventeenth century were dominated by a humoral conception of the body, one that does not privilege any of its component fluids. The body's physiological complexion is governed by the interplay and balance of the four humors: blood, phlegm, choler (yellow bile), and melancholy (black bile). Dating back to Galen (Claudius Galenus, A.D. 130–200?), this humoral conception presents an understanding of the body that is flexible and transitive based on the specific combinations and particular mixture of these four fluids.[3] The dominance of any particular humor creates an imbalance that shifts the individual's complexion from health to disease. In Montaigne's *Essays,* this humoral conception of the body inflects its embodied character and reflects its analogical relations to nature, as the juncture of the microcosm and the macrocosm. If the body is defined transitively, that is because its definition shifts in regard to its position and demeanor in the world. Like rivers or seas whose borders fluctuate and shift, the body is neither bounded nor defined as a fixed, self-enclosed entity. Montaigne's fluid interpretation of the body reflects an understanding of its shifting complexion, the result of the interplay of natural and cultural forces. Perceived in the mode of signature and citation, the body is the site of multiple reinscriptions, marking the imprints of both nature and culture and thus reaffirming its vital connections to the world.[4] Rather than being a mere object of observation, the body disposes of forms of agency; it has the capacity to inform and transform the knowledge that the self seeks to attain. The body in Montaigne is not merely the physical body, based on experience, but also the imagined one, constructed by personal desire and mediated by social and cultural institutions.

In contrast to Montaigne's scriptorial body, whose fluid complexion is defined by the interplay of humors, as well as of the personal, social, and cultural imaginary, Descartes presents a radically new interpretation. The Cartesian body is no longer defined by experience, custom, or habit. Reason is its sole guide and defining principle. The role of perception, imagination, and memory will be devalued by their association with the body and notions of embodiment. Their capacity to inform and shape the mind will be in question. I will argue that Descartes's affirmation of the separation of the mind from the body reflects not merely a metaphysical position, but a technological one as well, since it implies the objectification and instrumentalization of the body through its reduction to a mechanical device—a machine. Descartes's definition of the body is based on two newly emergent systems of reference: Harvey's anatomical discovery of the circulation of blood, and mechanical analogies that rely on the mathematization of nature. As this study shows, Descartes's appropriation of Harvey's model for the circulation of blood results in the disembodiment of the body as flesh and its reconstitution as a mechanical analogue. The mechanical organization of the organism supplants its organicity, so that the logic of the automaton as a simulacrum displaces the priority of the lived, experiential body. Descartes's prioritization of rational consciousness based on epistemological principles, as alluded to in the *Discourse* and elaborated exhaustively in the *Meditations,* leads to the errancy and subsequent loss of the body as a site for knowledge. In this and the next two chapters, I demonstrate that it is precisely this convergence of the anatomical, technological, and metaphysical models that generates a new understanding of the body as a virtual entity, an entity whose spectral legacy will continue to haunt the destiny of modernity.

From the Circulation of Blood to Bloodless Machines

> The soul of all flesh is in the blood.
> —Leviticus 17:14

Descartes's account of the circulation of blood in *The Discourse on Method,* part 5, is significant not merely because it purports to give a description of the body based on anatomical principles. Rather, the effort to valorize blood, as opposed to other bodily humors, involves a fundamental shift in the conception of the body. To privilege blood as the defining paradigm of the body is to effect a shift away from its former symbolic centrality in a society founded on the link between sanguinity and nomination, such as we find in kinship structures and paternity, toward a new symbolic order that valorizes blood not only as a figure of hereditary transmission, but also as a system that defines the self-enclosure of the body.[5] Descartes's selective appropriation of Harvey's model for the circulation of blood will lead to the redefinition of the intelligible essence of the body in terms of its material and mechanical functions.[6] Harvey's discovery reflects the emergence of a new concept of medicine, one that no longer relies on the "supposed isomorphism between the cosmic order and the equilibrium of the organism" reflected in nature's presumed powers to correct its own disorders.[7] In contrast to this therapeutics of watchfulness and self-regulation, Harvey's and Descartes's interventions exemplify the emergence of a modern medicine that is activist in orientation, since it relies on an operational approach to the body understood as an autonomous entity.

As opposed to earlier concepts of blood, which did not involve the notion of circulation, in *De motu cordis et sanguinis* (1628) Harvey describes the circulation of blood as a closed circle, thereby preserving blood against consumption. This self-enclosure of blood within the pathways of the arterial-venal system establishes it as an autonomous system of exchange within the body. The continuous and circular movement of blood insures both the preservation and regeneration of the body.[8] Moreover, as a microcosm the circulation of blood reflects the movements of the macrocosm, that of the circular motion of celestial bodies. This analogy of circular motion inscribes the circulation of blood within the framework of the Renaissance and baroque worldviews that sought to establish analogical relations between the microcosm and the macrocosm.[9] Within Harvey's system, the heart emerges as the true sovereign of the body, the guiding principle of life whose movements are perceptible throughout the body in the tangible form of the pulse.[10] Although Harvey compares the heart, in passing, to various mechanical devices (a pump, fire engine, or hydraulic device), these mechanical analogies still reflect an Aristotelian vitalist view regarding the centrality of the heart, rather than a mechanical worldview.[11] It is interesting to note that despite his mechanist tendencies, Descartes does not appropriate Harvey's interpretation of the heart as a pump. He explains the motion of blood as a result of the generation of heat in the heart, a position that he believes to be different from Aristotle's prior formulation.[12]

What may have interested Descartes in Harvey's anatomical model of the circulation of blood is precisely its autonomous character, a closed and self-regulating system of exchange, which redefines the physical closure of the body as material fact. The circulation of blood defines the body as a self-enclosed system whose network character provides the pathways for its mechanical functions. The circulation of blood provides a map for the body; it enables its schematic and figurative representation as a virtual ground-plan that autonomizes the logic of the body, dislocating, separating, and isolating it from the external world as its frame of reference. The capacity of the body to mirror and reflect analogically the macrocosm still present in Harvey's account is disrupted, since Descartes's objectification of the body reduces its capacity to sustain and generate meaning. The body is no longer a mirror of the larger cosmos; it is a mere object whose mechanical logic and material definition reflects his philosophical understanding of nature as inanimate, defined purely as matter, extension, and motion.[13]

The autonomy, centrality, and circuitous nature of the arterial-venal system enables Descartes to provide a physical analogue to the philosophical reflections regarding the centrality and autonomy of the cogito in part

4 of the *Discourse*. Here, Descartes describes the discovery of the cogito as a hypostatic moment based on a fiction of total negation: "And then, examining attentively that which I was, I saw that I could conceive that I had no body, and there was no world nor place where I might be; but yet I could not for all that conceive that I was not."[14] The validity of the cogito is founded on its radical denial of all bodily and material qualities, on their elimination in order to affirm the identity of thought with a new form of existence. The artificial veracity of the cogito supplants, in the realm of existence, the material reality of the body and its place in the world. By defining the cogito purely "as a substance the whole essence or nature of which is to think," and independent of "any place" or "material thing," as well as "entirely distinct from body" (*HR*, 1:101), Descartes removes it from the realm of worldly existence.[15] Thus when the body is brought back to be rejoined to the cogito, its own reality no longer references the same order of existence as the cogito. The body, as described in the *Discourse*, part 5, returns not as an organic entity but as a dissected corpse, whose mechanical logic is associated with the artifice of automata (*HR*, 1:116). The anatomical description of the body in terms of the circulation of blood thus provides a blueprint, an understanding of the body as an apparatus, the intelligibility of which will be governed by material and mechanical laws.[16]

The Automaton as a Spectral Model

> Every metaphysics of man as the protagonist in the *natural theatre* of creation is embodied in the automaton.
> —Jean Baudrillard

The analogy of the human body to mechanical devices was not new to the seventeenth century, but dated back to the late Middle Ages. In his treatise on surgery (1306–20), Henri de Mondeville compares surgery to the mechanical arts, specifically to architecture.[17] More importantly, he goes on to define the body as the "instrument of the soul" and dismembers this instrument, its constituent parts analogous to various mechanical devices involved in artisanal production: the lungs are compared to the bellows of a blacksmith, the elbow to a pulley, et cetera.[18] However, Mondeville's instrumentalization of various body parts preserves the overall organic character of the body, to the extent that these specific parts function by analogy to a generalized understanding of artisanal modes of production, including metaphors that cover the diverse utensils, materials, and products entailed. Moreover, this anatomical description of the body as an organism involves notions of cohesion and social solidarity among the component parts, so that the anatomical body mirrors in its composition the hierarchical structure and bonds of obligation and debt that define the social body.[19] This homology between the human body and its social organization preserves its organic character, since the component parts are connected and tied together under the aegis of the social contract.

Other sources for Descartes's analogy of the organism and the machine date back to Thomas Aquinas's passing metaphorical comparison of animals and clocks, as well as to Gomez-Pereira's claim that animals are machines, lacking any sensitive soul.[20] Sources may even include literary references.[21] Descartes's analogy of the human organism to a machine departs from these earlier formulations, in that the Cartesian machine acquires a new network of meanings. It designates an instrument for the transformation of natural forces or an ordered arrangement of parts that can function autonomously. It can also signify a combination of machines of varying degrees of complexity. In Descartes's time the word *machine* also has an additional meaning, that of a ploy, ruse, or a machination. This latter meaning is implicit in Descartes's use of the machine as an heuristic device, insofar as it functions as the insignia of human ingenuity, of its capacity to manipulate nature and deploy artifice.[22] The machine in Descartes's works is not merely a technical and mechanical analogue of nature; rather, its marvelous, quasi-artistic character attests to the erosion of the distinctions between nature and art. It represents an usurpation of the Aristotelian interpretation of the *organon,* which designates a functional part of the animal, toward a wider notion of functionality by erasing any distinction between organization and fabrication.[23] The Cartesian machine results from the dismemberment of the natural body and its resynthesis, manipulation, and control according to the dictates of a rational model.

In his *Treatise on Man* (written during 1629–33 alongside the *Discourse* and the *World* and published posthumously in 1662), Descartes does not speak directly of man. Rather, when speaking of men he refers to "fictional men," hypothetical analogues intended to cast light on "real men" in the same way that the axiomatic "new world" in the *World* is invoked to illuminate the nature of the "real world."[24] This ghosting and doubling of the human, by positing the priority of a fictional hypothesis in order to elucidate the real, emerges as a strategy of virtualization that enables Descartes to speak of the body not as a lived entity, but as a disembodied technical and mechanical thing. What are initially presented as mere tools for conceptualization, the "fictional men" of the *Treatise,* or the "new world" of the

World, become the theoretical prototypes that will dictate what can be known about "real men" or the "real world." Commenting on the *Treatise,* Canguilhem underlines the deception that Descartes's theory effectuates, since the analogy of the organism with the machine ignores the concrete existence of the lived body in order to substitute for it a rational reconstruction:

> The theory of the animal-machine would, therefore, have the same relation to life that a set of axioms has to geometry, that is, nothing more than a rational reconstruction. Thus the theory operates by deception: it pretends to ignore the concrete existence of what it must represent, and it denies that what it actually produces comes only after it has been rationally legitimized.[25]

But this rational reconstruction of the organism as a machine is itself a construction based on mathematical, geometrical principles. Its legitimacy is derived not from the body that it putatively represents, but from the general mathematization of nature. Its priority relies on the preeminence of epistemology, which, as a theory of knowledge, must precede all other understanding of the world.[26]

Having inaugurated his *Treatise* with the claim that these (fictional) men are composed like us of a soul and a body, Descartes in effect separates the two by considering the body alone. Although he briefly mentions the union of the body and the soul, this topic will be left largely untreated, for the *Treatise* focuses on the workings of the body alone, considered not as a real entity, but as hypothetical, virtual construct:

> I suppose the body to be nothing but a statue or machine made of earth, which God forms with the explicit intention of making it as much as possible like us. Thus God not only gives it externally the colors and shapes of all the parts of our bodies, but also places inside it all the parts required to make it walk, eat, breathe, and indeed imitate all those of our functions which can be imagined to proceed from matter and to depend solely on the disposition of our organs.
>
> We see clocks, artificial fountains, mills and such other machines which, although man-made, have the power to move of their own accord in many different ways. But I am supposing this machine to be made by the hand of God, and so I think you may think it capable of a greater variety of movements than I could possibly imagine in it, and of exhibiting more artistry than I could possibly ascribe to it. (*PWD*, 1:99)

Briefly alluding to the biblical creation of the body as a statue made of earth (Gen. 2:7), Descartes rewrites this mythic origin by suggesting that this body is also a machine deliberately made to resemble the human. His description of the human body as a statue and then as a machine undermines its biblical status as a vessel that is animated by the breath of God. Endowed with the external semblance of the human body, this artificial replica mechanically imitates human functions, such as walking, eating, and breathing. The fact that Descartes includes breathing among these mechanical functions alerts us to the secularization of the body, insofar as it is removed from the sacred purview of the *pneuma* (breath, or soul).[27] This secularization, implicit in the removal of the body from the realm of the creation, is accompanied by its dehumanization. By describing human functions in purely mechanical terms, as proceeding from matter and depending solely on the disposition of the organs, Descartes dehumanizes them to the extent that they cease to refer to the organic reality of the lived body. These mechanical analogues simulate elements involved in the organization of the lived body only to sublate them technologically. This conflation of the material and mechanical aspects of the organization of the body with its overall definition as an organism will lead to the reassignment of the human to the mind, instead of the body.

Descartes's subsequent mention of man-made machines, such as clocks, artificial fountains, and mills that have the power to move of their own accord, serves to underline human technical ingenuity. This allusion to the power of machines as artisanal products in turn is a testament to God's superior productive capacity to fabricate the human body as an infinitely complex mechanical device. According to Descartes's account, God the creator becomes God the fabricator, the consummate artisan who disposes of infinite resources and artistry. The gesture of divine creation that constitutes the realm of the natural world is now redefined as a form of fabrication that indelibly conflates technique and art. The natural world is thus sublated by the artificial logic of the artifact, just as the body is replaced by its mechanical specter—the automaton. As Canguilhem points out: "The intention behind the construction of an automaton was to *copy* nature, but in the Cartesian theory of life the automaton serves as an intelligible *equivalent* of nature. There is no room in Cartesian physics for an ontological difference between nature and art."[28] The Cartesian automaton does not copy nature, but seeks to gain ascendancy over it by becoming its intelligible equivalent. In so doing, it conflates organization with fabrication and erases the distinctions between nature and art. This can be seen in Descartes's claim in *Principles of Philosophy* that "it is not less natural for a clock, made of the requisite number of wheels, to indicate the hours, than for a tree which has sprung from this or that seed, to produce a particular fruit" (*HR*, 1:300).

But Descartes is not content merely to secularize divine creation by equating it with human technical and artistic ingenuity. Nor is he satisfied with eroding the distinctions between nature and art. He goes a step further by suggesting that nature itself, in making animals, has created automatons superior to artificial ones: "Since art copies nature, and people can make various automatons which move without thought, it seems reasonable that nature should even produce its own automatons, which are much more splendid than the artificial ones—namely, the animals" (letter to More, February 5, 1649, *PWD*, 3:366). While Descartes appears to recognize the superior powers of nature, insofar as it produces animals, he considers them to be nothing more than automata that are more accomplished than man-made, artificial ones. In the process, nature as source of creation for animate life is replaced with an interpretation of nature as consummate artisan, whose superior technical achievements represent merely a higher degree of virtuosity measured in terms of a human scale. Descartes's analogy thus suggests that just as art copies nature, so does nature produce artistic artifacts. Considered from this perspective, when art copies nature, it only reproduces processes of production attributed to nature itself. This instrumentalization of nature as technical producer of automata-animals removes from its purview the evidence of its animate character, divesting it of life and vital action.[29]

When Descartes mentions machines to explain how the organism works, he relies on the technical devices of his time: clocks, artificial fountains, water mills, et cetera. But in the *Treatise*, Descartes frames his mechanical analogies for the human organism by presenting them in an elaborate garden setting.[30] Here, grottoes and fountains, constitutive elements of landscape architecture, function as marvelous embodiments of the human body represented as a mechanical system:

> Similarly you may have observed in the grottoes and fountains of the royal gardens that the mere force with which the water is driven as it emerges from its source is sufficient to move various machines, and even to make them play various instruments or utter certain words depending on the various arrangements of the pipes through which the water is conducted.
>
> Indeed, one may compare the nerves of the machine I am describing with the pipes in the works of these fountains, its muscles and tendons with the various devices and springs which serve to set them into motion, its animal spirits with the water that drives them, the heart with the source of water, and the cavities of the brain with the storage tanks. Moreover, breathing and other such activities which are normal and natural to this machine, and which depend on the flow of the spirits, are like the movements of a clock or mill, which the normal flow of water can render continuous. (*PWD*, 1:100–101)

If God created man in the Garden of Eden, Descartes re-creates the body using the marvelous artifices of the gardens of his time as a paradigm for the human body.[31] Instead of simply describing the body in mechanical terms, he now stages its workings as the unfolding scenography of a garden landscape. The mechanical complexity that underlines Descartes's description of the human body is represented as a veritable feat of landscape architecture and engineering, a complex system that weaves in its conceptual fabric various kinds of machines, the structural and hydraulic principles of which ensure continuous motion. The human body is represented as a composite of various technical devices, parts of it operating like springs and others operating like channels and storage tanks, that is, conduits for the flow, pressure, and circulation of blood and the animal spirits.

What is notable in Descartes's discussion is the fact that the system for the circulation of blood also doubles as the carrier of animal spirits. The animal spirits represent the most rarefied and subtle parts of the blood that are separated through a process of mechanical filtration (based on the smallness of pores) into the pineal gland situated in the brain cavity (*PWD*, 1:100).[32] These minute corpuscles "cease to have the form of blood," since they attain an almost immaterial status. Their subtlety or fineness is such that they take on the character of a "very fine wind" or rather a "very lively and pure flame" (*PWD*, 1:100). Descartes also makes an analogy between the nerves and the system of pipes underlying a garden. He models the nervous system on the arterial-venal system, suggesting that neural circulation follows a hydraulic model involving tiny doors or valves placed in nerves (*PWD*, 1:107). The nerves are animated by the passage of animal spirits that have the power to change the shape of muscles (*PWD*, 1:100). Descartes thus mechanizes the nervous system by automating its functions, in order to explain its physiological processes in terms of the activity of the animal spirits. What is ingenious about the Cartesian model for the human body is that its hydraulic circuitry simultaneously accounts both for the circulatory and the nervous system, at the same time that it serves as a conduit for the animal spirits, intangible substances that visibly animate the body.

Descartes pursues his analogy of the human body with the gardens of his time, comparing external objects and their capacity to stimulate sense organs with garden visitors who unwittingly trigger mechanisms that set an elaborate spectacle in motion:

External objects, which by their mere presence stimulate its [the body's] sense organs and thereby cause them to move in many different ways depending on how the parts of its brain are disposed, are like visitors who enter the grottos of these fountains and unwittingly cause the movements which take place before their eyes. For they cannot enter without stepping on certain tiles which are so arranged that if, for example they approach a Diana who is bathing they will cause her to hide in the reeds, and if they move forward to pursue her they will cause a Neptune to advance and threaten them with his trident; or if they go in another direction they will cause a sea-monster to emerge and spew water onto their faces; or other such things according to the engineers who made the fountains. (*PWD*, 1:101)

Instead of presenting sense perception in technical terms, Descartes restages it as an elaborate spectacle whose theatrical character is intended to illustrate its mechanical underpinnings. The artifice of the hydraulic machine functions here as an analogue for the human, displacing the priority through the display of the illusionistic artifice that mimics it. The choreographed movements of these devices triggered by the movements of the spectators suggest not only their autonomous existence, but also the illusion of personality and even psychology, insofar as these figures appear to respond and interact. The seemingly autonomous movements of these machines create the illusion of agency, they mechanically ghost the human, since they appear to be moving as if by their own accord.

Descartes's representation of the workings of the human body by means of this scenographic garden display recalls the presentation of the anatomical body made available through the spectacle of display afforded through dissection.[33] In both these cases, the human body itself is rendered invisible insofar as it makes itself available as a display of complex mechanisms composed of specific mechanical parts and devices.[34] For Jean-Claude Beaune the Cartesian automaton is a theoretical instrument, a virtual model that elides through its mechanical displays its intervention as a heuristic device: "Most of all, the automaton is a spectral model, a sort of *theoretical microscope* enabling a 'sighting of depth': the anatomy and the internal movements are *seen* across the corporeal envelope, supposedly negligible, as one would see the wheels of a machine."[35] The opacity of the body as a corporeal entity is rendered transparent by the automaton, its spectral and mechanical analogue. Considered from this perspective, the body is no longer the means for the world's disclosure, for its autonomization as a machine supplants its corporeal character by substituting for it an organizational, mechanized logic.

In the conclusion to his *Treatise on Man,* Descartes returns to his earlier elaboration regarding the relation of bodily parts to their requisite functions by reiterating his materialist and mechanist position: "these functions follow from the mere arrangement of the machine's organs every bit as naturally as the movements of a clock or other automaton follow from the arrangements of its counter-weights and wheels" (*PWD*, 1:108).[36] These functions proceed solely from matter and the disposition of the organs, understood as the wheels and cogs of a machine. The capacity for movement, which generates the illusion of agency, is based solely on the internal arrangement and disposition of bodily parts and does not require an external principle of animation. As Descartes subsequently explains, these organic functions permit the machine to be conceived without recourse to a "vegetative or sensitive soul or other principle of movement and life, apart from its blood and animal spirits" (*PWD*, 1:108).[37] Descartes here rejects the medieval conceptions of the soul as vegetative and sensitive entities that animate the body, in order to emphasize the purely material and mechanical nature of the body. According to Stephen Gaukroger, Descartes's aim was to show that certain psychophysiological functions that had already been recognized as corporeal could be accounted for in a manner that did not render matter sentient.[38]

Ferdinand Alquié observes that Descartes's rejection of these medieval conceptions of the soul prepares the mechanized body for the reception of the soul, understood as a unique entity whose sole function will be that of being rational and intellectual.[39] Descartes's identification of the soul with reason alone goes against the Renaissance vitalistic or animistic interpretation of nature, where the soul permeates the universe and is identified with life.[40] Earlier in the *Treatise* Descartes notes that "when a *rational soul* is present in this machine it will have as its principal seat the brain, and reside there like the fountain-keeper" (*PWD*, 1:101). The rational soul resides in the mechanized body as the ghost in the machine, the centralized fountain-keeper, sole agent and administrator of the mechanized functions of the body. The immaterial presence of the rational soul that haunts the automated body controls its bodily and material manifestations. As Descartes later explains to Regius (letter of May 1641), "There is only one *soul* in human beings, the *rational soul*; for no actions can be reckoned human unless they depend on reason" (*PWD*, 3:182).[41] The rational soul becomes the only point of reference for the human, for all forms of agency achieve their humanity through their dependence on reason alone. Thus the locus of the human becomes the mind alone, defined as consciousness, intellection, and volition. The removal of agency from all aspects of the body and its equation with a machines will bring it within the purview of animality, understood no longer as a natural phenomenon but as the ultimate embodiment of artifice and mechanics. Descartes considers animals to be like clocks, that is, machines governed by the disposition of their organs and not by reason (*HR*, 1:117).[42] Thus the reification and secularization of the human soul to a purely rational entity, accompanied by the total mechanization of the corporeal body, runs the risk of a materialist reduction, of the evacuation of all spiritual elements, since they may be perceived purely as effects engendered through material causes. Although Descartes denies that his rejection of the sensitive and vegetative soul will open the way for atheists to deny the presence of even a rational soul in the human body, the rise of French materialism in the eighteenth century, as attested by the writings of Julien Offray de La Mettrie and the marquis de Sade, will prove otherwise.[43]

In part 5 of the *Discourse on Method*, Descartes proceeds to recapitulate the mechanical analogies elaborated in his *Treatise on Man* by reaffirming the equation of the body to automata and moving machines. He also reiterates his earlier contention, elaborated in the *Treatise*, regarding the analogy of the body to a machine, as product of human industry and invention, only to reaffirm the superiority of the human body as a product of divine industry (*HR*, 1:115–16). The perfectibility of the human body as a machine brings Descartes back to the question of how to distinguish the human from its mechanical analogues. If there exist such machines, capable of both resembling our body and simulating its actions, then a fundamental question arises regarding how to distinguish the human from its inhuman, mechanical doubles:

> On the other hand, if there were machines which bore a resemblance to our body and imitated our actions as far as it was morally possible to do so, we should always have two very certain tests by which to recognize that, for all that, they were not real men. The first is, that they could never use speech or other signs as we do when placing our thoughts on record for the benefit of others. . . . And the second difference is, that although machines can perform certain things as well or perhaps better than any of us can do, they infallibly fall short in others, by the which means we may discover that they did not act from knowledge, but only from the disposition of their organs. (*HR*, 1:116)

In this passage, the machine-body analogy reveals its troubling implications, insofar as the possibility of mechanically simulating the human body raises the specter of an inhuman double that could come to haunt it. The body's dispossession of its human qualities by the machine implies that the human must be forcefully relocated and redefined as an attribute of the immaterial mind—the "ghost" in the machine.[44]

Descartes's appeal to speech or signs as the distinguishing mark of the human relies on his valorization of reason. However, the reason in question here is no longer the disembodied thought of the cogito, defined by its self-identity and transparency, but rather of an embodied reason that makes itself visible and perceptible precisely because of its communicative, representational, and intersubjective character. As Jean-Pierre Séris points out: "The *loquela,* the speech, performance and usage proper to human language is the unique and certain indicator of the presence of a soul that thinks in the bodies of others."[45] Séris's emphasis on language as the defining characteristic of the human is based on Descartes's explicit references to language in the *Discourse* and in his correspondence.[46] However, Descartes's appeal to speech and signs suggests a more general appeal to the subject's capacity for representation understood as the manipulation and recording of signs, be they verbal or nonverbal. As Descartes observes in the *Discourse,* even the deaf and dumb are able to use signs to make themselves understood (*HR,* 1:117). Descartes's statement regarding man's use of speech and other signs locates the humanity of the subject within the realm of representation. However, the representation of ideas involves the use of material signs and thus modes of linguistic or nonverbal embodiment. Despite Descartes's earlier denial of the body as the locus for the human, his affirmation of the subject's humanity through representation inescapably reintroduces the material traces of the body and embodiment within the purview of rational subjectivity.

Descartes's second distinction between the human and the machine relies on his critique of the machine as a thing whose capacity to act is limited precisely because of its purely instrumental character. But it is important to keep in mind that when Descartes criticizes the instrumental nature of the machine, he is also necessarily alluding to his earlier equation of the body to the machine. He goes on to claim that, while reason is a universal instrument that can serve all contingencies, organs need special disposition or adaptations for each particular action.[47] Hence, Descartes concludes, it is impossible that there would be sufficient diversity in any machine to act in all events of life (*HR,* 1:116). Thus while machines may be able to perform certain functions better than we do, in the end they are limited by the fact that they do not act out of knowledge but simply out of the disposition of their organs. Descartes's critique of the machine serves as a strategic device to highlight the omnipotence of reason as the true and sole referent for the human. It also underlines the subservience and dependence of the body on reason, that spectral entity which informs and controls the body's workings.

Struggling against the simulacral verisimilitude of the automaton, Descartes locates the human in a knowledge that derives not from the logic of the organism, but rather that supersedes the organic, since it governs its very mechanisms. In so doing, he underlines the superiority and autonomy of reason as a faculty that is independent of the material and mechanical organization of the body, since the rational soul "could not be in any way derived from the power of matter" (HR, 1:118). While Descartes recognizes that it is insufficient to think of the rational soul as "lodged in the human body like a pilot in his ship," and that it is "necessary that it should also be joined and united more closely to the body" (HR, 1:118), the Discourse will provide no further details about how their conjoined nature could even begin to be thought. Descartes's final conclusion that "our soul is in nature entirely independent of the body" (HR, 1:118) will make it all the more difficult to envisage and mediate their relation. The rational soul's ultimate autonomy from material and bodily reality implies that it functions in an entirely different realm of existence. Having radically severed the relation of the mind to the body, Descartes's subsequent efforts to suture their division will continue to pose problems throughout his later works.[48]

Descartes's insightful and powerful comments regarding the distinctions between the human and the machine bring out the fundamental paradoxes that underlie his conception of the body, and that continue to haunt contemporary discussions as well. Descartes's first test for identifying the human with the capacity for representation, understood not merely as speech but as the ability to communicate and embody ideas through non-verbal signs, enters into conflict with his second test, which involves the limited instrumentality of the machine as material artifact.[49] If representation signifies the capacity for embodiment, for attaining material manifestation through signs, then the limited or specialized performance of the body as material artifact could no longer be construed in opposition to the mind. The material limits of the body would merely reflect a condition to which reason is subject as well, to the extent that it seeks to define and communicate its own nature. For the capacity of the mind to engage in representation is not a virtual event, but becomes perceptible and communicable through material signs, thereby bringing reason within the horizon of the body. Thus Descartes's insightful and pioneering effort in the Discourse, his test to distinguish between the human and the machine raises questions that will remain implicit in his subsequent elaboration of the mind-body dualism in the Meditations.

As the next chapter will demonstrate, the problem that continues to haunt the Cartesian system is that of conceptualizing the notion of embodiment, finding a mediation between a disembodied reason and the mechanized body. Descartes's initial anatomical schematization of the body through the circulation of blood, and his subsequent resynthesis of the natural body as a machine dismembered from the mind, emerge as instances of a process of virtualization that document the ascendancy of the automaton over the experiential body. This virtualization of the body attains its philosophical culmination in the *Meditations,* where Descartes elaborates a metaphysical framework that first casts into doubt, only to supersede altogether, the horizon of the experiential body. Haunted by an errant, disembodied mind, the triumph of these virtual bodies over the lived body will raise the specter of the inhuman as one of Descartes's most significant legacies to the modern age. As the later chapters will demonstrate, this virtualization of the body as physical entity will entail the aggressive resolidification of the body as the object of practical discourses that will attend to its administration.[50] The dehumanization of the lived body, as physical organism, by the machine will enable its instrumentalization and incorporation into the discursive and institutional frameworks of newly emergent disciplines in the sciences, politics, and the arts.

Chapter 4

Spectral Metaphysics:
Errant Bodies and Bodies in Error

> For I am one of those who deny that man understands by means
> of the body.
> —René Descartes

Descartes's *Meditations on the First Philosophy* are puzzling to the extent
that the ostensible aim of demonstrating the existence of God and the distinction between the mind and the body is underlain by the haunting invocation and recurrent appearance of errant, spectral, and mechanical bodies.
From Descartes's insistent appeal to the presence of his own body, seated by
the fire with paper in hand, we find increasingly estranged representations of
the body, ranging from sleeping bodies to mad bodies haunted by specters
of automatic men.[1] This insistent focus on bodies in the context of meditations is surprising, to the extent that its earlier counterparts, such as Loyola's spiritual exercises, used contemplation exclusively to gain access to the
divine.[2] Descartes's *Meditations,* however, present a philosophical account
of a mental journey the stages of which are marked by a process of progressive disembodiment, toward the inauguration of the birth of a rational, sec-
ular subject.[3] Given the metaphysical thrust of the *Meditations,* as evidenced in its efforts to define subjectivity according to rational criteria, the
persistent denunciation of the natural body as a site for error and its concurrent reappearance in the form of alienated or mechanical bodies is troubling and invites further inquiry.[4]

In this detailed reading of the *Meditations,* I follow the trajectory of the
body both as a conceptual construction and as a rhetorical and metaphorical figure. From the very inception of the *Meditations,* the radical critique of
the lived, experiential body emerges as the pivot that enables the emergence
of a metaphysical discourse that seeks to define human ontology within a
theological horizon. The progressive philosophical virtualization of the
lived body, culminating in its material disappearance, coincides with the

lived body's insistent reappearances as spectral, disembodied, or mechanical apparitions. The proliferation of errant bodies in the *Meditations* will be examined as a function of Descartes's derealization of the body and, hence, as a manifestation of the larger problem of embodiment that haunts the work. The reintroduction of the body and the material world at the end of the *Meditations* will not resolve, nor correct, the initial erasure of the body from the content of rational subjectivity. Having defined the scope of rational subjectivity outside the purview of the body, the difficulty of addressing the issue of embodiment will emerge as one of the most troubling legacies of this compelling work.

Rather than reexamining and recapitulating the major arguments regarding the passage from ordinary doubt to hyperbolic doubt, the *sum* argument, or the arguments for the existence of God, which I have treated extensively in my earlier work on Descartes's elaboration of subjectivity, this study of the *Meditations* examines them as a function of the body and notions of embodiment.[5] For instance, the analysis of the hyperbolic doubt argument will focus not merely on Descartes's radicalization of doubt, but rather, on the form that doubt will take in the guise of the evil genius. This propensity for error that defines the condition of the natural subject will be resolved by an appeal to a fictional and axiomatic entity, the evil genius, whose capacity for total embodiment and deception will remove the burden of doubt associated with the ordinary condition of the subject as an embodied entity.

Similarly, the "piece of wax" argument will not be read simply as an argument for the unreliability of the senses, but as evidence of the difficulty of conceiving the body, not as mathematical abstraction, but as an embodied nature. This mechanical reduction of perceptual processes will foreclose the possibility of a phenomenological access to the horizon of perception. Descartes's belated efforts at the end of the *Meditations* to reembody the rational subject through the reintroduction of the senses, along with imagination and memory, will prove to be a failure given the fundamental incompatibility between the definition of the nature of the mind and that of the body. Although not specifically intended as a reflection on the body, the *Meditations* suggest powerful new insights into the representation and legacy of Descartes's conception of the body. They make visible the pivotal role that the erasure of the lived body plays in the elaboration of the metaphysical underpinnings of a subjectivity that can only sustain itself by containing the representation of the body as a virtual entity, defined by the confines of a mathematical-geometrical system.

From the very beginning of the *Meditations,* the question of doubt and error is inalienably linked to the body. The quest for certitude, for the foundations of a discourse of truth counters the evidentiary obstacle presented by the body and the senses: "All that up to the present time I have accepted as most true and certain I have learned either from the senses or through the senses; but it is sometimes proved to me that these senses are deceptive, and it is wiser not to trust entirely to any thing by which we have once been deceived" (*HR*, 1:145). Descartes begins by recognizing the significance of the body as a conduit for knowledge, insofar as learning proceeds from or through the senses. This momentary affirmation of sensorial experience is quickly supplanted by the ghostly traces of possible deception or error. The fact that the senses are sometimes deceptive leads Descartes to call them into question altogether and thus remove the body from the purview of knowledge.[6] This initial affirmation of the body and of experience as a source for knowledge is particularly interesting, since it represents Descartes's unique, albeit provisional recognition of knowledge as embodied experience. The removal of the body as an obstacle to true knowledge engenders not merely its loss to a theory of knowledge, but the corollary loss of embodiment as a constitutive paradigm.

This disqualification of the body, not merely as instrument but as conduit for knowledge, reflects the impact of scientific developments in the seventeenth century, those of the Copernican revolution, and the research and production of new scientific instrumentation.[7] The counterintuitive discovery that the earth moves around the sun is supplemented by optical experiments with lenses that prosthetically enhance and expand the horizons of the senses. The testimony of the senses is undermined by forms of mathematical or technical evidence that supplant experience and the immediacy of perception.[8] The living body ceases to function as a site both for knowledge and as a generator of meaning, since the perceptual realm is being replaced by notions of cognition that function in either purely virtual or technical realms. The knowledge that the body supplies will be found to be contingent and partial, and thus irreducible to a universal paradigm or governing model. This is why perception in the *Meditations* will be in question both as external and as internal fact, for its evidentiary nature will be deemed to be deficient and disruptive, and thus fragmentary and insufficient for any rational philosophical synthesis.

The First Meditation is marked by the paradoxical interplay of two opposing representations of the body. On the one hand, Descartes's advances the immediacy of his own bodily presence as evidence of the persuasive power of the senses; on the other hand, he uses his bodily presence as a representation intended to cast doubt on the validity of all sense perception. In this second instance, his bodily presence functions as a site for deception, ranging from madness to dreams, suggesting that all forms of sensorial evidence must be cast into doubt:

> For example, there is the fact that I am here, seated by the fire, attired in a dressing gown, having this paper in my hands and other similar matters. And how could I deny that these hands and this body are mine, were it not perhaps that I compare myself to certain persons, devoid of sense, whose cerebella are so troubled and clouded by the violent vapors of black bile, that they constantly assure us that they think they are kings when they are really quite poor, or that they are clothed in purple when they are really without covering, or who imagine that they have an earthenware head or are nothing but pumpkins who are made of glass. But they are mad and I should not be any less insane were I to follow examples so extravagant. (HR, 1:145)

Presented in the first person, this passage reinforces the reader's attention not merely on the present, but on the bodily presence of the speaking subject of the *Meditations*. The fact of Descartes's bodily presence brings into focus the author of the *Meditations* as an embodied subject whose evidence as a material and physical entity is presented as a rhetorically unassailable fact. I say rhetorically, rather than philosophically, since it is precisely the evidence of the senses and of the body that have already been in question and placed under radical erasure through the bias of a totalizing negative fiction in the *Discourse*. Descartes asks us rhetorically as to how he could deny the evidence of his bodily presence. He is quick to reassure the reader that such a denial is in the order of madness.[9] But the threat of madness that Descartes conjures up in regard to the denial of the senses is a purely rhetorical gesture, since that precise denial was enacted very simply and categorically in the *Discourse,* in the hypostatic formulation by which he could feign that he had no body, that there was no world, "or any place he might be" (HR, 1:101).[10] Thus what is interesting about the *Meditations* is precisely the fact that bodily presence is affirmed first as the evidence of the sensorium, as an affirmation of the persuasive powers of the perceptual realm, only to be denounced later as a dangerous lure capable of deluding the perspicacity of the mind.

The question that Descartes asks in this passage is, however, crucial to his philosophy. Let us repeat this question as we read along with the text: "And how could I deny that these hands and this body are mine?"[11] How in fact can this denial be operated, for it would imply not merely the threat of alienation or even madness, but an even more radical gesture of dispossession, that of the loss not merely of our own body as we know it, but of its facticity as it is experienced by others. However, the evocation of self-deception and madness in this passage takes place in the context of a strangely reassuring experience; for Descartes relies on the performative evidence of his own intimate representation, attired in a dressing gown, pen and paper in hand to suggest the difficulty that he, and by extension the reader, would encounter in its denial.[12] The madness that Descartes is invoking here has as its precise object the possibility of the subject's disavowal of its own body, a maddening contention that Descartes will audaciously pursue, against the reassuring background of his self-presentation and performance as an embodied subject.[13]

If denying the evidence of the senses risks the threat of madness, their naive affirmation will be proved to be a matter of illusion or even delusion. Descartes pursues his argument by reminding himself of his own humanity, particularly by suggesting that he can conjure up representations of himself by the fire or even more extravagant ones in his sleep than in a state of madness.[14] The sensorial evidence of his own presence by the fire is now framed by the doubt that such a representation does not refer to the external world, but to the interior world of dreams leading him to conclude that "there are no certain indications by which we may clearly distinguish wakefulness from sleep" (HR, 1:147).[15] However, the problem is not merely one of distinguishing the states of sleeping and wakefulness, but of accounting for the veracity of the sensorial content present both in wakeful and dreaming states. Whether it is a question of the physically experienced or imagined body, these representations of embodiment are equally compelling in their respective realms of wakefulness or sleep, thus casting into doubt the reliability of all sensory data. Descartes's invocation of dreams here is particularly interesting, since during sleep the body becomes in a certain sense "disconnected" from the mind. It is precisely the body's physical immobilization and its shutting down of the external world that coincides with its mental errancy, its illusionary freedom to embody itself in different guises by defying the conventions of space and time.

Descartes goes on to hypothesize that he is asleep in order to consider the nature of the sensorial representations he experiences in dreams, while recognizing that "possibly neither our hands nor our whole body are such as they appear to us to be" (HR, 1:146). Having uncovered the doubtful character of external sense perception, he now proceeds to explore the nature of doubt as it applies to internal perceptions. While denying any direct reference between the waking and sleeping world, Descartes suggests that the "things which are represented to us in sleep are like painted representations," which could only be formed as "counterparts of something real and true" (1:146). Pursuing this painterly analogy, Descartes goes on to suggest that these imaginary representations of eyes, a head, and hands refer less to actual bodies in the external world, since they may be merely a composite medley, than to "some other objects yet more simple and more universal that are real and true" (1:146).[16] Thus the imagined body in dreams is disembodied and virtualized, insofar as its referential reality comes to be constituted less by its perceptual semblance than by its abstract generalization as a corporeal nature. As Descartes explains: "To such a class of things pertains corporeal nature in general, and its extension, the figure of extended things, their quantity, magnitude and number" (1:146). But this notion of universal corporeality no longer references the reality of the lived body as an embodied entity, but rather the certitude of a mathematical system that schematizes the body in the same way that it treats all other objects of inquiry. Descartes proceeds to reify the lived body, first by undermining its veracity through association with the errors of sense perception; and second, by questioning its reality as the imaginary entity of dreams, only to suggest its tenuous existence as a virtual entity whose hypothetical character is that of a mathematical object, a disembodied thing lacking the very indices of corporeality.

As Descartes is quick to admit, those sciences that have for consideration the nature of "composite things are very dubious and uncertain," whereas arithmetic and geometry treat things so very simple and very general that without ascertaining whether things are "actually existent" they can attain some measure of certainty and indubitability. It would seem that the difficulty of determining the existence of the body, be it the physical or the imagined one, is a consequence of its composite, embodied character. Only the disembodiment of the body and its reduction to a hypothetical thing can guarantee, not necessarily its existence in the world, but its virtual existence within a system of mathematical certitude. Given this fundamental dismissal of the body as a phenomenological and psychic entity, due to its consistent identification as the site of error, the meditating subject must now contemplate the ultimate deception, the fact that it may not be the subject, but rather the object of a deception enacted by someone else. This shift in agency between being subject, as opposed to object, of doubt is essential insofar as it reveals the fundamental epistemological impossibility of resolving the question of doubt within the confines of the embodied subject. It is only by positing an exteriority that exceeds the limits of the lived body, by fictionalizing doubt in the guise of the evil genius who acts as supreme deceiver, that the lived body will be purged of the specters of error attached to the manifestations of its own agency.

The Evil Genius: Fiction and the Loss of the Body

> Thinking, like writing and painting, is almost no more than
> letting a givable come towards you.
> —J-F. Lyotard

It is in the context of the hyperbolization of doubt that the possibility of a total doubt imposed by an exterior agent arises. First identified with God, only to be later conveniently reassigned to the fictitious persona of the evil genius, the possibility of a total, all-encompassing doubt comes into view:

> Nevertheless I have long had fixed in my mind the belief that an all-powerful God existed by whom I have been created such as I am. But how do I know that He has not brought it to pass that there is no earth, no heaven, no extended body, no magnitude, no place and that nevertheless [I possess perceptions of all these things and that] they seem to me to exist just exactly as I now see them? (*HR*, 1:147)

Descartes concludes that although it is contrary to God's goodness that he should thus be deceived, yet it is also true that he does "permit me to be sometimes deceived" (1:147).[17] It is from the fact that he is subject to occasional error that Descartes proceeds to produce the fable, first of God, and later the "double of God": the evil genius whose function is to enact upon the meditating subject the possibility of a total deception.[18] This fictitious being removes the burden of agency from the meditating subject, as well as the problem of occasional error tied to its ordinary existence as an embodied subject, by inflicting upon the subject from the outside the incapacitating web of an absolute and totalizing deception.

Descartes goes on to suppose the existence of the evil genius, who employs all his energies to deceive him and renders the world and all external things mere illusions or dreams, elaborate traps of his credulity: "I shall consider myself as having no hands, no eyes, no flesh, no blood, nor any senses, yet falsely believing myself to possess these things" (*HR*, 1:148). This hypothetical disavowal by the meditating subject of its own embodied nature, involving the progressive self-mutilation of its body and senses, enables the meditating subject to escape precisely those errors and deceptions to which it is subject by virtue of its embodied character. The meditating subject annuls, as it were, its condition as subject of error and experience, by submitting itself to the agency of the evil genius. As an agent of total deception, the evil genius possesses an infinite capacity for embodiment, since it can mislead the subject that considers itself as having no hands, no eyes, or no body, into believing that he or she is still so incarnated. Such a deception is no longer in the realm of human error, but within the purview of a metaphysical deception whose fictive character undermines the referential capacities of the real.[19]

Thus the creation of Cartesian subjectivity in the *Meditations* is mediated by a special representation, that of the evil genius—a representation of fiction par excellence. Its totality is not in the order of error, deception or madness, but rather in the hyperbolic leap of reason through which the meditating subject attempts to escape the possibility of error attached to its embodied condition. The hypothesis of the evil genius is no ordinary hypothesis, not merely for theological reasons, but for philosophical reasons as well. As a self-posited and self-defined proposition this hypothesis shares affinities with other types of axiomatic discourse, such as we encounter in mathematics and logic. However, this hypothesis also has a figurative and fictional character, insofar as the figurative reach of the hyperbole becomes the basis for a contract that the subject enacts with the evil genius, its fictive counterpart, through the medium of rhetoric in order to posit itself as an originary point before all determinations of its particular modes of existence. The totalizing power of the hyperbole as a rhetorical gesture thus arches both before and beyond subjectivity and becomes the index of its purely rhetorical existence. The hyperbolic audacity of the evil genius is to postulate the possibility of a totality that spares nothing, neither bodily "or intellectual perceptions, thus overriding the limitations of the meditating subject as an embodied and reasoning entity."[20]

In the Second Meditation, Descartes obsessively returns to his earlier formulations of hyperbolic doubt by stating again that he has persuaded himself that nothing exists of all that fallacious memory represents to him.[21] His passing mention of memory expands his earlier critique of the senses and dreams, since memory contains and preserves the traces of the meditating subject as an embodied entity. He restates that he possesses no senses, and that body, figure, et cetera are but fictions of his mind. Descartes then proceeds to elaborate the *sum* argument, establishing the certitude of his existence no longer by relying upon thought as a founding premise, as he did in the *Discourse,* but by virtue of the deception perpetrated by the evil genius:

> I myself, am I not at least something? But I have already denied that I had senses and a body. Yet I hesitate, for what follows from that? Am I so dependent on body and senses that I cannot exist without them? But I was persuaded that there was nothing in all the world, that there was no heaven, no earth, that there were no minds nor any bodies: was I not then likewise persuaded that I did not exist? Not at all; of a surety I myself did exist since I

persuaded myself of something [or merely because I thought of something]. But there is some deceiver or other, very powerful and very cunning, who ever employs his ingenuity in deceiving me. Then without doubt I exist also if he deceives me, and let him deceive me as much as he will, he can never cause me to be nothing so long as I think that I am something. So that after having reflected well and carefully examined things, we must come to the definite conclusion that this proposition: I am, I exist, is necessarily true each time I pronounce it, or that I mentally conceive it. (*HR*, 1:150)

In the articulation of the *sum* argument, Descartes moves quickly away from an argument for existence based on a model of self-persuasion, which would be liable to internal deception, toward a determination of existence founded on an external deception enacted upon him by the evil genius.[22] The *sum* argument strips away not only all bodily qualities, but also mental attributes, since the earlier arguments regarding dreams and madness have rendered even mental content suspect to deception.[23] Defined as a proposition of pure existence, "I am, I exist," the representation of subjectivity fostered by the *sum* argument represents an impossible reduction, a hypothetical zero point, attained through the fictional and rhetorical virtualization of the notion of subjectivity.[24]

Engendered through the decentering figurative reach of the hyperbole, this zero point of subjectivity, defined as pure existence, is so general that it makes it difficult for the subject to properly identify itself and not mistake itself for some other object: "But I do not know clearly enough what I am, I who am certain that I am, and I must be careful to see that I do not imprudently take some other object in place of myself" (*HR*, 1:150). Descartes's expressed prudence, however, is not merely a reflection of his fear of contaminating the indubitable nature of the certitude attained regarding his existence. Rather, the problem is that this certitude regarding existence does not provide one with any particular knowledge about oneself. This proposition regarding existence is so general that it makes it impossible for the meditating subject to locate and identify its own specific content. The purely virtual existence of the subject endangers its capacities for recognizing itself as a specific entity, thereby generating the possibility of both error and errancy, of mistaking oneself for something else. For this reason, Descartes must backtrack in his argument to what he formerly believed, to his belief in being a man, in order to reconstitute the content necessary to reembody or reincarnate himself as a particular subject.

Eschewing the Scholastic definition of man as a reasonable animal, which would require further inquiry into the meaning of these terms, Descartes proceeds to consider his own thoughts in order to derive an understanding of his own being.[25] He begins with a description of his body that is so clinically remote as to suggest that he is speaking in the third person. The body is itemized with such complete detachment that its personal attachment to the speaker comes into doubt: "In the first place, then, I considered myself as having a face, hands and arms, and all that system of members composed of flesh and bones as seen in a corpse which I designated by the name of a body" (HR, 1:151). Thus, when the body is brought back in the *Meditations* in order to be rejoined to the subject, defined as pure existence, its own nature has changed, for the body returns not as an animate entity, but an artificial, mechanical one. Thus another body comes onto the scene, one whose prosthetic logic organizes mechanically a cadaver. Having been derealized as subjective agency, the body returns as brute physical fact, as a thing whose purely material and mechanical nature excludes all forms of agency and memorial imprints, such as we saw in Montaigne's formulation of the body.

When Descartes goes on to specify the nature of his existence, he focuses on thought as the sole attribute that belongs inseparably to him.[26] Thought is now reintroduced into the *sum* argument, no longer a founding premise that enables the elaboration of the existence of the subject as in the case of the cogito argument, but as an attribute or characteristic that defines the existence of the subject as a thinking thing *(sum res cogitans).*[27] In the context of the *sum* argument thought itself is objectified, since it returns in the guise of a thing. The reintroduction of thought here serves to preserve it from contamination by forms of error and deception that the meditating subject encountered earlier in the *Meditations.* However, the problem is to identify the nature of this thinking thing, or as Marin Mersenne argues in *Objections II:* "but you do not know what this thinking thing is" (HR, 2:25). This thought that appears in the mode of a thing is one that is difficult to know precisely because its disembodied character does not reference any corporeal natures.[28] If Descartes begins to speak about the imagination at this point, this is precisely because he seeks to identify clearly the disembodied nature of thought.[29] Descartes goes on to specify that the knowledge and certitude he possesses of his own existence does not depend on the imagination, nor those things he can feign in imagination:

> An indeed the very term *feign* in imagination *(effingo)* proves to me my error, for I really do this if I image myself as something, since to imagine is nothing else than to contemplate the figure or image of a corporeal thing. But I already know for certain that I am, and that it may be that all these images, and, speaking generally, all things that relate to the nature of body are nothing but dreams [and chimeras]. (HR, 1:152)

This dissociation of thought from the imagination is very significant insofar as Descartes seeks to preserve thought from the errors and illusions of the imagination. However, since Descartes defines the imagination as the contemplation of a figure or image of corporeal things, its removal from the realm of thought associated with certitude suggests that his definition of thought is disembodied, for nothing corporeal is known to exist in it.[30] It is only later in Meditation Six that the separation of the body and soul will be formalized, culminating in the assertion that the essence of the soul is in thought alone and that the body cannot think.

In trying to specify further the nature of his content as a thinking thing, Descartes modifies his earlier formulation by introducing the imagination and the senses as powers or modes by which the mind thinks. But this reintroduction of the imagination and the senses not as faculties but as modes of thought is confusing to the extent that it appears to cast into question the incorporeality of the mind: "What is a thing which thinks? It is a thing which doubts, understands, [conceives], affirms, denies, wills, refuses, which also imagines and feels" (HR, 1:153). In this second formulation of the *sum res cogitans* argument, understanding is included as a mode alongside imagination and sensation. Stephen Gaukroger notes that this second characterization of the thinking thing must be qualified, since the inclusion of such corporeal faculties as imagination and sensation (which also pertain to animals) threatens the specificity of the human mind. He identifies the distinctive character of human cognition as an awareness of one's mental states.[31] However, this modal expansion of thought does not redefine the priority accorded to the disembodied mind, for to do so would imply, as Guéroult suggests, the substitution of an ordinary psychological consciousness for mathematical-rational intelligence.[32] Descartes's subsequent demonstrations in the *Meditations* support this contention, insofar as he maintains the indivisible nature of the mind as opposed to the divisibility of the body (HR, 1:196). Moreover, the elaboration of the wax argument, which immediately follows this discussion, will prove that the understanding alone, and not the imagination and the senses, belongs to the true order of the mind.

Descartes advances the argument of the piece of wax as a means of testing the naive belief that objects known through the senses and the imagination are better known than those truths that he has established regarding his "real nature," such as his definition of the subject as a thinking thing. The argument pits the limits of sensorial and imaginative evidence against the abstract cognition of the understanding. In so doing, Descartes elucidates the nature of the thinking thing through a particular analysis of the modes of thinking in relation to external bodies. The tangibility of the piece of wax becomes paradigmatic of the immediacy and presence of corporeal bodies, of their rhetorical force as bodies available to the senses:

> Let us take, for example, this piece of wax: it has been taken quite freshly from the hive, and it has not yet lost the sweetness of the honey which it contains; it still retains somewhat of the odor of the flowers from which it has been culled; its color, its figure, its size are apparent; it is hard, cold, easily handled, and if you strike it with the finger, it will emit a sound. Finally all the things which are requisite to cause us distinctly to recognize a body, are met within it. (*HR*, 1:154)[33]

The piece of wax represents the total gamut of perceptual qualities in all their immediate eloquence: those of taste, odor, color, figure, size, and sound.[34] The clarity and distinction of these perceptions is, however, quickly undermined once Descartes brings this piece of wax into the proximity of fire, since taste is exhaled, color altered, figure destroyed; size increases and the wax liquefies to the point where it can no longer be held. While Descartes ascertains the permanence of the wax after this change, he concludes the impermanence of the senses to provide us with reliable information, since what was perceptible in one form is now perceptible under others.[35] When he proceeds to abstract "all that does not belong to the wax," he discovers that "nothing remains except a certain extended thing which is flexible and moveable" (1:154): that is, an abstract conception that he will assign to the mind alone, rather than to the senses or the imagination.[36]

Before being altogether swept away by the persuasive elegance and simplicity of this argument, let us backtrack for an instant, for the argument of the piece of wax proves less the unreliability of the senses than the problem of thinking the body not as a mathematical abstraction, but as an embodied nature.[37] The difference in perceptual experiences that qualify the two states of the wax reflects precisely the fact that the wax is not only matter defined abstractly as extension, flexibility, and movability, but that it has particular configurations in its various physical manifestations. The differences in perception involving the particular states of the wax at two different moments attest less to the deceptive or illusory aspects of perception than to the problem of universalizing perception across time. The problem posed by the piece of wax as a body is its multiplicity in its various physical states and temporal manifestations. The choice of wax in this context is particularly telling, since its malleability and flexibility as a substance implies that it can take on multiple configurations or embodiments. Whereas earlier in his writings Descartes argued for the passivity of the senses by using the analogy of the imprint of a seal on wax, here in the *Meditations* he uses the wax in its multiple embodiments to argue the failure of perception to provide meaningful information about the world. In so doing, he redefines the wax as a thing that is no longer a body. Now defined as an "extended thing," this "same wax" no longer references the phenomenal world, but rather the immaterial reality of a geometric and mathematical schematism. This geometric description of the wax as an extended thing does not describe it as a body in the world, since this geometrical notion of thinghood is so general as to defy embodiment. This reification and disembodiment of the wax, through the removal of its perceptual qualities as a body, leads to its mathematical virtualization. As it recedes from the realm of perception, it becomes ghostly and spectral, since its reality is no longer defined by the physical world, but rather by its capacity for being instrumentalized in order to confirm and find adequation in the virtual realm of mathematical schematism. Thus the validity of the senses and experiential reality are radically undermined through this homology between the mind and the order of mathematical schematism.

Following the wax argument, which concludes with the affirmation of the powers of the understanding or the mind, Descartes returns in a last-ditch effort to consider the power of vision. As the noblest sense, vision is singled out precisely because its perceptual qualities of clarity and distinction rival the mind's own ambitions to attain such mental intuitions in its search for certitude.[38] Since the perceptual clarity of vision stands in competition with the mind's conceptual clarity, Descartes will suggest that the validity of perceptual vision is based on an ultimate illusion, an elaborate, artificial chimera engendered by automatic machines pretending to be human.[39] He concludes the wax argument by positing a highly theatrical and contrived spectacle:

> From this I should conclude that I knew the wax by means of vision and not simply by an intuition of the mind; unless by chance I remember that, when looking from the window and saying that I see men who pass in the street, I really do not see them, but infer that what I see is men, just as I say that I see the wax. And yet what do I see from the window but hats and coats which may cover automatic machines? Yet I judge these to be men. (*HR*, 1:155)[40]

This spectral parade of automata that mimic humans by appropriating their vestments in order to pass by Descartes's windows is disconcerting, not in terms of its deliberate intent to cast doubt on our faith in vision, but because it reveals something fundamental about Descartes's usurpation of the senses, the body, and what it ultimately means to be human. What is inter-esting about Descartes's example is precisely the fact that it is paradigmatic of his general strategy in the *Meditations,* since the invocation of the virtual or the machine as fictive entities functions to reveal the deceptive and illu-sionistic character of visual and other forms of perception. These automatic machines are in fact embodiments of Descartes's reductionist account of the body, with the exception that they are here given an agency and the ability to haunt the human by impersonating it. The simulacrum appears to gain on the real, not merely by supplanting it, but by mimicking it so successfully as to destroy reality itself as a frame of reference. Like the evil genius, the double of God who can perpetuate the ultimate fiction of a total deception, so do these automatons undermine through their fictional verisimilitude the human world of perception and the material world that it references.

As Descartes's attempts to strip the automatons of their hats and coats, in order to denounce the artifices and deceptions perpetuated by vision, the body has ceased to be in question, having been replaced by a machine. Descartes's subsequent claim to strip the wax to its bare essentials as a body, to "distinguish the wax from its external forms" as if he "had taken from it its vestments" in order to consider it in its "naked" form, reveals that both the notion of the body and that of embodiment are evacuated in the process.[41] Ostensibly an argument about the force of perception, insofar as it engages with the world in the guise of bodies in order to affirm the valid-ity of the mind alone as the site for true knowledge, the wax argument sun-ders both the subject's relation to the world, and by extension to its own body, effectively evacuating it from the world. The world is thus derealized, transformed into chimeras whose spectral and ghostly nature taunt and undermine the possibility of any human reality. These automatons and machines adumbrate the anamorphic, virtual reality of a posthumanist world whose technological essence defines itself through impossible fictions, hypotheses of inhuman conceits.

Is It Human?

> For the exclusive prioritization of consciousness is of course a
> kind of madness.
> —Francis Barker

What then remains of the human, when it has been stripped not only of per-ception but of its very connection with and embeddedness in the world? The

Third Meditation outlines this new condition of the subject, as it meditates upon its own solipsistic, almost apocalyptic existence:

> I shall now close my eyes, I shall stop my ears, I shall call away all my senses, I shall efface even from my thoughts all the images of corporeal things, or at least (for that is hardly possible) I shall esteem them as vain and false; and thus holding converse only with myself and considering my own nature, I shall try little by little to reach a better knowledge of and acquaintanceship with myself. I am a thing that thinks. (*HR*, 1:157)

The meditating subject blinds itself to the world by closing its eyes, it cancels the intrusion of the world by stopping the ears, and more radically, it even erases the internal traces of the world in the mind by effacing from thought all images of corporeal things (as if this were possible) by esteeming them as vain and false. The attempt to efface all images of corporeal things is intended to erase the imprint and memory of the bodily traces of the world that populate the mind of the introspective subject. Thus this self-mutilatory stripping of the subject through the severance of all connective ties to the world is enacted both externally and internally. This violent and forcible removal of the subject from the fabric of the world coincides with the introspective closure and enfolding-over of the subject onto itself into a private conversation that the subject undertakes with itself. However, this radical deracination of all bodily things from the subject and denial of its embodied character uses a model of introspection, only to deny alterity as possible content or result of self-reflection. It is important to recall that in Augustine's *Confessions*, introspection is a model for faith, rather than self-understanding, and that it functions as a vehicle for an encounter with the alterity of the divine.[42] Moreover, as the earlier discussion of Montaigne's *Essays* indicated, the introspective examination of the self leads invariably to the discovery of the other, to the redefinition of the self in an intersubjective mode. For Montaigne, it is precisely the solitude and isolation of the self that reveals to the self its embodied character in the writings of others, bearing within itself the estranging script of its worldly and cultural history.[43] Breaking with these traditions, the Cartesian model for introspection seeks to establish through self-reflection the rational essence of the meditating subject.

Descartes's effort to get to know himself "by holding converse only with myself," recalls the Platonic definition of thinking as a discourse that the mind carries on with itself without spoken sound. But as Merleau-Ponty reminds us, the meditating subject's effort to engage with itself through conversation, by seeking an invisible intimacy with itself, implies an impossible transparency: "We must accustom ourselves to understand that 'thought' (cogitatio) is not an invisible contact of self with self, that it lives outside this intimacy with oneself, *in front of us,* not in us, always excentric."[44] His reminder serves to alert us to the fact that the transparency that the Cartesian subject seeks with itself is illusory, insofar as thinking, understood as this internal conversation or dialogue, necessarily implies the use of signs, of forms of material mediation that are "excentric" to the extent that they imply the alterity of intersubjective exchange and the use of embodied signs. The subject's effort to come to know itself as a thinking thing thus brings back the previously excluded world, insofar as the internal reflection of thought cannot sustain itself without the support of some form of worldly embodiment.[45]

It is interesting to note that Descartes's contemporaries Arnauld and Gassendi, in their objections to the *Meditations* questioned the wisdom of Descartes's account of the mind to the exclusion of the body. In the Fourth Objection, Arnauld cautions that it is not clear to him that a knowledge obtained by excluding the body from one's essence is either complete or adequate (HR, 2:83). Gassendi in the Fifth Objection is even more pointed, for he questions Descartes's exclusion of all corporeality from his thinking essence, including the introspective, self-reflective turn of the mind: "But what if the mind is unable to turn towards itself or towards any idea without at the same time turning itself towards something corporeal, or represented by a corporeal idea?" (HR, 2:192). Gassendi's question addresses the very fallacy of the Cartesian account of the mind presented above, to the extent that it sought to autonomize thought and affirm its transparency. Although Descartes affirms the self-identity of thought by severing its relations to the body and carries this operation to its hypothetical extreme by effacing from the mind all images of corporeal things in order to deny its embodied character, his thought remains within the inescapable horizon of the body. But the philosophical and rhetorical illusion that the mind can free itself of the body, that there can be a thinking without the body, will continue to persist both for him and for the tradition.[46]

Although Descartes tries, through the reintroduction of other elements of his subjective existence as modes of thought, to specify his nature as a thinking thing, as one who doubts, affirms, denies, wills, desires, and also imagines and perceives, this reintroduction of modal content is secondary to his primary claim regarding the self-identity of thought. This strategy of reintroduction is by no means intended to restore our conventional understanding of the subject as an embodied entity. Rather, the belated reintroduction of the material world and the body in the Sixth Meditation coincides with their reappearance as mathematical objects and takes place in the context of the elaboration of the separation of mind from the body.[47] Descartes opens the Sixth Meditation with the claim, "Nothing further now remains but to inquire whether material things exist. And certainly I at least know that these things may exist insofar as they are considered as the objects of pure mathematics, in this aspect I perceive them clearly and distinctly" (HR, 1:185).[48] The reintroduction of the material world in the guise of mathematical objects—that is, as virtual entities devoid of any sensorial or embodied character—signals Descartes's persistent effort to maintain the separation between the virtual world of cognition and that of the material world made available through imagination and perception.

When Descartes considers attentively the imagination, he finds that "it is nothing but a certain application of the faculty of knowledge to the body which is immediately present to it, and which therefore exists" (HR, 1:185).[49] This passing comment that derives the existence of the body from the imagination is deceptive, given Descartes's initial rejection of the imagination as a foundational term and his later qualification that the existence of the body can only be derived from the imagination as conjecture or probability (1:187).[50] Having attempted to recognize the imagination as a mode of thought in the Second and Third Meditations, he now goes on, however, to establish a radical distinction between the imagination and intellection.[51] Taking the example of the chiliagon, a thousand-sided geometric figure, Descartes underlines the limited capacity of the imagination to visualize this virtual figure, as opposed to the conceptual grasp attained through pure intellection (intellectionem).[52] This leads him to remark that "this power of imagination which is in one, inasmuch as it differs from the power of understanding, is in no wise a necessary element in my nature, or in [my essence, that is to say, in] the essence of my mind; for although I did not possess it I should doubtless ever remain the same as I now am" (1:186). Compared to the understanding that comes to constitute the essence of the mind, the imagination is marginalized because of its turn toward the world, since "it depends on something which differs from me" (1:186).[53] The imagination is presented as extrinsic, even incidental, to the essence of the subject defined in terms of the self-reflexive mind.[54]

Descartes's critique of the imagination references directly the question of the body. He goes on to specify that the imagination differs from pure intellection precisely because of its engagement with the body: "as mind in its intellectual activity in some manner turns on itself, and considers some of the ideas which it possesses in itself; while in imagining it turns towards the body and there beholds in it something conformable to the idea which it has either conceived of itself or perceived through the senses" (*HR*, 1:186). The mind's self-reflective inspection of itself excludes the body, which is relegated to the domain of the imagination.[55] For Descartes, the imagination involves this turn toward the body, in order to confirm something previously conceived or perceived through the senses. However, as Descartes subsequently notes, the existence of the body cannot be deduced from the imagination other than as probability or conjecture (1:186–87). Hence the idea of corporeal nature derived through the imagination proves to be insufficient for the elaboration of a philosophical argument regarding the existence of the body. While the reintroduction of the imagination into the subjective content of the meditating subject involves the recognition of its bodily character, this claim does not modify in any substantive sense Descartes's previous philosophical position regarding the self-identity of the mind and its distinction from the body.

Upon their reintroduction by an appeal to commonsense experience, the senses and the body fare no better than the imagination. While Descartes admits to having persuaded himself that he "had no idea in his mind that had not formerly come through the senses" (*HR*, 1:188), this insight rapidly leads him to a radical critique of the unreliability of the senses. Similarly, his admission that his body belongs to him is undermined by the subsequent affirmation of the separation of the mind from the body. It is through the senses that Descartes forms the belief that his body belongs to him, and that he cannot be separated from it, as from other bodies: "Nor was it without some reason that I believed that this body (which by a certain special right I call my own) belonged to me more properly and more strictly than any other; for in fact I could never be separated from it as from other bodies" (1:188). This sense of belonging that qualifies the sensorial experience of the body affirms less the inseparability of the body proper than the sense of separation experienced in relation to other bodies. Descartes's difficulty in articulating how the body belongs to him and his inability to describe the nature of that bond other than by an appeal to a "certain special right" whose nature is left unelucidated reveal the dilemma posed by embodiment. It also serves to alert us to the absence of a system of mediation that would bridge the gap between the senses and the subject's experience of itself.

The reintroduction of the senses in the Sixth Meditation results in their final dismissal, since Descartes uses his experiences to uncover the errors and illusionism of sensory perception:

> But afterwards many experiences little by little destroyed all the faith which I had rested in my senses; for I from time to time observed that those towers

which from afar appeared to me to be round, more closely seemed square, and that colossal statues raised on the summit of these towers, appeared as quite tiny statues, when viewed from the bottom; and so in an infinitude of other cases I found error in judgments founded on the external senses. (*HR*, 1:189)

The multiplicity of experiences with their various even contradictory sensory content leads him to conclude their total unreliability.[56] It is precisely because experience is embodied as multiple and apparently discontinuous representations, that he is led to conclude the error of the senses.[57] But the problem here concerns less the senses than Descartes's incapacity to conceive the variable and changing nature of experience.[58] Descartes uses experience both to claim the deceptive nature of the senses and to cast experience itself into question, as an evidentiary system capable of generating an objective—that is, a universal and consistent—understanding of the world.[59] The multiplicity of experience fragments, by its partial and framed perspectival character, the illusion of a unified and coherent subjective vantage-point that would be continuous temporally and spatially. The error in the judgment based on the senses suggests not only the embodied nature of sensorial experience, but also a fundamental discontinuity and cognitive incoherence in the viewing subject insofar as it is also an object in the world.

If the senses prove to be deceptive with regards to the external world, the internal perceptions regarding the body's own awareness and knowledge of itself prove no less unreliable.[60] The internal experience of the body is proved to be as much the subject of error as that experience provided by the external senses. Taking as an example the mutilated body of an amputee, Descartes derealizes the referential reality of pain by describing it as the effect of a phantom limb:

And not only in those founded on the external senses, but even in those founded on the internal as well; for is there anything more intimate and more internal than pain? And yet I have learned from some persons whose arms and legs have been cut off, that they sometimes seemed to feel pain in the part that has been amputated, which made me think that I could not be quite certain that it was a certain member that pained me, even though I felt pain in it. (*HR*, 1:189)

He attempts to show that the reality of pain does not reference the body directly, since pain is experienced by the amputee as a reflection of the subject's prior embodied condition.[61] Despite its immediacy, its intimate and personal character, the experience of pain appears to designate not merely the reality of the physical body, but also that of the imagined body.[62]

Descartes's example thus suggests less the unreliability of internal sensorial experience than the fact that the body it references may be a multiple entity. Internal sense perception disrupts the unity of both the subject and the body not through deception per se, but by making visible the embodied condition of the subject in terms of multiple referents. The undecidability between the physical and imagined body renders the evidence of the internal senses problematic, insofar as it disables the subject from grasping the certitude of its own body as a single and unified totality. Thus the question regarding the doubtful character of internal sense perception reveals a far more fundamental problem concerning both the referential instability of the body and its plural existence as diverse modes of embodiment. After having disqualified the senses, both in terms of external and internal perception, Descartes returns to his earlier elaboration of the subject as a thinking thing by noting that no other thing necessarily pertains to his essence: "my essence consists solely in the fact that I am a thinking thing [or a substance whose whole essence or nature is to think]" (1:190). This reaffirmation of his earlier conclusion that he is a thinking thing, however, is intended not only to define the essence of the meditating subject, but also to establish definitively the separation of the mind from the body:

> And although possibly (or rather certainly, as I shall say in a moment) I possess a body with which I am very intimately conjoined, yet because, on the one side, I have a clear and distinct idea of myself inasmuch as I am only a thinking thing, and as, on the other, I possess a distinct idea of body, inasmuch as it is an extended and unthinking thing, it is certain that this I [that is to say, my soul by which I am what I am], is entirely and absolutely distinct from the body and can exist without it. (1:190)

While restating the possibility that he possesses a body to which he is intimately conjoined, Descartes reiterates the two things that he knows with certitude, since he possesses a clear and distinct idea of them: on the one hand, that he is a thinking thing, and on the other hand, that he has an idea of the body as an extended, but unthinking thing.[63] However, Descartes is not content to merely affirm these two notions separately; he goes on to emphasize explicitly the distinct separation of the soul from the body and concludes by stating that the soul can exist without the body.[64] This latter conclusion does away with the body as material support by upholding the soul's independence and autonomy from the body and suggests its immortality, its capacity to escape, by virtue of its immaterial nature, all material and worldly constraints.[65]

This radical claim regarding the separation of the mind from the body makes it difficult, even impossible, to think the nature of subjectivity as an embodied entity. Given the chasm between the immateriality of the soul and the materiality of the body, the effort to mediate between them by thinking their union emerges as one of the most problematic sites in Cartesian philosophy.[66] Although a few pages later Descartes will stress the substantial union and intermingling of mind and body, this effort to reintegrate the two remains unconvincing:

> Nature also teaches me by these sensations of pain, hunger, thirst, etc., that I am not lodged in my body as a pilot in a vessel, but that I am very closely united to it, and so to speak so intermingled with it that I seem to compose with it one whole. . . . For all these sensations of hunger, thirst, pain, etc., are in truth none other than certain confused modes of thought which are produced by the union and apparent intermingling of mind and body. (*HR*, 1:192)[67]

As opposed to his *Treatise on Man*, where he described the rational soul in its relation to the body-machine as a fountain-keeper, Descartes seeks here to change his position. In his reply to Arnauld's objection, Descartes explicitly states that he wants to avoid the inference that "man was merely a spirit that makes use of a body" (*HR*, 2:102).[68] Such an inference would imply precisely what Descartes has suggested all through the *Meditations*, that the mind as pure spirit "haunts" the body by disposing of it as a mere vehicle. Moreover, given Descartes's prior critique of internal sensation, and especially of the doubtful nature of pain insofar as it references the body, it now becomes difficult to recoup pain as the insignia of the substantial union of the mind and the body.[69] The fact that there may be an interaction between the mind and the body does not clarify, nor does it necessarily attest to, their substantial union.[70] Thus Descartes's attempt to reembody himself, so as to compose a whole with his own body, conflicts with his prior claims regarding the philosophical centrality and metaphysical exclusivity of the mind.[71] The mind's essential definition in terms of thought and exclusive of corporeality renders the conceptual task of reinfusing it and intermingling it with the body difficult, if not altogether impossible.[72] For it is precisely the description of the body as an unthinking and extended thing, and the lack of a theory of embodiment, that hinders the body's substantial reconnection to the mind.

Descartes's subsequent analogy of the human body to a clock observing the laws of nature, his description of the body as a machine, reveals tangibly the dilemma of integrating the mind into a mechanical system: "if I consider the body of a man as being a sort of machine so built up and composed of nerves, muscles, veins, blood and skin, that though there were no mind in it at all, it would not cease to have the same motions as at present, exception being made of those movements which are due to the direction of the will, and in consequence depend upon the mind [as opposed to those that operate at the disposition of its organs] . . ." (HR, 1:195). The analogy of the human body with a machine, where the organic components are reduced to mechanical counterparts, implies an objectification of the body that deprives it of any possible agency. Operating purely as a mechanism, such a body functions by virtue of the disposition of its organs, independently of the mind.[73] The appeal to the will, and thus by extension to the mind, only serves to underline the difficulty of locating these forms of human agency within the logic of the mechanism. These forms of agency appear to haunt the mechanism, as an afterthought. The disembodiment of the body into a machine, a purely mechanical analogue of an organism, removes the body from the surrounding world and undermines its ability to inform and communicate with the mind. While the mechanization of the body renders it available as an object of knowledge, it forecloses the possibility that the body may function as an agent and site for mediating knowledge. It is precisely the objective clarity of the mechanized body that elides its capacity to be reconnected either with the mind or with the world. When Descartes later specifies that the body is by nature divisible and the mind indivisible (1:196), this fundamental re-affirmation of their difference makes it even more difficult to imagine how two such different natures may be intermingled and connected so as to attain a substantial union.

At the end of the *Meditations* something surprising happens. Descartes mentions laying aside hyperbolic doubt, not only to recognize that the senses may indicate more truth than falsehood, but more significantly to reflect on the role of memory, a term previously devalued in the text.[74] But Descartes is not interested in considering memory itself as a faculty, but rather in positing memory as an answer to the earlier question that he posed himself regarding the distinction between waking and sleeping states. Memory proves to be instrumental to the identity of the rational subject, for it provides the temporal continuity necessary for the perceived existence of the meditating subject in time.[75] According to Descartes, the role of memory is that it "can never connect our dreams with one another or with the whole course of our lives, as it unites events which happen to us awake" (HR, 1:199). It is memory that provides the bridge for the Cartesian subject to extend and expand its rational dominion, by providing a horizon for both synthesis and continuity otherwise unavailable to it. It is memory that supplies the temporal horizon of the waking subject:

And, as a matter of fact, if someone while I was awake, quite suddenly appeared to me and disappeared as fast as do the images which I see in sleep, so that I could not know whence the form came nor whither it went, it would not be without reason that I should deem it a specter or phantom formed by my brain [and similar to those I form in sleep], rather than a real man. (1:199)

The specter or phantom that haunts Descartes, the sudden apparition and disappearance of a man that he is unable to contextualize either in terms of origin or destination, captures the very drama of the Cartesian text. At issue is less the manifest distinction that he seeks to draw between the states of wakefulness and sleep than the far more fundamental problem that the very subject of the *Meditations*, as it is defined to date, is like the spectral entity that he conjures up as the effect of his dreams. Without memory, without the capacity of dwelling in time, the rational subjectivity of the *Meditations* remains purely punctual and discontinuous.[76] It is only by contextualizing perceptions and connecting them with the course of his life through memory that Descartes can assure the position of the waking, rational subject.

This appeal to and inscription of memory, which appears almost as an afterthought at the end of the *Meditations*, alerts us not merely to its significance, but also to the impossibility of maintaining the rational subject in its disembodied condition. Although throughout his earlier writings and his correspondence Descartes has denounced and even rejected the role of memory, his reintroduction of memory at this point demonstrates precisely how necessary memory is, both in terms of locating the subject in time, and in enabling it to connect a variety of experiences. Memory ensures the perpetuation of the self-identity of the rational subject. As the faculty that makes it possible for an individual to retain and recall past experiences into consciousness, memory involves images, impressions or thoughts, embodied imprints capturing the semblance of the experiential world, which Descartes up to this point has radically called into question. Along with the imagination, which Descartes associates with the body, these memorial traces record the condition of the subject as embodied nature.

By severing the relation of the mind and the body in the *Meditations*, and reintroducing only belatedly and as an afterthought the imagination and memory into the content of subjectivity, Descartes undermines the possibility of their functioning as a site of mediation for the mind-body duality. It is precisely the exploration of the sensorial character of the imagination that could provide insight into the embodied nature of the subject. Considered as a system of inscription and transcription, memory offers a scriptorial model that would enable the subject to record and transmit its embodied nature.

Without imagination and memory to capture and transmit its embodied imprints, the Cartesian body is bereft of any ability to communicate with, inform, or connect with the mind. By depriving the body of any agency through its summary equation with a machine and by overlooking the conceptual implications of both the imagination and memory insofar as they may provide models for embodiment, Descartes reduces the body to a mute existence as a pure, material thing. Despite his insistence on the substantial union of the mind with the body in the *Meditations,* his metaphysical definition of the subject as a thinking thing will undermine his subsequent efforts to reintegrate it within the material and technical fabric of the body. The effort to think and situate the body and its relation to the mind would require a theory of embodiment whose representational character would imply the radical redefinition of both the body and the mind.

Insofar as the *Meditations* represent the metaphysical culmination of his earlier elaborations of the body in the *Treatise on Man* and the *Discourse,* they make explicit Descartes's progressive virtualization of the lived, experiential body. Ranging from the anatomical schematization of the body through the circulation of blood, to its technical reorganization as a machine, and to its ultimate philosophical reduction to a material entity devoid of all agency, the priority of the lived body and its experiential realm are systematically eroded. As this study has shown, the elaboration of the metaphysical framework of the *Meditations* relies not only on the progressive erasure and dehumanization of the body, given its associations to error, but also on its ultimate disappearance, insofar as it ceases to be essential to the definition and existence of the thinking subject. Thus, it is precisely the metaphysical framework of the *Meditations* that constitutes the decisive obstacle toward the reintegration of the body into the Cartesian system.

If bodies, be they sleeping, mad, automatic or spectral, persistently haunt the *Meditations,* their errant and elusive traces attest both to the erasure of the experiential body and to its inevitable return in the guise of virtual and spectral apparitions. Just as Plato's cave functioned as the allegorical apparatus for the projection of truth, so does the body in Descartes's *Meditations* function as a horizon and apparatus of projection that stages the elaboration of rational subjectivity. Plato's effort to free truth from its simulacral and deceptive semblances, those of shadows, phantoms, and reflections on water, is echoed in Descartes's own attempt to free subjectivity from an error by disengaging it from its deceptive semblances and errant apparitions. Thus, the virtual, spectral bodies that haunt the *Meditations* emerge as the insistent traces and reminder of subjectivity as an embodied condition. For this condition to become not only explicit, but also philosophically necessary and inevitable, will require the overturning of the Cartesian meta-physical edifice and its subsequent legacies.[77] As chapters 6 and 7 will demonstrate, the development of French materialism in the eighteenth century, as elaborated in the writings of La Mettrie and Sade, while appearing to undermine the Cartesian mind-body dualism through a materialist reduction, will challenge but not overturn its authority. It is only later, in the writings Nietzsche and Merleau-Ponty, that the philosophical authority of the body will be reclaimed as a necessary condition of a subjectivity reembedded into the fabric of the world.

Chapter 5

Incorporations: Royal Power, or the Social Body in Corneille's *The Cid*

The concurrent publication of the *Discourse on Method* (1637) with the performance of Pierre Corneille's *The Cid* (1637) affords a special opportunity for observing how seventeenth-century French culture represented and understood the body. *The Cid* provides a literary counterpart to René Descartes's anatomical and philosophical analysis of the body in the *Discourse* and thus enables a broader understanding of the cultural and social context in which his ideas were elaborated. The play's ostensible concerns with heroism and the competing demands of love and honor are staged in terms of reflections on the body, documenting the submission of the physical body to the larger interests of the body politic, and they involve explicit discussions regarding its social and political significance.[1] The literary representations of the body in the play reflect a veritable obsession with blood, its genealogical transmission and heroic expenditure, providing a social context to Descartes's anatomical account of the circulation of blood. Corneille's focus on the body is less physical than social, for the play explores changes associated with the social and symbolic significance attached to blood. Corneille's figurative fragmentation and reification of the physical body in the service of an emergent notion of the body politic echoes in social terms issues of objectification and instrumentalization implicitly associated with the Cartesian virtualization of the body in its analogy to a machine. These concerns internal to the play resonate in the extensive debates surrounding its performance (the so-called Quarrel of *The Cid*), thereby supplying us today with historic insights into the play's reception and its anomalous use of figurative language to represent the body. Given this literary and critical evidence, modern readers can begin to understand how the body is conceived, the competing meanings attached to it, and the dilemmas it poses for the broader cultural framework of seventeenth-century French society.

In his "Judgement of *The Cid*," (1637) Charles Sorel draws attention to

Pierre Corneille's use of metaphorical figures *(pointes)* in *The Cid*.[2] Instead of focusing on questions of genre, specifically Corneille's observation of the classical theatrical rules of the three unities of place, action, and character, Sorel comments on Corneille's anomalous use of blood, body, and valor as interchangeable metaphors. He observes that blood is personified in the play, through its endowment with subjective qualities such as thought, speech, and writing.[3] Sorel's observations on Corneille's style, echoed by other critics such as Georges de Scudéry and Chapelain, demonstrate that the objections against the play cannot be resumed as mere complaints of the play's formal structure. They involve arguments about Corneille's inappropriate use of figurative language in regard to the body, and the inclusion of juridical and economic terminology and discourse deemed unsuitable for the context of the tragicomedy genre.[4]

The problem for Sorel is that abstract notions such as valor are given agency through personification, thereby creating unintended effects. Not only does valor "speak," even after the death of the protagonist who incarnates it, but more surprisingly, the valor of the dead hero proceeds to "borrow" the voice of his daughter in order to make heard its demand for revenge. The Corneillian passage central to Sorel's discussion is as follows:

> Rather, his valour, now reduced so low,
> Spoke to me through his wound, called for revenge.
> And, to appeal to the most just of kings,
> Borrowed by these unspeaking lips *(triste bouche)* my voice.
> (Vv. 677–80)[5]

Taking the logic of the Corneillian text literally, Sorel satirizes its circuitous representation and transformation of valor, since valor is no longer presented as being embodied by any particular person:

> This valor, firstly, takes on a fantastic body, then it places itself at the opening of this wound, it speaks through this hole and calls to Chimène; then the author checks himself, and says, however, that this valor does not speak, but uses the mouth of this wound in order to speak, and finally through this mouth it [this valor] borrows the voice of Chimène. What detours! This dead man, no longer able to speak, borrows the voice of his valor, his valor borrows the mouth of his wound, and the wound borrows the voice of Chimène.[6]

At issue here is more that a question of literary style and the use of figurative language, involving the personification of blood, body parts, and abstract values. Rather, Sorel's objections focus on Corneille's figurative language, his indiscriminate mixture at the metaphorical level of abstract and concrete, organic and inorganic, and natural and social categories. Sorel's parodic reading reveals the logical implications of Corneille's figurative language, which assimilates values (man-made categories) to organic metaphors in so exaggerated a fashion as to defy even the mortality of the body. The scandal of valor as a ventriloquist free-agent, speaking through the dead body, itself reduced to the status of a fantastic megaphone, only to later borrow the body of Chimène to make itself heard, epitomizes a denial of the natural character of the body as a proper and private entity. It seems that the physical body is merely the vehicle for abstract values such as valor or virtue, the expression of which exceeds its material limits and thus its physical facticity whether alive or dead.

As the present analysis of *The Cid* will demonstrate, the scandal that Sorel identifies in the play's figurative language represents more than mere poetic or stylistic license. The figurative structure of *The Cid* will be examined as a symptom of the larger cultural and political forces at play in seventeenth-century French society. The metaphorical fragmentation of the body and its circulation and recuperation within the body politic indicate a shift in the way the body is conceived both as a private and as a public entity. Reflecting the consolidation and centralization of monarchic power in the seventeenth-century France, begun under Cardinal Richelieu and later followed through on by Mazarin, we see an emergent emphasis on social identity and the recuperation of the individual as agent and instrument of the state.[7] The figurative structure of the Corneillian text reflects this historical and social shift in its metaphorical representations of the body. As this study will show, in *The Cid* the body's identity as a physical organism is consistently violated by the indiscriminate exchange of bodily parts, which are traded as currency in the service of personal glory or for the sake of the king. This disarticulation of the body as a physical organism will coincide in the play with its social reorganization and incorporation in the body politic of a monarchy whose political economy inaugurates the emergence of the absolutist state.

Jacques Ehrmann's seminal study of structures of exchange in *Cinna* has brought to our attention the extent to which notions of obligation, gift, prize, and exchange govern the language of Corneillian text.[8] The persistent presence of concepts of exchange in the Corneillian theater will be considered as an index of the significance of social exchange, as the social body is being restructured in relation to the emergence of a new, absolutist concept of monarchy. Taking into account Serge Doubrovsky's dialectical analysis of the Corneillian hero, it becomes clear that the concept of exchange that governs the play cannot be viewed from a purely structural perspective, but rather must be specified in order to account for the different kinds of bodily and social exchange that function in the play.[9] Although Doubrovsky identifies in the play the trace of feudal aristocratic values, based on a system of obligation that relies on individual prowess and physical force, this study will show its paradoxical coexistence with a mercantile and emergent bourgeois interpretation of value, since value is also presented as payment and accrued interest from the husbanding of resources. In order to demonstrate the coexistence of these apparently mutually exclusive systems of value, this study will examine the circulation of blood, as a figure of social exchange—that is, the fragmentation of the body and its artificial recuperation in terms of its social function—as a means of explaining the constitution of royal power. The physical body in the Corneillian text no longer functions as a microcosm of the state.[10] The prominence of blood, the circulation of which demarcates the closure of the physical body and its reduction to an artificial mechanism, marks the emergence of a new concept of statehood in which the law establishes principles of bonding and social organization that replace blood bonds.

This transformation in the conception of blood is reflected in the Corneillian hero's dilemma regarding the authentic character of his nobility. The question of the political efficacy of heroic valor and its duration mirrors the dilemma in the position of the king, whose power is marked by two competing systems of social exchange. The king in *The Cid* is an absolute subject, whose position is assured through a process of nomination tied to his issue from a princely, that is to say "divine," bloodline. But in addition to being the symbolic guarantor of the collective social body of his subjects through consanguinity, the king is also an individual who is subject to historical and political pressures.[11] Consequently, the king can maintain his political power only through the economic management and expenditure of heroic acts that will affirm his symbolic role—that is, to say his valor—as interest accrued from the wise management of the bodies and blood of his subjects.

Legible Blood versus Legible Bodies

The play opens with the question of how to judge valor within an aristocratic system, where nobility is "naturally" inherited through consanguinity, so that valor can be shared by two people of equal genealogical descent.[12] The count (Don Gomès) attempts to make a choice between two potential grooms for his daughter. He is unable to discern a legible distinction between the suitors, since their comparable social status undercuts the effort to single out one of them as worthy. This dilemma is reflected in the remark of the count, who attempts to read their eyes to divine their valor: "They're young, but in their eyes already shines *(mais qui font lire aisément dans leurs yeux)* / The glorious mettle *(vertu)* of their ancestors" (vv. 27–28). The count's inability to distinguish the particular merit of the two contenders on the basis of genealogical descent and physical considerations leads him to shift from nominal to historical considerations. Rather than rely on the given name as guarantor of nobility, his judgment of the suitors will also reflect the acquired heroic valor of the fathers, that is, their capacity to make a name for themselves. Genealogical standing is thus enhanced through the heroic valor that accrues to the hero's name.

The imposition of a performative criterion, that of making a name through particular deeds instead of merely inheriting it, redefines the body's legibility in terms of its social and political contribution. Valor ceases to be consubstantial with the body; it can longer be genealogically inherited but must be earned. The count chooses Don Rodrigue (Don Diègue's son) as his daughter's groom because his perceived genealogical worth is increased by the accrued value of his father's heroic acts. The son represents the embodiment of both his father's name (genealogy) and his social history (performative acts). For the count, Don Diègue embodies a legible monument, one that has engraved upon it the glories of its historical feats. He describes the wrinkles on Don Diègue's forehead as the living trace of his past exploits, which, despite the passage of time, "speak" to [*disent*] the count: "His feats are graven on his wrinkled face / Which still reflects his might in former times / The son may be what once his father was" [Ses rides sur son front out gravé ses exploits, / Et nous disent encore ce qu'il fût autrefois. / Je me promets du fils ce que j'ai vu du père] (vv. 35–37). The body is presented as the stage for historical acts, where the traces of past exploits give voice to heroism as a performance in the present. History is written upon the body, and its legibility in the act of interpreting its value enacts the speech of the past, thus creating the illusion of the present. The father's past existence thus becomes that of a "living" monument, legible in the present.

The count's affirmation of wrinkles as an unambiguous monumentalizing trace prompts Sorel to comment on their dubious legibility as absolute proof of heroism: "these wrinkles that have graven Don Diègue's exploits on his forehead, cause me to imagine that one sees in them the battles won, and the positions taken and traced by the lines that make up the wrinkles: as though those of a warrior and those of a laborer were very different."[13]

For Sorel, the figurative trace of heroism on the body cannot be interpreted as an absolute sign of heroism, since this engraving on the body outlines the natural passage of time, rather than individual heroic acts. The universality of wrinkles among men, be they heroes or ordinary laborers, renders this figure an inappropriate and even ridiculous embodiment of heroism. Sorel's critique of Corneille's abuse of figurative language touches on the problematic status of heroism in the play in relation to both language and history. For Sorel, the legibility of the human body cannot be reduced to the abstraction of valor by becoming consubstantial with it, for the aging body's physical traits ill serve the effort to portray the embodiment of a heroic ideal.

The count's effort to interpret the heroic promise of his daughter's suitors is echoed by the subsequent dispute and duel between the two fathers, Don Diègue and the count, regarding their own heroism. Paradoxically, their quarrel takes place in the context of their potential union, that is, the mixture of their blood through the marriage of their children. While Don Diègue recognizes their comparable standing as heroes of equal stature, he attempts to mark their hierarchical difference, since he has been awarded a higher position in the king's administration. Don Diègue argues: "You are today as great as once I was. / You see that nonetheless a king has drawn / A certain difference between us two" (vv. 212–14). Although Don Diègue recognizes the count's current valor, he understands the king's award of governorship as a reward for his past valor. The count, on the other hand, interprets the king's reward as a measure of his political fallibility, observing that "kings reward not *(savent mal payer)* present services" (v. 160). The count challenges Don Diègue's aristocratic ethos by suggesting that the king's failure to reward or pay for services performed in the present may endanger his political viability. For the count, the traditional system of aristocratic exchange based on obligation that defers payments for the past into the present represents a failure to reward valor in the present. As such, it does not reward those who presently embody valor and who assure the protection of the state.

The debate between the two heroes regarding their heroism past and present reflects different interpretations of valor as regards history and time. When Don Diègue suggests that the story of his past life suffices to explain to his son his present glory ("he / Need only read the story of my life" [v. 186]), the count responds, "Living examples are of much more power. / No prince can learn his duty in a book" (vv. 191–92). The count's response indicates that a prince cannot merely rely on recorded past history, since he needs more than books *(livres)* to defend his present glory, in order to be delivered *(délivrer)* of his enemies. When the recognition of his own valor is at issue, the count redefines his earlier position, since he views valor as an objective embodiment in the present, rather than as a nostalgic category. Although he was willing to "read" and thus infer Don Rodrigue's potential heroism in the acts of the father, the father's aged body is dismissed as incapable of bearing any longer the inscription of heroic activity.

The count's interpretation announces the emergence of a new system for measuring valor, one whose terms are based on mercantile, rather than aristocratic, categories. A worthy name and a heroic past do not guarantee effective intervention in the present. The count underlines his position by concluding: "If you were valiant, I am valiant still *(aujourd'hui)*" (v. 195). The count challenges the king's interpretation of valor and thus his power, since he feels unjustly excluded by this aristocratic system that favors tradition and thus past performance over heroic action in the present. In so doing, the count challenges not merely Don Diègue's position within the hierarchy, but also the principles of its function and its transmissability. His insistence that his heroic acts be rewarded through present recognition marks a reinterpretation of symbolic exchange in mercantile terms as direct payment, as opposed to deferred reward in a gift-based economy. Thus, despite its ostensible feudal appearance, the Corneillian ideology of power also has a mercantile, even bourgeois character. Jean Starobinski observes: "In the face of such an ideology, typically feudal in structure, Corneillian psychology seems to define, in contrast, the attitude of the upper bourgeoisie *who make a name for themselves* on the strength of their exploits and of their service to the king and to France" (emphasis added).[14] This mercantile system of social exchange will compete with its earlier feudal models in order to establish its own ascendancy.

Value and Systems of Social Exchange

As we have demonstrated, the quarrel that defines the play is hinged upon two different, but concurrent, interpretations of valor. On the one hand, valor is defined aristocratically as inherited through nomination and transmitted through genealogy, so that the past symbolically informs the present. On the other hand, valor is interpreted as a function of an act performed and recognized in the present, so that past valor no longer serves as a measure of current worth. This interpretation of valor breaks with aristocratic traditions, since it is no longer genealogically or nominally coextensive with the past. The redefinition of heroism in performative terms affirms the coincidence of valor with the exercise of immediate force, so that heroism is revalued in terms of its pragmatic impact in the present, rather than its deferred symbolic value. The immortality of heroism as an aristocratic symbol is brought into conflict with pragmatic and utilitarian considerations that subject it to the demands of history and time. This interpretation of heroism reflects a new understanding of kingship, understood not merely in divine terms, but also in worldly and thus political terms.

It is important to note, however, that this equation of heroism with pure performativity, while mimicking traditional heroism, actually usurps the traditional aristocratic concepts of genealogy and obligation. The self-invented character of this new interpretation of valor is summarized in the count's words, "And all alone ensure the victory" [ne devoir qu'à soi le gain d'une bataille] (v. 183), and his conclusion, "Explain to him your lessons by your deeds" (v. 184)]. The count sees himself as the executive political arm of the king, and his own name as the rampart whose symbolic stronghold preserves Castille. The king's power is represented as being mediated by the count's actions, or in the count's words, "under my protecting arm" [à l'ombre de mon bras] (v. 204). The count's demand for direct "payment" for his services represents a transformation of the traditional aristocratic structure of obligation, since the obligation of the noble to the king is no longer conceived in symbolic terms involving retroactive or deferred payment. Thus, two competing interpretations of the value of heroism are at work in the service of the king: the first representing traditional aristocratic values, and the second representing the emergence of mercantile and bourgeois values. These competing systems of exchange embody the paradox of the king's symbolic role in the social system, reflecting his dual nature as a "twinned person." The king's position is double: he is man by nature, subject to history, mortality, and the possible loss of power; but as the genealogical inheritor of kingship, he represents divine rights, whose symbolic character make him immortal. As the creator and guarantor of human laws, kingship places him above those very laws of which he is the supposed executor.[15]

In order to settle the affront to his honor, Don Diègue places his quarrel with the count in better hands, those of his son. Appealing to his genealogical link with his son, he "borrows" his son's arm in the service of their common cause as a means of redressing the injustice done to their shared name and to the heroic purity of their shared blood. Paternity enables the father to overcome the physical limits of his body by appropriating his son's body, as an extension of his own being.[16] The conceit upon which this communal body is based involves the total erasure of the female body that mediates paternity through its physical intervention. This can be clearly seen in Don

Diègue's exclamation: "Come, O my son! my blood!" (v. 266), as if the shared blood with his son rendered them indistinguishable as separate persons. This erasure of the distinction between persons marks decisively the absence of the female body as mediating force. The legal claims of the physical body are elided by paternal claims of social reproduction. The reification and fragmentation of the physical body in the play corresponds to its reduction to a function in a system of social reproduction, where paternal filiation mediated through nomination substitutes for the natural attributes of the physical body.

It is important to note that it is the exclusion of the female body that marks the coincidence of both the feudal and the mercantile systems of social exchange. Both systems rely on a disenfranchisement of the female body in favor of a symbolic, socially reproduced body, either through force or through commodification. But this socially sanctioned body is no longer identical with the physical body. This can be seen in Don Diègue's expedient solution to correcting the loss of the count through the heroic gains of his son: "Come, follow me, to fight and show your king / What in the Count he's lost, he's gained in you" (vv. 1099–1100). Don Diègue hopes to recompense the king's loss of the count through the deeds of his son, as if the two were interchangeable bodies in his service without any particular identity. Identity is thus reduced to a function, privileging use value over an aristocratic definition of value based on inherited value. Don Diègue's functional solution must be understood as the logical extension of the patriarchal position that underlines both the feudal and the mercantile traditions. The exclusion of the female body coincides with the more radical erasure of the physical body in general. If Rodrigue can replace the count, it is because the count's body has no meaning in and of itself, other than as the embodiment of political exigencies.

The erasure of female body in the Corneillian text will lead to a crisis of legitimacy in the later plays. As Anne Ubersfeld has shown, the denial of the female body will prevent direct access to kingship and thus to the possibility of reintegrating the law and divine rights.[17] This crisis of legitimacy is prefigured in *Rodogune* (1645), since Queen Cleopatra can reign only through the mediation of men, who embody the political force of the state. Her body as a queen, while the legitimate medium for the transmission of royal power, does not represent an adequate symbolic substrate of political power; hence her reign quickly becomes assimilated to tyranny. In the later plays, such a *Héraclius* (1647), *Nicomède* (1651), and *Sertorius* (1662), the queen represents a medium of legitimacy without power. She is, as Ubersfeld observes in her analysis of *Sertorius*, "kings of names" [rois de noms], that is, a nominal but powerless agency.[18] The only power left to her is a potential one, that of reinstituting legitimacy through heredity and thus guaranteeing the reproduction of the monarchy.

The King, the Law, and the Social Body

The king interprets the duel between Don Diègue and the count as a challenge to his own absolute power. The independent use of force by the two nobles threatens the law of the monarchy, since it raises the specter of illegitimate and even tyrannical power. The king reminds the count, through his spokesman Don Arias, that his legitimacy is above the circuitry of social exchange, even if his actual power is established through human feats. To serve the king is a matter of duty and not personal glory: "Whatever glorious deeds a subject does, / These never put the monarch in his debt *(Jamais à son sujet un roi n'est redevable)*" (v. 370). The king suggests that his obligation to his subordinates is not reciprocal, since his duty is symbolic and thus beyond direct measure and recompense. However, the count's perspective is that the scepter of the king would fall without the intervention of his own arm, thereby underlining once again the impossibility of separating the king's symbolic and political power. The conflict of power between the two nobles, while embodying the paradox of the king's twin nature, also menaces its system of law and order.

The king recognizes the challenge posed by the count's interpretation and redefinition of social exchange in mercantile terms. His vehement response to the count's persistent desire to engage in a duel underlines the threat presented by the count's claims about heroism in relation to his own power:

> Heavens! this overweening subject, then,
> So lacks respect or eagerness to please
> He slights Don Diego and he scorns his king.
> Here in my court he even dictates to me *(il me donne la loi)*.
> He may be brave and a great general,
> But I will take his haughty humour down.
> Were he value itself *(la valeur même)*, and the god of war,
> He'll see what it can mean, not to obey.
>
> (Vv. 561–68)

As the giver of the law, the king questions the count's autonomy and his efforts to impose his own laws, challenging as an individual subject the king's unique position as absolute subject. The count's act of disobedience in attempting to settle by force a dispute to which the king provided a diplomatic solution is perceived as a challenge to the king's legal authority as the sole maker of new laws. The count's arrogant gesture infringes on the divinely sanctioned authority of the king, for it affirms the triumph of nobiliary self-interest over the authority of the state.

The king values acts of individual glory in terms of their potential service to the state, whose political economy cannot tolerate the gratuitous expenditure of its agents.[19]As the representative of the state, the king presents himself as the preserver and manager of the blood and bodies of his subjects:

> A king whose wisdom aims at better things
> Is far more sparing of his subject's blood *(meilleur ménager du sang de ses sujets).*
> I watch over my people, keep them safe *(mes soucis les conservent),*
> As does the head the members serving it.
> So what is right for you is wrong for me.
> You speak as a soldier. I must act as a king.
> . . . To slight my choice is to attack myself
> And seek to weaken my authority *(le pouvoir suprême).*
>
> (Vv. 595–606)

The king's analysis reveals his extraordinary standing in relation to his subjects. His position is defined by prudence, not by force. As king, he is the steward managing the blood and bodies of his subjects by conserving and preserving them, even against their own private predilections. As the symbolic head of the social body, the king views himself as its extension, its reason. But his reason is not an ordinary one, since it is the reason of the state, with him as its figurehead. Thus, the count's challenge to the king's reason is not an ordinary gesture, as between one subject and another. It is, rather, an attack on the king as supreme Subject, as the maker and giver of universal and divinely sanctioned laws to ordinary subjects.

In the play, the king's power is represented as great enough to challenge and exceed human limits, such as death. When Chimène presents her plea of vengeance for her dead father, the king appeals to his own immortality through kingship, in order to suggest that he will take the place of her dead father: "Your king will be your father in his stead" (v. 672). This symbolic assurance to Chimène is intended to pacify her desire for vengeance, since the king as the representative of the social body can substitute himself for any of the missing parts. By taking on her legal tutelage, he cancels the demand for Rodrigue's head and thus conserves his arm in his own service. However, Chimène is not seeking protection from a substitute father, but the vengeance of her real father. She refuses to accept the king's tutelage unless its legality can be defined in terms of interpreting the king as both father and executor of the law.

Femininity, Desire, and the Law

Chimène's demand for justice is expressed in legal terms that echo the king's logic, in order to show that Rodrigue's victory against her father menaces the very structure of the state.[20] Chimène's argument mediates between the feudal and the mercantile systems of exchange, in order to show that Rodrigue represents a danger to both. She creates an analogy between her own vengeance, her demand for payment "blood for blood"—an allusion to the feudal system—and the threat that Rodrigue's heroism presents to the power of the king and to that of the state within a mercantile system:

> In short, my father's dead. Vengeance I cry
> More in your interest *(intérêt)* than for my relief.
> You suffer *(perdez)* by the death of such a man.
> Avenge it by another's, blood for blood.
> Sacrifice *(Immolez)* not to *me*, but to your crown,
> And to your greatness, to your person, Sire;
> Sacrifice *(Immolez)* to the welfare of the State
> All that so great an outrage swells with pride.
>
> (Vv. 689–96)

Chimène argues that by not punishing Rodrigue, the king will lose in terms of all his interests, whether personal, symbolic, or political. If Rodrigue must be sacrificed, this is because the Crown and its interests have already been symbolically immolated. The private aspirations of the hero and his use of illegitimate force represent a feudal perspective and are here presented as the challenge of potential tyranny to the order of the state. The threat of tyranny that haunts Corneille's plays is embodied in this struggle between nobility sanctioned by force, and the king whose power is assured through divine rights.[21] Plays such as *Horace* (1640) and *Cinna* (1641) represent in explicit terms the danger that the heroic ethos and its individualistic character present to the legitimate power of the state, since they challenge privileges of heredity by the use of political force.

Chimène's demands for justice are answered by the plea of Rodrigue's father, Don Diègue, who claims that his son had merely lent him his hand and that he, Don Diègue, is the true "head," the one worthy of punishment:

"I am the head; he, Sire, is but the arm" (v. 724). In other words, the father asks that his son be recognized as a mere instrument, as the extension of their common incorporated feudal body. The problem is, however, that it is exactly this feudal body and its principles of incorporation based on force that present a menace to the modern state understood as a social body, whose legal and administrative principles of incorporation exceed genealogical bonds.

The scandal of this endless circulation of body parts is put to an end when Rodrigue confronts Chimène and asks her to kill him in order to avenge her father. He offends her by presenting his sword to her, which Chimène perceives to be covered with the blood of her father and thus, following the implicit logic of the scene, to be tainted with her own blood. Don Rodrigue's solution to Chimène's internal conflict between the competing demands of filial and erotic love is to insist on the possibility of his own elimination, in order to efface, as it were, the stains of her own blood on his sword: "Plunge it in mine, / And thus efface the stain of your own blood" [Plonge-le dans le mien / Et fais-lui perdre ainsi la teinture du tien] (vv. 863–64). This final mixture of the blood of the two protagonists in the act of death performs a mock marriage that would settle the differences of their delayed marriage. The erotic subtext of the play indicates the only possible issue for reconciling social differences: either by shedding blood or by marriage.[22] But the solution that marriage can provide by reconciling the differences between the demands of genealogy and those of personal history is not available to the protagonists, since this is not a ceremony that they are free to authorize and perform by themselves.

Rodrigue's recourse to a heroic ethos, that of a direct encounter and confrontation with Chimène, is challenged by Chimène's appeal to the law, since she recognizes the mediated character of their social encounter. Her use of legal terminology challenges the critical tradition that has sought to feminize Chimène by describing her as a victim of passion.[23] Chimène presents her claim as a case would be presented before a judge, thus countering the illusory freedom of Rodrigue's heroic intervention that assimilates the judge and the criminal: "I wish to prosecute, not execute (je suis ta partie, et non pas ton boureau). / Is it for me to lop your proffered head? (Si tu m'offre ta tête, est-ce à moi de la prendre?) / I must attack, you must defend yourself. / I must obtain it from another's hand. I must pursue you but not punish you" (vv. 940–43).[24] Chimène's reminder to Rodrigue that her quarrel is of a juridical, rather than personal, nature defers any immediate solution. Their quarrel is of a symbolic order, involving the principle of the law and thus not open to heroic intervention. Chimène's reply to Rodrigue's challenge represents her denial of force as a socially valid principle. She refuses to assume the position of executioner that would bring her within the very order and logic of heroism within which she has already suffered the loss of her father, and which now threatens her with a new loss, that of her lover.

Chimène's solution involves neither the denunciation of the patriarchal system nor the refusal to participate in it. Rather, she attempts to maintain the law and its symbolic order and thus contain legally Rodrigue's heroic force-based ethos. Her refusal to kill Rodrigue can also be seen as an implicit critique of a heroic order founded on force, within which the claims of her own body have been excluded. Chimène's appeal to justice in the play will only be recognized because her drama echoes the king's own dilemma regarding the conflict between a nobiliary heroic ethos and the authority of the state. Her use of juridical terms reflects the very principles that govern the king's administrative stewardship, that of upholding the abstract legitimacy of the law over the political forces at play within society.

Residues of the Body: Death

Since the public appreciation of Rodrigue's valor is also the vivid reminder and living emblem of her father's death, Chimène is not free to forget her quarrel with her lover. The reality of her father's death is not an abstract fact, since it is tangibly inscribed upon her own body:

> If he's enslaved two kings, he's killed the Count [my father],
> And these sad garments which proclaim my woe
> Are the first outcome of his gallantry [valor] *(valeur)*.
> Elsewhere this lionheart may be extolled;
> Everything here speaks to me of his crime.
>
> (Vv. 1130–34)

The objective reality of her father's death, which corresponds to her own physical appearance marked by mourning, makes it impossible to erase his death by abstractly incorporating him in a system of exchange that would trade him for Rodrigue's valor. Chimène cannot accept Infanta's suggestion that her father is resuscitated, as it were, through Rodrigue's heroic performance: "Your father lives again in him alone" [Que ton père en lui seul se voit ressuscité] (v. 1180). Her father cannot be reborn as another person and, particularly, not in the guise of his assassin. The attempts on the parts of the king and the infanta to appeal to the welfare of the state in order to console Chimène for the loss of her father demonstrate the challenge that the body of the dead father and its remembrance pose for the well-being of the state.

Chimène's refusal to allow the incorporation of her father's body into the social body of the state, by recognizing that his heroic traits are now embodied by Rodrigue, indicates her persistence in ensuring his recognition. She continues to affirm her father's individual existence and rights before the law. It is interesting to note that the question of the claims of the count's dead body are echoed by Corneille's own dilemma as author, as he attempts to justify his elision of extensive references to the funeral and other ceremonial treatments of the dead body in the play. In his "Examen du 'Cid'" (1660), he elaborates the logistical difficulties of alluding to the count's dead body, since such references make the possible marriage of Chimène and Rodrigue at the end of the play seem implausible:

> The funeral of the Count was still a very burdensome matter, be it carried out before the end of the play, or be it that the body remained present in the palace, awaiting someone to put it in order. The least word that I were to let fall of it would have broken the heat of attention, and would have filled the spectator with this cumbersome notion. And I believed it more appropriate to hide it from the imagination by my silence. . . ; I finish with a remark on what Horace said, that that which one exposes to sight touches much more than that which one only learns of through a tale.[25]

However, the scandal that the dead body poses for Corneille is not merely one of maintaining, through silence, a plausible ending for the play. Rather, the residual presence of the body challenges the very logic that seeks to incorporate the body within the state apparatus and thereby silence its former existence and legal claims. Corneille's quote from Horace, affirming the precedence of sight over story, and thus the precedence of present over past performances, is ironically a reiteration of the count's valorization of performative over narrative representations of heroism. Corneille thus doubly silences the claims of the physical body. He first excludes it from the stage, the scene of the representation, and then he elides it again by attempting to silence its legal claims. This double erasure of the count's dead body enables Corneille to perform on stage its subsequent incorporation within the interests of the state, as symbolized by the marriage of Chimène and Rodrigue.

The Economy of Absolutism

> The name "Leviathan" is only too significant of this monster of a state.
> —F. A. Lange

Rodrigue's subsequent victory over the Moors leads to the resolution of the crisis between the feudal and mercantile interpretations of heroism. By his victory over two pagan kings, Rodrigue establishes himself in a new relation to the king and acquires a new identity, a new name, the Cid, a name that unlike *Rodrigue* is no longer associated with crime. The king's summation renders this explicit: "The Moors in flight have carried off his crime" [Les Mores en fuyant ont emporté son crime] (v. 1414). The king represents crime in physical, rather than legal terms, so that it can be "objectively" removed and replaced by valor, as if it were a physical object, rather than a legal entity. The removal of the count's legal claims through Rodrigue's victory over the king's enemies indicates the priority of the legal claims of the state over the rights of any private subject. Moreover, it signals the economic reinscription of the body, which, having no intrinsic value in and of itself, can now be traded for the higher values represented by those of an incorporated state.

By battling the Moors, Rodrigue/the Cid establishes himself as a new kind of agent, one whose valor exceeds the domain of the king's compensation. Through his victory over two pagan kings, the Cid becomes the head of a new system of merit and exchange. Within this new system, Rodrigue, alias the Cid, has been named and thus legally recognized by two pagan kings as their supreme leader. By bringing the pagan kings within the governance of his own king, the Cid marks the affirmation of his own subjection to the order of the state. Rodrigue's submission of his own victory to the king, which he brings within the dominion of the king proper, is recognized by the king as a gesture that has legal consequences:

> But your reward *(récompense)* comes from two captive kings.
> They've named you both in front of me the Cid.
> Since in their tongue Cid is as much as lord,
> I'll not begrudge you this fair title. Be
> Henceforth the Cid. Sweep all before you. Fill
> Granada and Toledo with affright,
> And let it show *(marque)* to all beneath my sway
> Both what you are and what I owe to you *(Et ce que tu me vaux, et ce que je te dois).*
>
> (Vv. 1221–28)

By acknowledging the legal claims of the captive kings, the king recognizes Rodrigue/the Cid's new legal position, which is at once within his own jurisdiction and also outside of it. Whereas Rodrigue has committed a crime, the victorious Cid is a hero; that is, he has become a "new" person, despite the fact that he shares the same body with the criminal. Rodrigue's new name, the Cid, or "Sire," from the Arabic *el Sayyid,* no longer designates him merely as an individual, but also indicates his newly acquired social standing. Rodrigue/the Cid's divided social and legal status, which echoes the king's own position as a "twinned person," enables the king to recover the Cid's victory and his body as interest or surplus value in the economy of his royal organization and power. The king's recognition of the Cid's heroism is not merely a sign of generosity, but the sign of the recognition of the political and historical contingencies of kingship. Although the Cid's heroism exceeds the sphere of his social body, the king is able to incorporate and preserve this excess within his own economy of obligation and power. The legal differences between the king and Rodrigue/the Cid are resolved through this appeal to a new referential system. As the Cid, Rodrigue can no longer be held legally accountable to the king, since he is also now a king in his own right, and thus free to dispose of his power over the bodies of his subjects.

The king's legalistic solution, which upholds the interests of the state, does not resolve the moral claims of the two protagonists, Chimène and Rodrigue, since they must continue to argue and uphold their personal duties and valor. Chimène persists in her demand for justice, since she considers Rodrigue's death to be the only appropriate punishment for murder. Although she recognizes Rodrigue's value to the state, she insists on the validity of her own legal position by asking for his death for her father: "And for my father, not the fatherland" (v. 1365). Rodrigue must be punished for his crime, so that he may not triumph over crime in the same way that he triumphed over his enemies. Chimène's call for justice is reinforced by Rodrigue's own father, who is afraid that the king's refusal to judge Rodrigue may tarnish his glory (v. 1421). When he insists that the law be observed, "What! Sire, for him alone you flout *(renversez)* your laws" (v. 1415), his appeal is based on recourse to heroic, rather than to legal codes. Rather than attempt to mitigate the crime of his son in court, he would like him to defend it by force in a duel. Don Diègue's appeal to a heroic solution marks the shift in his political position. His speech represents his partiality for his own interests, which he now upholds, like the count before him, above the interests of state.

Having proven his valor to the state, Rodrigue offers to uphold his duty to his love by sacrificing himself to it. He once again offers to be sacrificed by Chimène, even if this sacrifice must be mediated through the hands of his rival. He tells Chimène, "I shall, in fighting him, lay bare my breast, / Revering in his hand your instrument *(Adorant de sa main la vôtre qui me perd)*" (vv. 1499–1500). By offering his body to Chimène to be immolated by Don Sanche's hand, Rodrigue attempts to distinguish between his love for his country and his love for Chimène. In so doing, he seeks to resolve the impossible difference produced by competing demands—of his honor and of his love—upon his body, "Preferring still in his enamored heart, / Honour to his beloved and her to life" [Préferant quelque espoir qu'eût son âme asservie, / Son honneur à Chimène, et Chimène à sa vie] (vv. 1541–42).

But Rodrigue's proposal to a solution mediated through the hands of Don Sanche is also unacceptable, for Chimène recognizes that she would be objectified as the prize awarded to the victor. Rodrigue's appeal to a mercantile ethos, where value is generated through exchange, does not structurally alter her position. When she urges that Rodrigue fight and even that he fight to win her, she is not merely expressing her passion, as the critical discussions of Corneille would have us believe. Rather than the pure expression of affect, Chimène's gesture represents her refusal to be objectified and traded within systems of both feudal and mercantile exchange. This is because such a gesture would imply a double sacrifice: in addition to giving up her love, she would also be given away by her lover to his rival, "to a man whom I abhor" [à l'objet de mon aversion] (v. 1552). In so doing, she would betray both her love and her honor, unlike Infanta, who earlier in the play gives away Rodrigue to Chimène in exchange for her personal glory, "This youthful knight whom I bestowed on her" [cet amant que je donne] (vv. 82–83).

The end of the play resolves the differences that divide Chimène and Rodrigue. The king upholds the legality of the marriage of Chimène and Rodrigue, noting that Chimène has been freed by her obligation to her father by having upheld her call to justice over her own passion: "Honour's redeemed and duty is discharged *(Ta gloire est dégagée, et ton devoir est quitte)*. / Your father's satisfied. He is avenged / By hazarding Rodrigo's life so oft" (vv. 1766–68). Chimène recognizes that she now must submit to the law whose very terms violate the obligation that she owes to her father. Her response to the king projects her own internal differences onto him, by questioning how the king can accommodate within his legal structure such irreconcilable differences:

> And when a king commands, I must obey.
> But whatsoever was your sentence, Sire,
> Can you allow this marriage and look on?
> And when you call on duty to submit,
> Does all your injustice harmonize with that?
> Rodrigo is a pillar of the State *(à l'état devient si nécessaire)*,
> But must I be the wages *(salaire)* of his deeds?
> Must I incur for ever the reproach
> Of having stained hands in a father's blood?
>
> (Vv. 1804–12)

Chimène's question to the king addresses the fundamental dilemma of the play: the impossibility of recognizing at the same time the exigencies and values of two different systems of social exchange. However, by placing herself in the hands of the king, Chimène places her personal difference in the public domain. The scandal of her personal demand for justice now becomes a scandal within the law, one that the king must reconcile within his order without destroying it.

The king's decision to defer the marriage of Chimène and Rodrigue/the Cid as a means of reconciling their differences brings into the play a new dimension, that of time. The introduction of time through the postponement of the marriage to the following year functions as the legal recognition of Chimène's personal claims, but also as the sign of the transcendent logic of the state:

> Time has repeatedly legitimized
> What seemed at first could not be innocent *(sans crime)*.
> Rodrigo won you *(t'as gagnée)*, and you must be his.
> But, though you are the prize of valor, I
> Would have to be your glory's enemy
> To grant the fruits *(le prix)* of victory at once.
> Deferment *(hymen différé)* still accords with my decree
> Which destines you, at no fixed time, to him.
>
> (Vv. 1813–20)

The king asserts his power in the play by introducing an element not available to any of its players, that of the symbolic power of duration. The king, whose position is guaranteed in time, will now invoke temporality to legitimate differences that cannot be resolved in the present. Whereas at the beginning of the play, the conflict between the count and Don Diègue showed that heroic acts in the past cannot be effective if they cannot be performed again in the present, the king's invocation of time demonstrates the transcendence of kingship over the limited duration that defines the bodies of his subjects. Heroes may live or die, but their existence depends on the existence of the monarch as guarantor of the state. Even when the king dies, kingship lives on.

The king's statement at the end the play marks the coincidence between time, valor, and kingship: "Leave it to time, your valiance and your king" [Laisse faire le temps, ta vaillance et ton roi] (v. 1840). The legitimacy of time mediated through kingship challenges the legality of crime and erases its performative character. The deferral of the marriage, authorized by the king, resolves the differences between individual subjects and their temporality, construed as a pure present. With the passage of time, the crime loses its "legibility." After the prescribed period of mourning there will be no physical traces that attest to its legitimacy. By exercising his power not merely as the executor of the law, but also as the manager of his own representation and thus of the duration implicit in his authority, the king is able to conserve both his political efficacy and his symbolic position. Although subject to history, the king upholds his power, available to him through his title, to use time as a representation in order to consolidate his rule in an even more absolute sense. The original difference that marks the representation of the king as a "twinned person" has now been recuperated to his advantage, since this difference marks the possibility of a deferral, that is, the king's recovery of his political fallibility within a system of power, more absolute than originally made possible by the traditional definition of kingship.

The emergence of this concept of absolute monarchy corresponds, as we have shown, to the redefinition of the body as a social entity subject to laws of mercantilistic exchange. In Corneille's *The Cid*, the body reduced to its social function becomes objectified and reduced to currency. This reduction of the body to its use value corresponds to its assimilation within the order of an administrative and economic system of exchange. The legitimacy of the body is thus subsumed within its social function, so that it can be politically saved or expended according to the law and beyond the intervention of contingent individual forces. The submission of the body to a set of rules that governs its administration independent from it leads to the redefinition of its organic character. As this study has shown, the body is reinterpreted in the Corneillian text, so that it no longer signifies the physical body, but the artificial and socially constructed body of the state, that of the body politic.

Within this system of social exchange, the body ceases to possess individual meaning and value, since its social commodification recoups its individuality in the survive of a larger symbolic order. As this study has shown, its reduction to its social functions, whose norms are governed by the state apparatus, results in its figurative mutilation. In his study of the body in the seventeenth century, Francis Barker argues that the decorporealization of the body and its subjection are tied to the emergence of an absolutist concept of the subject:

> The mastery of the body in which subjectivity is predicated by these texts by no means depends wholly on the violent decorporealization of the flesh, but also on the equally aggressive solidification of the object-body and of the practical knowledges—discourses—which attend to its philosophical status, its psychic and physical administration, the organization of its sexuality and

the definition of its gender. Even if that solidification is abstractly coded as analytic, diagnostic, diagrammatic, conceptual.[26]

Although less immediately concerned with the incorporation of private bodies into the state apparatus, Barker's remarks underline the fundamental tendencies that this study has isolated in the Corneillian text. They indicate the paradoxical coexistence of a process of decorporealization of the body, with the redefinition of its solidity within the bonds and disciplines of the state, as an incorporated social body. This schematization of the body redefines corporeality in terms of the practices of its social administration, rather than as an expression of individual subjectivity.[27]

The most striking analogy to Corneille's redefinition of the body in social terms can be found in the writings of his English contemporary, Thomas Hobbes. In *Leviathan* (1650), Hobbes describes man as a mechanism and the state as an artificial mechanism that embodies to a higher degree the principles of incorporation that the individual body possesses in only a limited fashion. In his introductory passage, Hobbes develops his definition of the state by redefining the organic character of the body in social terms that are equated with artificiality:

> Nature, the art whereby God hath made and governs the world, is by the *art* of man, as in many other things, so in this also imitated, that it can make an artificial animal. For seeing life is but a motion of limbs, the beginning whereof is in some principal part within; why may we not say that all automata . . . have an artificial life? . . . For by art is created that great LEVIATHAN called a COMMONWEALTH, or STATE, in Latin CIVITAS, which is but an artificial man.[28]

Although Hobbes proceeds to enumerate the functions of the state by analogy to those of the body, it is clear that the principle of organicity that governs the social body represents the literal "commonwealth," that is to say, the total workings of its "corporate" rather than "corporeal" character. If the state represents "artificial man," this supreme automaton is clearly superior to ordinary man, who is merely a cog in the state mechanism. The principle of incorporation of the state, the "commonwealth," presents the inscription of a system of exchange whose power is located beyond actual physical limits of the individual body and its internal system of circulation, its "blood." The incorporated body reflects the imprint of social and economic principles that open up its sphere of power toward political and administrative efficacy. This technologization of the social body suggests that royal power can also be understood in mercantile terms, as the accrued interest of wealth from the totality of the "commonwealth."

If Louis XIV was an ardent admirer of Corneille's works, we can now begin to understand why. The lesson of *The Cid* is that the power of the absolute monarch lies in the ability to understand that all representation, including the body, is artificially produced. By manipulating the mechanisms of representation, the king can conflate the aristocratic and mercantile systems of exchange for the effective management of the social body. The surplus power available at the disposal of the absolute monarch is the result of the recognition of the uniqueness of his position as a sovereign guarantor of the totality of the social order. The exchange and the circulation of individual bodies within this symbolic order involve economic effects that exceed, because of their totality, particular individual interests. The king's power comprehends individual rights, only to exceed them, since he embodies both the legal and executive powers of the state. Consequently, the king can expend or economize the social body and thus control its symbolic order and expenditure. The emergence of absolute monarchy involves the recognition that value is both inherited and earned, and that the "true" body is *not* the physical body, but the socially viable body incorporated in the ideology of the state. This redefinition of the social body in the context of the absolutist state thus announces the paradoxical coexistence of royal absolutism with an emergent mercantile ideology. The coincidence of these seemingly disparate historical ideologies is visible in their interpretation of power as interest, whose function as capital is reified by and economized through representation. Along the way, the physical, corporeal body has lost its meaning, since its viability is defined solely in terms of its virtual, but no less powerful or tangible, social manifestations. The organicity of the physical body thus gives way to its social organization, and the commonwealth subordinates the logic of the organism. It is this sublation of the physical body into a rational system of laws governing its administration that marks the peculiar convergence of the Cartesian and the Corneillian project. Although operating with entirely different agendas, since Descartes's concerns are scientific and philosophical, while Corneille's are social and political, their representation of the body reflects a common repression of the flesh in favor of an abstracted body, one whose purely schematic character can be recuperated in the desiccated organizational logic of a machine, or the incorporated and depersonalized logic of the state apparatus. Thus instrumentalized and reified, the physical body is reduced to abjection. Its obdurate persistence, however, serves to remind us still of a subjectivity once understood as an embodied condition.

Part 3
Materialist Machines

Chapter 6
Men-Machines

Man is a historical idea and not a natural species.
—Merleau-Ponty

Does the cogito have a sex? This question might appear to be absurd or at best irrelevant, given that the discussion of the Cartesian cogito in chapter 3 established the disembodiment of subjectivity and the virtualization of the body by its reduction to a machine. If the question of sexuality and sexual difference appears to be moot in regard to Cartesian subjectivity, this is because the metaphysical definition of the subject as a thinking thing *(res cogitans)* and the concomitant reduction of the body to a material and extended thing *(res extensa)* radically exclude the question of embodiment. Although Descartes attempted later in the *Meditations* to argue the formal union of these two substances, insofar as they mutually inform human functions, the meaning of their union remained unintelligible.[1] This radical disjunction implicit in the Cartesian mind-body dualism, which posits the autonomy of mind and body as distinct substances, makes it difficult to raise the question of sexual difference as a subjective, rather than as a purely material, phenomenon. For the reduction of the body to matter, governed by mechanical laws, restricts the purview of embodiment and of sexuality, as one of its signatory manifestations, to purely material and physiological considerations.

How then are we to think the notion of sexual difference within the material confines of the Cartesian definition of the body? More troubling still is the question of the relation of sexual difference to the notion of ontological difference that underlies Cartesian dualism and its elaboration of subjectivity. In the pages that follow, this troubled and confusing legacy of the Cartesian conception of the body is at issue, in terms that seek to clarify both its decisive influence and the difficulties encountered in challenging it. Starting with an examination of La Mettrie's expansion of the Cartesian mechanistic account from the body to man as a whole, this study then proceeds in chapter 7 to inquire into Sade's violent and parodic representations of sexuality. While relying on La Mettrie's materialist and mechanist assumptions of man and nature, Sade will challenge the definition of the body, sexuality, and sexual difference, through violent parodies that undermine both the premises of rational thought and the logic of representation.

Discussing the legacy of the Cartesian metaphysical dualism to the development of French materialism in the eighteenth century, Aram Vartanian underlines its paradoxical effects:

> By the distinction of two substances, *res cogitans* and *res extensa,* not only idealism was provided with a firm foundation: matter was raised to a revolutionary status by comparison to its former position at the rock-bottom of Aristotle's scheme of entelechy.[2]

In order to argue for the emergence of a double philosophical legacy, he takes as a point of departure Descartes's dualism with regards to the fundamental distinction between the subject defined as a thinking substance and the body defined as matter and extension. The first tradition, idealist and transcendental in character, will be founded from within the sphere of a subjectivity defined in purely rational terms, whereas the second, built on the substantialization of the body as material fact, will further the development of materialism. These two traditions imply two different scenarios for understanding the body, embodiment, and sexual difference.

The idealist account of rational subjectivity precludes both the body and embodiment from its purview, since it seeks to define thought alone as the universal foundation of subjectivity and humanity. The Cartesian equation of subjectivity with pure reason defines the emergence of the subject of knowledge, whose universal, impersonal, and thus neutered character becomes the condition of possibility for the existence of all other ordinary subjects in the world. This neutering of the rational, universal subject is echoed in François Poullain de la Barre's pronouncement, "The mind has no sex," in *The Equality of the Sexes [De l'égalité de deux sexes: Discours physique et moral]* (1673).[3] It is this universal subject that becomes in the eighteenth century the basis for the emergence of "man" as a generic category, whose supposed gender-free or neutered universality is intended to reference humanity as a whole.[4] However, it is precisely these transcendental claims associated with subjectivity that also entail the objectification and even abjection of the body, its enforced materiality as a manipulable, mechanical, and even disposable thing. Within this definition of subjectivity becomes perceptible an entirely new way of constituting human agency as an expression of thought alone, while the body is forcefully disenfranchised of the ability to act, since its materiality can neither inform nor act upon the mind. This disengagement of agency from the horizon of the body has significant consequences, insofar as it suggests its passive submission to a higher rational order that governs both its construction and functions.

Although Descartes's attempted to defend himself against his contemporaries' objections to the materialist implications of his definition of the body, based on his account of the body as extended matter, his efforts proved to be unsuccessful. The very fact that he sought to redefine the soul in purely rational terms (thereby extricating it from Scholastic antecedents that included, in addition, a sensitive and vegetative soul, that is, embodied notions of soul) established the effective disembodiment of the subject and led to the decisive removal of all spiritual aspects from its material sphere. According to Vartanian, this gesture inadvertently accomplished not only the decisive substantialization of matter but, more importantly, its elevation to a new and unprecedented status within an ontological order that had privileged the mind. Descartes's subsequent elaborations on the mechanical character of the material body, his analogy between animals and machines *(bêtes-machines)*, and the implicit analogy between the human body and a machine further contributed to materialist appropriations of his philosophy. Moreover, his insistence on explaining the functions of the body in terms of mechanical principles implies ascribing to its organization aspects that define it as an organism as a whole. Given this material and mechanical definition of the body, the question of embodiment, particularly as it pertains to sexual difference, becomes problematic to the extent that it reduces the horizon of sexuality to purely material concerns. It is this danger that becomes explicit in La Mettrie's and Sade's materialist interpretations of Cartesianism, since the substantialization of the body in terms of matter governed by mechanical laws forecloses an understanding of sexuality outside the deterministic sphere of physical phenomena and laws.[5]

A Materialist Critique of the Mind-Body Dualism

> We cannot separate thought from a matter that thinks.
> —Hobbes

The rise in eighteenth-century France of materialism, a set of doctrines concerning nature and the world that affirm the primacy of matter, attests to the legacy of Cartesian physics, particularly as regards its mechanist and automatist account of the human body.[6] This influence is most visible in Julien Offray de La Mettrie's *Man-Machine* (*L'homme-machine,* 1748), a pioneering work that presents a consistently materialistic account of man and that proved to be instrumental in the development of naturalistic biology in the eighteenth century.[7] It is important to note that in *Man-Machine*, La Mettrie is not content to restrict his materialist position to a discussion of the human body. Rather, this materialist thesis will be extended to nature as a whole in order to challenge the transcendental and theological foundations of the Cartesian edifice.[8]

La Mettrie introduces his treatise with a discussion of the systems of philosophy governing the understanding of man's soul, reducing them to two major traditions: materialism (the more ancient) and spiritualism. Alluding to John Locke's claim that matter might manifest the faculty of thinking (though he finds this formulation to be poorly expressed), he is quick to affirm that such a claim does not dishonor reason per se. La Mettrie dismisses the Leibnizians and their notion of preestablished harmony, which merely "spiritualized matter, rather than materializing the soul,"[9] and attacks the Malebrancheans for their doctrine of occasional causes that perpetuates the Cartesian idea that "man consists of two distinct substances, as though they had seen and counted them" (*MM*, 64). La Mettrie's agenda soon becomes clear: the materialization of the soul, since the excellence of reason does not depend on its immateriality (*MM*, 65), and the denial of the mind-body dualism through the affirmation of a material substance whose organization and laws would apply equally to the mind and the body, thereby acquiescing to the possibility of a "soul of mud" (*MM*, 65).

Reaffirming the validity of scientific method based on experience and observation, La Mettrie reclaims the rights of the physician-philosopher to truly inquire into the nature of man and reveal "man's springs hidden under coverings" (*MM*, 66). Rather than falling prey to the anxiety that Descartes expresses in the Second Meditation, his mistaking "hats and coats which may cover automatic machines" (*HR*, 1:155) for men, La Mettrie assumes man's mechanical essence as a given. His inquiry inverts the Cartesian order of argumentation by starting with an examination of the mechanics of the body, only to subsequently address the issue of the soul:

> Man is a machine so complicated that it is impossible at first to form a clear idea of it, and, consequently to describe it. This is why all the investigations the greatest philosophers have made *a priori*, that is by wanting to take flight with the wings of the mind, have been in vain. Only *a posteriori*, by unravelling the soul as one pulls out the guts of the body, can one, I do not say discover with clarity what the nature of man is, but rather attain the highest degree of probability possible on the subject. (*MM*, 66)

In this passage, La Mettrie makes a decisive leap from Descartes's animal-machines to state that man is a machine, so complicated in its workings as to defy efforts to form either a clear idea of it or to describe it. He then suggests that it is this very complexity that led philosophers to establish the a priori condition of the mind. La Mettrie, however, insists that the question of the soul must follow (a posteriori), rather than precede in a foundational sense an inquiry into the nature of man. Radically undermining previous theological precedents, he also suggests that the understanding of the soul must be situated in the same material and mechanical order as the body, enjoying no greater privilege than any other bodily organ. By observing that one unravels the soul as one pulls out the guts of the body, La Mettrie challenges its metaphysical priority as guarantor of certitude and clarity and settles instead for a probable understanding of man's nature.

Aiming pointed barbs at the Cartesian idealization of the mind at the expense of the body, La Mettrie perversely dismisses Descartes's hypothetical denial of the body through the rhetorical evocation of madness in the First Meditation (HR, 1:145), equating this rhetorical position with a statement of belief: "Why should I dwell on those who think their noses or other members are made of glass?" (MM, 68). His analysis abounds in examples that seek to relodge the soul within the body, from allusions to hysteria and hypochondria, to more ordinary instances such as sleep, when the soul and the body fall asleep together (MM, 68). Using the same examples as Descartes did in the *Meditations* to argue the priority and superiority of the soul, he redeploys their logic so as to claim the interdependence of the body and the soul within the organism of man defined as a machine: "The blood circulates too fast? The soul cannot sleep. The soul is agitated? The blood cannot calm down" (MM, 69). This material co-dependence of the body and the soul is further emphasized by his insistence on the role of food as the material substance that fuels and sustains the soul, thus elucidating the body's nature as a "self-winding machine" (MM, 70).

In order to demonstrate that the states of the soul always correlate to those of the body, La Mettrie appeals to the evidence provided by comparative anatomy. Noting the structural similarities, except for differences in size, between man's brain and those of animals, he attempts to bridge the Cartesian chasm between animal-machines and man-machine by establishing their shared material and mechanical organization. In so doing, La Mettrie challenges one of the fundamental tenets of the Cartesian philosophical and theological system. Descartes's definition of animals as machines devoid of conscious feeling and thought is founded on the privileged uniqueness of the rational human soul, as well as its purported immortality. It is this metaphysical interpretation of automatism that La Mettrie usurps by recuperating a notion of automatism based on mechanical causes that applies to all animate beings, thereby rendering the differences between man and animals a matter of degree and not a foundational or a constitutive difference. Given the great resemblance of man to apes, La Mettrie even raises the question of their possible education: "Why could not an ape through careful effort communicate with sign language just as the deaf?" (*MM*, 76). This latter question directly challenges the Cartesian interpretation of man as an entity that defines its very humanity through its symbolic capacity of manipulating and deploying signs. His suggestion that apes may be educated to meaningfully use signs by training through games or exercise usurps the cognitive prerogative previously reserved solely to designate the human.

La Mettrie emphasizes the material and embodied nature of human knowledge insofar as it implies the exchange of signs, where "words are the arbitrary signs" (*MM*, 79). This definition of knowledge is aimed not only at redefining cognitive materials, but more importantly at redefining cognition itself in material, rather than purely conceptual, terms:

> All that learning whose wind inflates the balloon-brains of our pedants is nothing more than a vast accumulation of words and figures which impress on our brains all those traces by which we distinguish and recall objects. . . . Words and figures designated by them [ideas] are so tied together in the brain that one rarely imagines something without thinking of its name or sign. I always say *imagine* because I believe that everything can be imagined, and that all the parts of the soul can be reduced to imagination alone. Imagination constitutes them all. (*MM*, 81)

Once again, La Mettrie's observations take Descartes's metaphysical edifice to task, especially as regards his efforts in the *Meditations* to isolate conception as an expression of reason, which, unlike the imagination, is not caught up with bodily forms. It is also important to recall that Descartes described the imagination as a faculty of the body and not of the spirit, precisely because of its involvement with figurative and visible forms. La Mettrie's claim that everything can be imagined and that the soul can be reduced to the imagination alone reintroduces the material and physical dimension that Descartes previously excluded in order to argue for the embodied character of both the soul and human knowledge in the machine. His conclusion that all parts of the soul can be reduced to imagination alone enables him to regroup judgment, reason, and memory as its constitutive parts. La Mettrie's attempt to integrate these faculties in the soul under the aegis of the imagination undermines Descartes's previous efforts to distinguish among them when he privileged judgment and reason alone as the condition of the understanding. Reason was defined as a conception independent of material constraints, as opposed to the imagination and memory, whose exclusion from rational subjectivity reflected their dependence on corporeal nature.

For La Mettrie, judgment, reason, and memory are parts of the soul understood as a physical and material entity, insofar as they are "real modifications of that *medullar canvas* onto which objects painted from the eye are projected as from a magic lantern" (*MM*, 81). If these faculties are indissociable from the imagination, this is because they share with it the same organic and material base, that of the "medullar canvas," as well as reflect in their various modifications the sensible and material reality of the external world. Attributing his privilege of the imagination to the organization of the human brain, La Mettrie concludes his critique of Descartes by questioning the very division of the mind in terms of a rational and sensitive principle: "But if such is the marvelous and incomprehensible result of the organization of the brain, if imagination explains everything, and if everything is conceived by it, why do we divide the sensitive principle that thinks in man's mind?" (*MM*, 81). His insistence on the organization of the brain explains in material terms the particular powers of explanation and conception that define the imagination. The imagination becomes that "sensitive principle that thinks in man's mind," that is to say, a principle whose intrinsic material and embodied nature precludes further distinctions. In other words, it is precisely the "sensitive" nature of the imagination, its indivisibility from the material world, that defies the efforts of any further philosophical reduction, such as earlier encountered in the "advocates of the simplicity of the mind" (81; i.e., Descartes and his followers). Mocking the use of terms such as *spirituality* and *immateriality*, La Mettrie attempts to overcome the Cartesian metaphysical legacy.

La Mettrie details the cognitive functions of the imagination by specifying its perceptual and representational powers:

> But it is still true that only the imagination perceives; the imagination represents all objects with the word and figures that characterize them; and, thus again, the imagination is the soul since it plays all the roles. Thanks to the flattering paintbrush of the imagination, the cold skeleton of reason takes on rosy, living flesh. (*MM*, 82)

Rather than denouncing the deceptive and incarnate character of the imagination, as did Descartes, La Mettrie locates both perception and representation among its functions, along with reason and judgment. Both perception and representation involve a materially concrete, rather than a purely abstract, engagement with the world. His privileging of the imagination thus reflects a recognition of its embodied character, insofar as the knowledge it acquires or purveys involves either the body (sensation) or material signs (representations) that embody its understanding of the world. La Mettrie's privileging of the imagination recalls Montaigne's emphasis on this all-important faculty (*Essays,* III, 13: 833).[10] By arguing, however, that the imagination is the soul, since "it plays all the roles," La Mettrie underlines its versatility to both embody and represent diverse forms of knowledge. It is through the imagination that reason becomes incarnate, both perceptible and representable: "the cold skeleton of reason takes on rosy, living flesh." The abstract nature of Cartesian ideas is recast by the "paintbrush of the imagination" into tangible representations. La Mettrie thus accords to the faculty of the imagination a philosophical priority and authority that is new compared to its subordinate position in Descartes due to its associations with the body. However, by declaring the imagination to be the "soul," La Mettrie reverses key terms in the Cartesian philosophical edifice without necessarily overturning the dualist logic that subtends them.

The task of the imagination, according to La Mettrie, is not only to "paint nature," but to "measure" it by noticing the relations among these representations: "Just as it cannot enjoy the pleasures of the senses without experiencing their voluptuous perfection, the imagination could not reflect on its mechanically conceived ideas unless it were identical with judgement itself" (*MM,* 82). This passage posits the experience of sensation and the pleasures associated with it as deriving solely from "mechanically conceived ideas" in order to suggest the imagination's reflective capacities to form judgments, rather than merely generating representations. At issue, however, is neither La Mettrie's attempt to bring judgment within the purview of the imagination nor his effort to rehabilitate the senses by insisting on their pleasurable effects. More notable is the fact that he attributes this experience of pleasure by the imagination to "mechanically conceived ideas," thereby redefining its nature as one that involves purely material and mechanical concerns. It is important to recall, in this context, that Montaigne's praise for the powers of imagination derived from its ability to mediate and make desire tangible as embodied forms (III, 13: 833). Its capacity for embodiment was not represented as a function of the search for knowledge, nor of the understanding, but as a way of expressing the power of desire to attain material semblance. Desire as a major motivating force of the imagination is entirely absent in La Mettrie's argument, precisely because its consideration would challenge the deterministic confines of his materialist and mechanical system.

While La Mettrie will go on to equate the imagination with the highest intellectual achievements, contending that it can be "elevated by art to the lofty and rare dignity of genius" (*MM*, 84), this revalorization fails to spell out its precise modes of operation. It will be the task of education to give free reign to or to restrain what La Mettrie calls the "lively springs of the imagination" (85), in order for individuals to attain either artistic or scientific (and philosophical) development. His argument regarding imagination as a source of genius is innovative insofar as it attributes a common source to intellectual development in both arts and sciences. Moreover, it suggests the shared affinity between poetic and scientific knowledge. La Mettrie's position is symptomatic of the rise of a new concept of intelligence in the eighteenth century, a concept that no longer privileges reason, but rather celebrates its powers under the aegis of the imagination and the multiplicity of forms that it may take, since it "easily embraces an astonishing host of objects" (*MM*, 84).[11] By celebrating the imagination and the multitude of forms it embodies, La Mettrie redefines the powers of intellect in terms of its material engagements with the world. However, this affirmation of imagination as the figure for human intellect takes place within a rational horizon that excludes considerations of desire.

Having emphasized the material dimensions of the intellect, La Mettrie will continue to argue for the material and organizational continuity between men and animals: "Man is not molded out of more precious clay than they. Nature employed the same dough for both man and animals, varying only the leaven" (*MM*, 90). His refusal to recognize any material distinctions between the two leads him to reaffirm that "organization is therefore sufficient to explain everything" (98). Insisting on the organization of man as a machine that simply disposes of a few more cogs and springs than animals, he refuses to explain aspects pertaining to man in terms that rely on previous philosophical or religious traditions. For instance, he will argue that the soul is simply an empty word to which no idea corresponds, and that it should be invoked only to name the part of the brain that thinks (*MM*, 98, 103), leading him to conclude: "Thus, the soul is only a principle of movement or sensible material part of the brain, which one can regard as the machine's principal spring without fear of being mistaken" (*MM*, 105). The soul is presented here as a principle of movement lodged in the sensible material part of the brain and thus implicit and inherent in its physical organization. Its former religious and philosophical autonomy and authority as a purely spiritual and immaterial agent are dismissed with no further consideration of the implications of assigning to material organization properties heretofore reserved to subjectivity and the definition of the human.

Sex and the Logic of the Machine

> To be a machine, to feel, think, know good from evil.
> —La Mettrie

Pursuing the analogy between the human body and the machine, La Mettrie compares its complexity to an "immense clock," constructed with so much artifice and skill that if particular parts of the mechanism break down, they by no means endanger its abilities to function as a whole (*MM*, 110). However, La Mettrie is not content to restrict this mechanical analogy to the body, as Descartes had done, but uses it as a way of describing man as a whole. This gesture has extremely significant consequences, since it seeks to reinscribe the entire horizon of the human within the logic of the machine. La Mettrie elaborates his analogy of man to the machine by introducing into its mechanical operations conscious feeling, thought, and even moral reflection:

> To be a machine, to feel, think, know good from evil like blue from yellow, in a word to be born with intelligence and a sure instinct for morality, and yet to be only an animal, are things no more contradictory than to be an ape or a parrot and know how to find sexual pleasure. And, since the occasion presents itself for saying so, who would have ever divined *a priori* that shooting off a gob of sperm during copulation would make one feel such divine pleasure, and that from it would be born a tiny creature who one day, following certain laws, would enjoy similar delights? (*MM*, 112)

All human functions, ranging from sensation to thought, and including the capacity to make moral distinctions, are posited as an extension of mechanical principles relocating the human within the realm of automatism and mechanical determinism. Regardless of their degree of complexity, these diverse functions that cover the gamut from perceptual to intellectual activities are assimilated indiscriminately to a mechanical order whose laws apply to both human and animal behavior.

In the passage above, however, La Mettrie is not merely content to state the mechanical character of perceptual and intellectual functions, but goes on to suggest that their logic is of the same order as the sexual behavior of animals. The introduction of sexuality at this point functions as yet another example of the overlap between human and animal bodily organization and behavior. However, this appeal to sexuality is particularly surprising, since it is difficult to understand how sexuality would reference the reality of the machine. For it is precisely sexuality and procreation that were invoked to distinguish inanimate machines from animate beings. It is useful in this context to recall Voltaire's ironic comment that clocks do not make little clocks. The incapacity of an inanimate machine to create other machines of a complexity and nature equal to itself is answered by La Mettrie through the mechanization of both sexuality and its procreative functions in all animate beings. By introducing "sex" into its workings, La Mettrie seeks to embody the machine as both a gendered and generative device.[12]

La Mettrie introduces sexuality within the purview of the machine by insisting on its purely material and mechanical nature in both men and animals. Sexuality and its "divine pleasures" are linked reductively to the mechanics of the animate body, its shooting of a gob of sperm. Sexual pleasure is represented as the mere effect of mechanical forces whose expression is contained within a system of material causality. Thus sexuality ceases to reflect an encounter between subjects, since their mechanical coupling attests to the mere performance of a logic inherent in the organizational blueprint of the machine. Both desire and the potential role played by the imagination, insofar as they have an impact on both the physical and the imaginary status of bodies in the context of human sexuality, are entirely left out of his discussion. Thus La Mettrie's efforts to "sex" the machine only result in the mechanization of sexuality itself, by reducing it to a purely organic and physical function that neither reflects nor has any bearing on the subjective makeup of man as distinguished from animals.

To speak about man, in this context, is no accident, since La Mettrie's focus is entirely on ejaculation and the male sexual functions and pleasure.[13] Although he does not broach the notion of sexual difference explicitly, his subsequent discussion regarding the animated nature of the male sperm and the supposed vegetative nature of female egg into which it plants itself and which provides its food suggests a very specific gender hierarchy. The anatomical difference between the sexes is analyzed by emphasizing the active nature of male sperm, leading La Mettrie to question the actual contribution and participation of the female egg: "For example, so rarely do male and female seeds make contact in sexual congress that I am tempted to think that the female seed is unnecessary for generation" (*MM*, 114).[14] Although he recognizes the sometime resemblance of children to the father or the mother, this physical evidence that attests to the "intercourse between the parts," does not prevent him from reiterating his prior conviction:

> On the other hand, why let the lack of an explanation rule out a fact? It seems to me that the male does all the work, both in a woman fast asleep as well as in the most lustful woman. From the beginning, then, the disposition of body parts comes from the male seed or tiny worm. (*MM*, 114)

Despite the concrete evidence of heredity attesting to the passage of both masculine and feminine traits, La Mettrie persists in maintaining the privilege of male sexuality as a generative and engendering principle. While the active and generative principle of human sexuality is ascribed to the masculine component, the female component is minimized to the point where its very existence and contribution comes into doubt. This is not altogether surprising, given that La Mettrie's mechanical description of nature valorizes motion in order to account for the generative and transformative aspects of matter. Although La Mettrie's analogy of man to a machine initially appears to exclude gender considerations, his efforts to embody the machine by providing an account of its sexual and procreative functions reinscribes the notion of sexual difference and the hierarchy of the sexes in his materialist system. La Mettrie's putative universalist account of sexuality based on mechanical and material causes is in fact male gendered, insofar as it claims the priority of both male orgasm and the male sperm as the fundamental features for biological generation.

Having outlined some of the most salient features of La Mettrie's materialism and his equation of man to a machine, it is important to consider whether the challenge that he extends to the Cartesian mind-body dualism is sufficient to overturn its rational order, particularly as regards its impact on his elaboration of sexual difference. Critics of Cartesian rationalism, such as Karl Stern and Susan Bordo, have described its legacy in terms of the "masculinization of thought."[15] For Stern, this notion of masculinization reflects the disembodiment of the Cartesian rational subject and thus the exclusion of embodiment from the purview of subjectivity: "Man is made flesh-less, as it were, and the Incarnation as the pivotal point of history becomes a meaningless myth."[16] Both man and nature cease to function within the horizon of incarnation, of a becoming whose character is irreducible to a purely mechanical causality. For Bordo, on the other hand, Cartesianism implies both the transcendence of the body, as chief impediment to objectivity, and the consequent diremption of the natural world from the human: "The dichotomy between the spiritual and the corporeal also established the utter diremption of the natural world from the human."[17] This diremption reflects both the rational subject's dispossession of its human character and the concurrent objectification of nature operated through its material reduction.

Descartes's objectification of nature as *res extensa* ("totally devoid of mind and thought") implies its subjection to rational subjects, whose stated ambition is to become "masters and possessors of nature." The equation of objective knowledge with mastery over nature inscribes knowledge within a dynamics of power inflected with gender overtones. This mechanical interpretation of nature not only overthrows what Carolyn Merchant called an "organic cosmology," where nature's generative powers are equated with female principles, but also restricts nature within a framework where the discovery of its mechanical laws coincides with its submission to a rational order.[18] Thus, while manifestly beyond gender, the Cartesian cogito and the representational order that sustains it evoke sexual difference not as an expression of the body, but as the expression of the power relations foundationally latent within representation.

The legacy of the Cartesian ontological blueprint proves to be extremely significant to La Mettrie's efforts to bring back the human in the guise of a machine within the framework of a natural world defined in materialist and mechanist terms. While at first sight La Mettrie's "materialistic monism," which rejects the soul's distinctness from the body by redefining it as something implicit in organized matter, appears to replace Cartesian dualism, the question lingers as to whether his gesture succeeds in overturning the Cartesian ontological blueprint.[19] As the preceding analysis of *Man-Machine* suggests, the valorization of matter as a foundational term does not undermine the Cartesian diremption of the human from nature. The shift from dualism to a materialistic monism does not reverse the initial hierarchy of these terms, insofar as the reduction of nature to materialist and mechanist principles follows out of Descartes's original reduction of the body to a machine. La Mettrie's attempt to grant to the laws of nature the universal status formerly ascribed to the rational mind only reinforces the fact that their material and mechanical character reflects an objectification of nature based on the privilege accorded to the scientific method.[20] Even though La Mettrie attempts to materialize reason by defining it within the purview of the imagination, this effort to reframe it by no means impacts on its methodical application and stated goal to attain scientific knowledge through "clear-sighted penetration" (*MM*, 86).[21]

La Mettrie's efforts to redefine man as a machine imply the impossibility of recovering a notion of embodiment as other than a function of mechanical principles. These mechanical principles subordinate all subjective expression to the deterministic logic of the machine. Embodiment emerges in this context as a function not of an organism, but of its material organization. Thus the logic of embodiment is institutionalized within the abstract rational and mechanical laws that govern the material foundation and administration of the body. Embodiment thus emerges as a feature of nature understood as a rational order, whose material and mechanical laws virtually configure the materialization of the body. Within this material framework, sexuality references not the organic body but a mechanical device, since embodiment merely attests to its material organization and submission to a rational order. La Mettrie's mechanical reduction of sexuality also objectifies human behavior, thereby simply expanding Descartes's original analogy of the body and the machine by generalizing it as universal law. While neutralizing the differences that separate man from machines, by assimilating the logic of their behavior to common material and mechanical laws, this eradication of difference that erodes mind-body dualism does not ultimately challenge the broader meaning of ontological difference understood as a rational and representational order. Hence it is not surprising that when La Mettrie evokes the notion of sexual difference in the context of his embodiment of the machine, its manifestations suggest the reinstatement of power relations and differences proper to the rational and representational order that subtends his mechanist account. The logic of sexual difference thus still remains within the horizon of ontological difference, thereby revealing the fundamental difficulty of thinking about embodiment as long as the machine functions as the determining horizon for the being of humans, animals, and nature as a whole.

The questions and problems raised by La Mettrie's materialist and mechanist interpretations of man and nature come to a head in the marquis de Sade's works, with their violent, perverse, and even criminal interpretations of sexuality. In the pages that follow, Sade's own engagement with materialism will be at issue. The exaggerated violence that Sade unleashes on the body of his novelistic protagonists will be examined as a function of both the mechanical reduction of the body and his efforts to undermine the very premises that underlie rational thought. Resorting to a strategy of both literary and philosophical parody, he will radically destabilize the generic and gender-referential aspects of classical discourse and thus challenge the very limits of representation. Attempting to destroy both notions of sexual and ontological difference, Sade will make manifest the violence and relations of power implicit in the Cartesian legacy—that of the technologization of man and nature. But this face-to-face encounter of thought with its limits, while radically challenging the Cartesian metaphysical legacy, will not succeed in restoring to the body either its corporeality or its capacity for agency.

Chapter 7

Sex at the Limits of Representation

The real is the impossible.
  —Jacques Lacan

The impossible is literature.
  —Georges Bataille

"It is necessary," wrote Baudelaire, "to keep coming back to Sade, again and again."[1] Baudelaire's injunction has been quite prophetic, since contemporary critics continue to return to Sade in order to assess his contribution to modernity. D. A. F. de Sade's novelistic work has been interpreted by critics since Bataille as a literature of transgression.[2] However, the limits that the Sadean text challenges are not those of sexuality alone. Rather, through his exhaustive exposition of sexuality, Sade succeeds in expanding its meaning to include not only perverse and even criminal modes of activity, but also to challenge all moral referents and thus fundamentally alter the very definition of the limits of thought.

As Michel Foucault suggests in "A Preface to Transgression," Sade's transgressive gesture posits through the language of sexuality an ontological and theological challenge to man's definition of and relation to God:

> From the moment that Sade delivered its first words and marked out, in a single discourse, the boundaries of what suddenly became its kingdom, the language of sexuality has lifted us into the night where God is absent, where all our actions are addressed to this absence in a profanation which at once identifies it, dissipates it, exhausts itself in it, and restores it to the empty purity of its transgression.[3]

Sade's extensive exploration of the boundaries of sexuality is interpreted by Foucault as the prototype of all transgressive gestures, since it stages the challenge of the limits of philosophy and religion. Based on Georges Bataille and Pierre Klossowski, Foucault's interpretation of the role of sexuality underlines the liminal character of Sadean thought, presenting him as the closure of classical, representation-based thought. Foucault suggests that

Sadean discourse is the last discourse that undertakes "representation," that is to say, defines its order through an exhaustive nomenclature and totalizing categorization.[4]

However, the encyclopedic character of representation in Sade's work in fact threatens, through its excessive display, to foreclose and thus to destroy the boundaries of classical representation. The question thus arises whether it is sufficient or even adequate to classify Sade's novelistic and philosophical works in terms of "transgression." This study will show that while embodying the principles of the Enlightenment, the search for totalizing categories and a universal order, Sade's representation of reason and humanity is in fact a parody of the ideology of the Enlightenment. His ostensible encyclopedic ambition to "say everything" and to "show everything" results both in the saturation of the classical order of representation and in its actual violation, through the production of an excess that challenges the notion of order itself. Everything that up to Sade constitutes the exterior of reason—evil, crime, monstrosity, and sexual perversion—is brought within its domain, thereby redefining the positive connotations that his contemporaries associated with reason. The very premises of eighteenth-century thought are systematically exposed and debased by Sade, so that the underpinnings of its logical foundations are pitted through parody against themselves. Sade's work thus emerges less as a literature of scandal than as the scandal of literature, insofar as his reflections on representation embody and stage the confrontation of thought with its limits. Sade's demythologization of reason as the substratum of representation involves, as this study will show, the violent expansion of its logical and systematic properties, so that thought itself becomes the figurative victim of the excesses of literary and philosophical parody.

The Misfortunes of Literature

> I state and affirm that I have never written any *immoral books,*
> and that I never shall.
> —Sade

In his *Reflections on the Novel,* Sade defines the novel *(roman)* as follows: "We give the name 'novel' to any work of imagination fashioned from the most uncommon adventures which men experience in the course of their lives."[5] Despite the somewhat Aristotelian tone of this pronouncement, which had been previously applied to the mechanisms of tragedy intended to evoke fear and pity, Sade's comments later in his pamphlet indicate that this statement should be taken "literally." That is to say, that Sade's novels will deal with adventures so uncommon that their implausibility will threaten the very definition of the novel. In the *Poetics,* Aristotle designates misfortune as an accident inspired by a character flaw or weakness *(hamartia),* intended to inspire sympathy and catharsis;[6] whereas for Sade, misfortune becomes a rule in and of itself—an ultimate challenge to any possible identification on the part of the reader. Since vice will reap the rewards of virtue, the process of identification with the character in a cathartic sense is precluded. The Sadean antinovel thus presents its reader with a paradox. On the one hand, these works refuse mimesis as a principle of imitation and identification that guides the reader's relation to the text. On the other hand, the Sadean antinovel will rely on a new concept of imitation. Rather than pretending to copy reality, his novels parody the very conventions that structure novelistic reality.

This strategy for appealing to identification on the part of the reader, while simultaneously rejecting mimetic conventions, can be seen in Sade's warning to his readers. Attacking other authors who make "vice seem attractive," Sade explains in *Reflections on the Novel* that the violence of his novelistic representations excludes all possible identification:

> I have no wish to make vice seem attractive. Unlike Crébillon and Dorat, I have not set myself the dangerous goal of enticing women to love characters who deceive them; on the contrary, I want them to loathe these characters. 'Tis the only way one can avoid being duped by them. And, in order to succeed in that purpose, I painted that hero who treads the path of vice with features so frightful that they will most assuredly not inspire either pity or love. In so doing, I dare say I am become more moral than those who believe they have licence to embellish them.[7]

Sade's works defy the reader's expectations since they refuse claims that rely on the traditional conception of the novel as a vehicle for imitation and as a model for truth. While Sade recognizes that the moral referent of classical novels is merely a subterfuge for presenting images that violate it, his condemnation, however, cannot be construed literally as a moral claim. Although Sade suggests that he is "more moral" than his contemporaries, his ostensible "moral" intention is immediately put into question by his disclaimer at the end of the essay that he is the author of the scandalous *Justine.* By challenging his own authenticity as the author of *Justine,* Sade parodies any simplistic inference regarding the authoritative and direct referential relation of the author and his text. His comment at the end of his treatise on the novel brackets the question of the identity of the author and reduces it to a parody of the authorial persona.

Sade's parody of his own authorial persona is made explicit in an attack on one of the critics of his *Crimes of Love*, Villeterque. Sade brutally admonishes his critic by accusing him of falsely identifying the author with the fictional characters:

> Loathsome ignoramus: have you not yet learned that every character in any dramatic work must employ a language in keeping with his character, and that, when he does, 'tis the fictional character who is speaking and not the author? and that, in such an instance, 'tis indeed common that the character inspired by the role he is playing, says things completely contrary to what the author may say when he himself is speaking?[8]

Sade's critique of Villeterque as a bad reader, who persists in conflating author and character, exposes the myth that underlies literature as a mirror of the identity of the author. Rather than interpreting the author as a naive referent for the literary work, Sade suggests that the author himself may be nothing more than a fictional character, that is, an invention or a convention through which the literary work is made intelligible. He taunts Villeterque by flaunting the one thing that he and his characters agree about:

> Ah, Monsieur Villeterque, what a fool you are! This is one truth concerning which both I and my characters will always be in complete agreement whenever we have the occasion to exchange views regarding your prosaic existence.[9]

By affirming his explicit complicity with his fictional characters, Sade underlines his refusal to be simply assimilated to his work. In so doing, Sade disrupts the mimetic relation between the author and the work, by having his characters mime him as comical mouthpieces that reiterate his putative claims. By both disengaging himself from his characters and by enlisting their support, through a perverse play with the notion of mimesis, Sade succeeds in distinguishing himself from what he calls Villeterque's "*mirror-authors*."[10] Sade's attack on Villeterque and his camp of "mirror" authors represents his own complex position as a parodist, who uses imitation only to destroy it as a category that has any referential relation to "reality." His response does not merely address Villeterque, but functions as a warning to all future critics who will naively persist in identifying him with his characters, and who will search for clues of his authorial identity by identifying the author with the literary work.

In *The Misfortunes of Virtue*, Sade systematically enacts his critique of the classical novel through strategies that disrupt identification with both mimetic and moral referents. In the preface, Sade forewarns the reader that the aim of the novel is to depict the misfortunes of virtue, rather than its rewards. By suspending moral claims, Sade challenges the limits of novelistic verisimilitude and plausibility. *The Misfortunes of Virtue* presents the reader with an implausible plot: that of the relentless, exaggerated, and caricatural description of the heroine's misfortunes. The heroine, Justine/Sophie, who can hardly be called such since she is nothing more than a compendium of banal moral maxims, is shown suffering from her unsuccessful attempts to reconcile her own beliefs and her worldly experiences. Her misfortunes are profoundly literary: they represent a classical discourse, a discourse of normative morality and good faith, and its violation through its explosive encounters and clashes with other types of discourse, representing various noble, scientific, religious, and mercantile institutions.

The discomfiture of the reader in the face of the erotic victimization of the heroine takes on a surreal, almost dreamlike character. As Blanchot has noted, Sade's eroticism paradoxically derives its brutal reality and exaggerated freedom from its fictional nature: "Sade's eroticism is a dream eroticism, since it expresses itself exclusively in fiction; but the more this eroticism is imagined, the more it requires a fiction from which dream is excluded, a fiction wherein debauchery can be enacted and lived."[11] Blanchot's observation regarding the deliberate fictional staging of eroticism in Sade's novels is helpful toward elucidating the reader's complicitous relation to fiction. The paradox, as Blanchot suggests, is that Sade uses fiction in such an exaggerated fashion as to challenge its limits and consequently to abolish through fiction the reader's sense of novelistic reality.

The reader's effort to identify with the protagonists of the novel is thwarted from the novel's inception. *The Misfortunes of Virtue* introduces two heroines, the sisters Juliette and Justine, who are remarkably different. Each represents in caricature the obverse of the other. Juliette is the character who though virtuous in her beliefs learns that virtue has no real currency in the social world. She sells the physical equivalent of her virtue many times over, thereby parodying and debasing it as counterfeit money. She considers virtue to be a mere sign, a convention that can be traded in the social domain in order to generate power, pleasure, and security. Her activities document her remarkable education from victim to master and passage from pleasure to crime, since her behavior shuns both the notion of social contract and that of a universal moral referent.

At the other end of the spectrum, Justine represents the epitome of virtue, a virtue that is so proud of itself that it invites violation. The reader is trapped, since s/he cannot identify with either character without a sense of moral complicity with one of two unacceptable sides—vice or virtue. This problem is exacerbated by the fact that although the story focuses entirely on the misfortunes of Justine (alias, virtue) the character is further removed from the reader through a linguistic displacement. Justine's real name is Sophie (wisdom, in Greek), a name all the more ironic since the heroine displays her magnificent virtue very unwisely, inviting violation and destruction. By upholding compulsively an ideal standard of behavior, Justine/Sophie invites transgression. The desiring structure of the text is constituted around the adventures of virtue, the narration of its consistent violation. The reader is thus freed from identification with the discourse of victimization and made aware of the complicity involved in the act of reading.

Justine's encounter with Bressac in *The Misfortunes of Virtue* emblematizes both her status as erotic victim and the reader's complicitous position as victim of novelistic conventions.[12] Hidden behind a bush, the heroine witnesses the verbal and physical exchanges between the aristocrat Bressac and his valet. Doubling the position of the reader, as a female voyeur, Justine discovers that the act of witnessing the discourse and act of sodomy involves complicity. Despite her sense of moral condemnation, she is literally drawn into the scene (like the reader); having been discovered by Bressac, she is tied to a tree and menaced with flagellation and sodomy. Thus from the very beginnings of the novel, Sade demonstrates that there can be no exterior or privileged position for Sophie, or for that matter the reader, as a voyeur. Having been literally "drawn" into the scene, both Justine and the reader discover that they risk being physically marked by this experience. By identifying with the heroine, the reader becomes a victim as well, since the act of reading governed by the mimetic relation of reader and text implies the risk of being marked by the punitive logic of the text. The physical violence unleashed by the text is thus directed not merely toward the heroine, but also to the traditional conventions that govern the classical novel. In other words, the reader may discover, like Justine, that the act of representation involves an inescapable complicity.

The consistent violence unleashed upon the body of the heroine becomes the index of a violence endemic to classical representation in general. The act of marking Justine's body, through sexual, perverse, and punitive acts, traces upon the body the script of the social and political ideology that the heroine consciously attempts to contain through her virtue. Just as characters such as Bressac and Du Buisson attempt to stamp their own demystified social ideology upon their victim, their inability to mark her ideas will culminate in Justine's body being branded falsely as a thief. This unjust punishment, however, is logically consistent with the heroine's structural position, since her victimization is due to her unconscious assimilation of popular ideology, her metaphorical "thievery" of a popular ideal of virtue. As an unconscious exponent of popular ideology, Justine refuses to reflect on or learn from her misadventures and thus to recognize the imprint of competing ideologies. This refusal to examine the social and physical implications of ideology leads to the increasingly violent tone of the novel as it attempts to literalize ideology and thus implicate an unwitting Justine in more heinous crimes such as murder and arson. Notwithstanding the heroine's ostensible innocence, her observance of virtue becomes the site of violence against the other, since its unreflected nature can be manipulated as an instrument of destruction of both the heroine herself and other protagonists. Passing from the position of spectator to that of unsuspecting actor, Justine is shown to be playing the role of the victim whose very innocence becomes complicitous with crime.

The trajectory of the unfortunate adventures of the heroine Justine (alias Sophie) involves successive encounters with several types of institutions: a noble or feudal model (Bressac); a scientific or experimental model (Rodin); a Christian religious model (the convent Sainte-Marie des Bois); and at the end, a false double of the noble and mercantile model (Dalville's château), which simulates the codes of both institutions in order to function as a "factory" for the production of false currency. Marcel Hénaff has shown that the economy of Sadean libertinage is a consumer economy that operates by reference to these three major models—feudal, monastic, and mercantile.[13] However, each of these social institutions has ceased to function in a traditional sense. Neither the castle, nor the monastery, nor the factory functions as a normal site of production. Instead their social, religious, or economic role has been subverted, since they have been appropriated and perverted for either sexual or monetary ends. Although sexuality appears to be the shared subtext of all these social institutions, since it represents its principles of social exchange or consumer economy, this perception is soon qualified. The last example in the book, that of Dalville's château, where he abuses his subjects both as laborers and as sexual objects, demonstrates that their status as autonomous subjects is totally in question, since the perversion of the social order is equated with the production of false currency. Thus the sexual referent, although universal, is no more privileged than any of the other terms of the novel, since it can also be subject to an economy of simulation. Just as money can be counterfeited and thus function within the social domain, so can sexuality be reified, objectified, and perverted from its legitimated reproductive functions. Social institutions whose previous aims involved the cumulative interest of social production or reproduction are demystified as purveyors of expenditure, that is to say, waste.

To these central models of social exchange we may also add the production of knowledge, whose ideological underpinnings are elucidated by Sade in his parody of scientific discourse. The methodology of scientific knowledge, particularly the experimental method, is caricatured in order to reveal that science, like religion, relies on a set of beliefs that blind the observer-believer to the scandalous implications of the method. Sophie's encounter with the surgeon Rodin, a researcher who practices vivisection of the sexual organs, reveals the fact that medical discourse relies on a concept of knowledge whose methods imply the reduction of subjects to objects. Rodin perversely derives pleasure from the objectification implicit in medical experiments insofar as they entail manipulation and power. Thus medical knowledge is equated with Dalville's counterfeit money, to the extent that they both instrumentalize sexuality as means to attain something else. In the first case sexuality enables the discovery of new ideas; in the second case, sexuality is a vehicle for the production of false currency that stands in for the ideas. Within this economy of total simulation, neither sexuality nor ideas can function legitimately. As simulated products of an economy of waste that dispenses with the subject, both sexuality and money are exchanged arbitrarily, thereby wreaking havoc on notions of both social production and reproduction.

The superimposition of these different institutional codes in the novel has profound effects on the conception of the individual as a social and private entity. As Justine learns, the social and the private become indistinguishable within the socialized context of the convent. There is no room either for privacy or ultimately for interiority. This can be seen in the advice offered to Justine by Omphale, who tells her that there are no excuses in regard to the law: one cannot say that one should not be punished for an infraction because one did not know the law. As Omphale explains, one must be either instructed by one's companions or guess everything by oneself; without any forewarning one is held responsible and punished for everything.[14] Omphale's warning is very clear: ignorance is no excuse in the eyes of the law. Consequently, in the Sadean text there is no space public or private that escapes the script of the law, since the individual even at the most private moments is still within the confines of the social scenario. Justine's useless efforts to retain her personal identity within the context of the perverted convent of Sainte-Marie des Bois represents Sade's radical critique of the humanist interpretation of man as an autonomous individual entity. Even the body, as the insignia of the personal, is victimized in such a way as to transgress the conception of the body as private property. It is not by accident that the Sadean body has often been equated to a machine, since its impersonal and mechanical character best represents the technical inscription of ideology upon the body. This is why the protagonists in Sade demonstrate a lack of self-consciousness in the psychological sense, or, from a theological perspective, a lack of spiritual interiority. Sade parodies St. Paul's dictum in Romans that the law is not the letter but the spirit. In his works, there is only the law as the letter and no spirit.

In *The Misfortunes of Virtue,* Justine's refusal to recognize the function of the law as an emblem of the social symbolic leads to her ultimate destruction, ironically by nature, rather than by society. This ironic ending, which we shall examine later in more detail, reflects Sade's exploration and final assimilation of the natural to the social. Justine/Sophie's death by a thunderbolt, which corresponds to her "unjust punishment" in the world of the novel, reflects her complicitous relation to popular ideology: her identification with the order of representation based on conventional moral principles. She represents the bad reader, the reader who mistakes the material and signifying levels of the text. In the novel, it is exactly her conceit regarding a certain way that representation behaves or its exemplarity that is constantly tested and negated. Despite the overtly sadistic victimization of the heroine, and by extension, the traditional reader, it becomes clear, following Foucault's observation, that the "object of sadism" in the novel is not ultimately the heroine, but "everything that might have been said," that is, conventional discourse.[15] Insofar as the heroine herself is a representation of the reader, it is her bad faith as a reader and good faith as a character that constitute the plot of the text and the texture of her misfortunes.

From the Bedroom to the Deathbed of Philosophy

> Sade lived through an ethical darkness similar to the intellectual
> night in which Descartes shrouded himself.
> —Simone de Beauvoir

If *The Misfortunes of Virtue* represents a heroine whose misfortunes derive from her inability to learn from her experiences, *Philosophy in the Bedroom* presents the counterscenario of a heroine whose erotic education leads to the facile equation of eroticism with perversion and crime. The title of the novel, *Philosophy in the Bedroom,* encapsulates the paradoxical content of the work, its effort to combine eroticism and philosophy. However, despite the overt affiliations of this novel to other erotic novels in the eighteenth century and to the materialist philosophy of La Mettrie, d'Holbach, and Helvétius, it soon becomes clear that neither eroticism nor philosophy is treated in traditional ways.[16] As this analysis will show, Sade is not simply using philosophy as a pretext for the presentation of erotic scenes, or vice versa. Rather, his exploration of perverse sexuality and crime corresponds to and reflects his effort to destroy the foundations of rationalist thought. Perversion, understood in these terms, takes as its point of departure the sexual referent in order to take to task the premises of rational thought itself.

The dialogue form of *Philosophy in the Bedroom* and its theatrical character present problems for the reader. The narrative level, or what is told, is enacted and staged for the reader, while providing at the same time theoretical justification. As Sollers has noted, word, gesture, and thought are brought together within a global theater that constitutes the "writing of the inadmissible."[17] The problem for the reader is that the identification with the erotic scene as the stage of desire is constantly interrupted by philosophical disquisitions that threaten to mislead the reader into a criminal relation to the text. The violation of the traditional norms that govern the relation between reader and novel and novel and reality corresponds to the perverse representation of sexuality and reason. As Michel Tort observes: "We find a correspondence in Sade's work between the theoretical law of maximizing perverse deviation, and a theory of the evolution of novelistic forms and their necessary exhaustion."[18] This correspondence in Sade's work between a theory of perversity and the use of deviant novelistic forms will be the springboard for our discussion of the status of representation and its philosophical conditions. A closer reading of the novel will demonstrate that perversity is not merely an incidental aspect of the novel, but rather that it reflects Sade's understanding of representation and his critique of classical reason.

Despite the overt erotic and licentious content of *Philosophy in the Bedroom,* the reader quickly becomes aware of the fact that both the erotic body and the nature of pleasure are being redefined. The problem is that the incessant couplings and scrambling of body parts defy not only our conventional notion of sexuality, but more importantly, the autonomy of the body as the bearer and purveyor of pleasure. Eugénie's initiation to sexuality by her two "teachers," Mme. de Saint-Ange and Dolmancé (who are brother and sister), rapidly progresses into perverse activities. The conventions that define both the anatomy and the functions of the "natural" body are willfully ignored in order to redefine the body and the pleasures traditionally associated with it. Sexuality becomes an expression of the maximized forms of mechanical coupling available to the body. But this saturation of all the orifices and positions of the body-machine is accompanied by its further virtualization and multiplication through mirrors. Mme. de Saint-Ange's explanation as to why there are so many mirrors in her bedroom clarifies the status of the libertine body in the novel:

> By repeating our attitudes and postures in a thousand different ways, they infinitely multiply those same pleasures for the persons seated here upon this ottoman. Thus everything is visible, no part of the body can remain hidden: everything must be seen; these images are so many groups disposed around those enchained by love, so many delicious tableaux where lewdness waxes drunk and which soon drive it to its climax.[19]

Mme. de Saint-Ange's reply elucidates the status of sexuality in the novel. Pleasure is no longer based on the natural body, nor on its conventional associations. The mechanical saturation of the body is supplemented here by the pleasures incited by its additional replication through images.[20] The limits of the body are extended through mirrors whose reflections generate an infinitely fragmented and deformed representation of sexuality. The effort to make the body totally visible, so as to reveal its sexual workings, results in the multiplication of the body as "delicious tableaux." These "mirror" images of the body redefine pleasure as a perverse excess generated through representation. Thus the "pleasure principle" governing the Sadean text no longer affirms the autonomy of the conventional body, but rather its deviation and multiplication through perverse representations. Perversion in this context no longer functions as the expression of particular forms of deviation, but emerges as a general attitude toward representation.

In the novel, the body is not presented according to classical conventions, asking to be deciphered, decoded or interpreted. As Hénaff observes, the body in Sade exhibits no symptoms, it is not enigmatic, and knows no content other than that of its libertine context.[21] The sexual expenditure of the body requires a language proper to expenditure—that of use-value, not the referential language of communication or interpretation. The body is defined purely by its functionality, and as such is reduced to a machine (recalling La Mettrie), but a machine that exists only as a hookup to other machines. Given this purely functional interpretation of the body, it is not surprising that cruelty may become equated with and supersede pleasure. Dolmancé explains that "it is purely a question of exposing our nervous system to the most violent possible shock; now there is no doubt that we are much more keenly affected by pain than by pleasure: the reverberations that result in us when the sensation of pain is produced in others will essentially be of a more vigorous character" (*PB*, 252). Pain is described in mechanical terms as a violent shock, recalling Sade's description in *Reflections on the Novel* of why he chose to write about subjects that inspire shock and terror. Following Sade's perverse logic, the representation of pain mechanically "reverberates" or mirrors sensation more effectively than pleasure. Cruelty can also be experienced as a function of mental representations that generate physical effects: "Look, Madame, do you see it? Do you see this libertine discharge *mentally,* without anyone having touched her?" (*PB*, 288). Sade supplements the mechanics of the body with virtual images, since the imagination can represent events whose shock value exceeds physical reality. Thus in addition to investing sexuality in the body in a mechanical sense, Sade supplements its materiality with virtual images, thereby inscribing sexuality in the order of representation. By positing cruelty as a new kind of pleasure principle, Sade perversely undermines conventional notions of sexuality in order to challenge, through representation, the limits of both reason and the natural body.

Undermining the hierarchical separation of the mind and the body by demonstrating their interchangeability as organs of pleasure, Sade proceeds to question further the identity of the body. In *Philosophy in the Bedroom,* the body is presented as an undifferentiated entity, whose orifices are indistinguishable by reference to pleasure: "For no one will wish to maintain that all the parts of the body do not *resemble* each other, that there are some which are pure, and others defiled; but, as it is unthinkable that such nonsense be advanced seriously . . ." (*PB*, 325–26; emphasis added). The traditional distinctions and hierarchies that describe the body are abolished, in order to define the body through the principle of resemblance. The cultural conventions that valorize certain parts of the body in order to exclude others are denounced, so that the entire body may become the purveyor of pleasure. By affirming the functional resemblance of all the parts of the body, Sade scrambles its conventional definition in order to constitute the libertine body through perversion and parody. Not content to question the identity of the body, Sade goes on to ask what man is, and why he occupies a privileged place in the world:

What is man? and what difference is there between him and other plants, between him and all the other animals of the world? None, obviously. . . . Since the parallels are so exact that the inquiring eye of philosophy is absolutely unable to perceive any grounds for discrimination *(dissemblance),* there is just as much evil in killing animals as men, or just as little, and whatever be the distinctions we make, they will be found to stem from our pride's prejudices, that which, unhappily, nothing is more absurd. (*PB*, 330)

By refusing to acknowledge a philosophical basis for man's distinctive place in the hierarchy of natural beings, Sade destroys man's foundational position. Recalling La Mettrie, his argument that man resembles all the other natural beings so closely that even philosophy is unable to establish any fundamental difference between them threatens all moral distinctions. The resemblance between men and animals endangers man's identity (or self-resemblance): his preservation and immunity from crime. Sade's overt refusal to appeal to reason as the distinguishing trait that separates men from animals reflects his philosophical position rejecting transcendental categories based on foundational difference.[22] As such, it represents both an attack on and a dismissal of the Cartesian definition of man. Sade's effort to assimilate man and animal reflects his concept of nature, which for him is both undifferentiated and indifferent. By denying man's privileged position in nature, Sade reopens the question of man's definition and relation to nature.

Sade's gesture represents an explicit attack on the theological foundation of man, made in the likeness of God, for the libertine is a new kind of (wo)man, whose likeness has been rendered incoherent by the incessant scrambling of all the different parts. The libertine does not resemble "man" as a universal type, lacking the internal coherence that defines the identity of the classical subject. Rather, the libertine resembles him or herself excessively, since identity is constituted through a play of simulations. The libertine's identity is conceived as a copy with no prototype, a subject that knows no originary or foundational moment. Consequently, Sade's definition of "man" differs radically from the criteria used during the Enlightenment. By questioning the specificity and the sovereignty of man, as a being different from other natural beings, Sade challenges the humanist interpretation of man, espoused by the tradition of Augustine, Montaigne, and Rousseau.

The Sadean critique of traditional humanism is based on his concept of nature, which is no longer simply an object for contemplation or manipulation, but rather a new source for poetic inspiration. Sade's elaboration of libertine philosophy is grounded in an understanding of nature that is free of moral connotations: nature is described as possessing no inherent distinctions in its organization. Vice and virtue are represented by Dolmancé as being equal in respect to nature:

one single motor is operative in this universe, and that motor is Nature. The miracles—rather, the physical effects—of this mother of the human race, differently interpreted by men, have been deified by them under a thousand forms, each more extraordinary than the other. (*PB, 360*)

This lack of difference or distinguishing traits in nature impairs man's effort to establish moral distinctions, as well as to uphold his sovereign status. The problem is that nature is both "motor" and "mother," that is to say, an originary principle that generates difference merely as a secondary "effect," while still resembling itself. According to Sade, difference only comes into play as men attempt to interpret nature, and thereby disrupt through this understanding the governing principle of resemblance. The space of nature is presented in terms of the excess generated through resemblance, thereby equating it with the space of parody.[23] Considered from this perspective, culture is no longer conceived as the obverse of nature, but becomes the mirror of its already perverse principles. Given this interpretation of nature, it is not surprising that Sade attacks the laws that affirm the preservation of humanity, either through marriage or the interdiction of crime.

Having redefined nature as an undifferentiated principle and thereby affirmed the arbitrary character of human conventions, Sade proceeds in *Philosophy in the Bedroom* to parody the law of incest, the very principle that separates nature from culture. His preposterous effort to valorize incest must be understood as the logical result of his pursuit *ad absurdum* to describe nature in a new way. By hypostasizing the undifferentiated and indifferent character of nature, Sade frees himself to make the most absurd fictional claims. This is because the notion of "natural law" is for him merely a projection of man-made fictions. In his pseudorevolutionary pamphlet, "Yet Another Effort, Frenchmen, If You Would Become Republicans" (which constitutes a dominant section of *Philosophy in the Bedroom*), Dolmancé outrageously contends that incest should be the law of all republican governments based on fraternity (*PB*, 242). Sade's bitterly ironic claim represents his violent attempt to parody revolutionary rhetoric. As an exponent of fraternity, Sade is haunted by his own precarious position as a victim who only accidentally escapes being guillotined during the Terror.[24] By interpreting the notion of fraternity literally as incest, Sade parodies and reveals the violent underpinnings of the discourse of the Enlightenment.

Dolmancé goes on to explain why incest may become the new law of the revolutionary state: "If, in a word, love is born of *resemblance,* where may it be more perfect than between brother and sister, between father and daughter? (*PB*, 236; emphasis added). Sade redefines the principle of erotic love as no longer being based on sexual or cultural difference. By positing *resemblance* as the principle of love, Sade perversely arrives at incest as the necessary conclusion of his social and philosophical parody. Filial and fraternal love is privileged, since as Sade explains elsewhere, an incestuous marriage provides "double reason to love."[25] His use of this phrase suggests that the scandal of incest is tied to the duplication and hence deregulation of heretofore socially incompatible categories. Thus both eroticism and writing share a similar fate in Sade's work: as discourses of resemblance, their true referent is the order of representation itself. But representation here no longer implies either a rational order or the imitation of reality according to convention, but rather their systematic destruction through the deviant movement engendered by parody.

The outrage perpetrated by Sade's incestuous discourse undermines the notion of nature by substituting for it the fictitious space of parody. His incestuous narratives transform the relation between theory and practice by valorizing fiction.[26] The originality of Sadean discourse resides less in its efforts to transgress social norms than in its success at redefining literature itself as a deviant and even criminal activity. By equating writing with perversity and crime, Sade redefines nature as the referent of his writerly project. Thus Sade's obsession with incest reflects his effort to rethink nature in terms of his theory of representation, which is based on resemblance. If incest is a privileged term, this is because it embodies the very scandal of representation. Incest is the index of a social and hence a linguistic crisis, insofar as it suggests the capacity to combine inassimilable social categories and thus generate fictitious predicates.

This attempt to violate the natural social order by mixing and scrambling social and linguistic categories can be seen in *Juliette,* where Noirceuil presents his ultimate fantasy of perverse marriage. He wants to marry twice the same day, impersonating both roles of man and woman, while imitated by Juliette, who transvested as a man would marry another woman:

> An extraordinary fantasy torments me since long ago, Juliette. . . . I want to get married . . . twice the same day: at noon, dressed as a man, marry a bardache as a woman. I want more . . . I want a woman to *imitate me* and what other woman could better serve this fantasy? Dressed as a man, you must marry a tribade at the same mass where, as a woman I marry a man! and that dressed as a man, when I have resumed the vestments of my sex, I marry, as a man, a bardache dressed as a woman.[27]

Sade's scenario represents the ultimate perversion of nature, since the false replication of gender roles generates the ultimate incest fantasy, that of a marriage of the like, where a transvested man and woman marries their own sex. Hénaff comments on this scene by noting Sade's desire to permutate and saturate all possible sexual positions.[28] However, this first type of chiasma, of saturation in an encyclopedic sense, is accompanied by an even more radical gesture. For the desire for totality is accompanied by the production of an excess *beyond* totality. Noirceuil's demand to be imitated by Juliette, as he imitates himself as a man, creates an excess of signification that can no longer be accommodated in the order of representation.[29] Marriage as the social union of difference, as an exogamous relation, is doubly reenacted the same day, each time with the same sexual partners. This fantasy of mimicry becomes the figurative index of incest as a space of pure parody. The free circulation of all the predicates of sexuality, their arbitrary accumulation and expenditure, de-essentialize both gender and the moral values attached to it. The sexual referent of the Sadean text thus emerges as pure simulacrum: a copy without a real referent; that is, as the principle of parody itself.

Unlike the other materialist thinkers such as La Mettrie, Helvétius, and d'Holbach, Sade does not simply revert to a naturalistic ideology.[30] He does not valorize nature as a new idol; on the contrary, he attempts to negate it and defile it, and yet nature eludes him.[31] Since Sade views even crime and evil as part of the workings of nature, the efforts to negate nature only confirm its principles. Nature thus represents a philosophical and moral scandal, since man can adopt neither an exterior nor a sovereign position in relation to it. The crisis that nature presents for the Sadean protagonists, as well as for the author, can only be resolved by subverting the notion of representation. Given the perversity that Sade ascribes to nature, Sade's solution is to copy it and thus infinitely perpetuate it:

> yes, I abhor Nature; and I detest her because I know her well. Aware of her frightful secret, I have fallen back on myself and I have felt. . . . I have experienced a kind of pleasure in copying her foul deeds. . . . Should I love such a mother? No; but I will imitate her, all the while detesting her, I shall copy her, as she wishes, but I shall curse her unceasingly.[32]

Almani's comment in *Juliette* summarizes Sade's dilemma as an author who, forced to copy nature, uses imitation as a form of denunciation. This copy, like any other representation, resembles nature and deviates from it at the same time. By presenting the task of copying nature as a burden, Sade parodies Boileau's injunction in *L'Art poétique:* "Imitate nature, only nature is true." Whereas for Boileau nature signifies an ideal of perfection, for Sade it signifies crime and evil, hence the burden of its representation. Rather than defining the task of the writer in terms of verisimilitude *(vraisemblance),* understood as the appearance of truth in fidelity to nature, Sade defies the conventions of novelistic plausibility. His "fidelity" to nature is no longer based on idealization; rather, it represents his perverse interpretation of literature. While claiming to copy nature, Sade chooses to depict its most deviant manifestations, thereby undermining its representation through parody.

Sade's perverse pleasure as an author replicating images of nature echoes Mme de Saint-Ange's description of the libertine's pleasure at seeing the body multiplied through reflections. For both, perversion is the figure of the excess generated through *representation,* understood as the copy of a prior or pregiven presentation. By simulating nature through parody, Sade opens up the exploration of a new novelistic space, one where the principle of fiction is elevated to a new "reality" that exceeds the constraints of the dichotomy of both nature and culture.[33] Rather than accepting the traditional division between theory and practice, Sade stages the contamination of philosophy through the writing of fiction. By elaborating a theory of representation based on parody, Sade mockingly stages the hypostasis of erotic and criminal pleasure: the coincidence of the "bedroom" and the "deathbed" of philosophy.

The Impossible as Literature

> The excesses of the Terror have dulled the taste of crime.
> —Saint-Just

Having outlined the most salient aspects of Sade's theory of representation, we shall now return to the question of why *transgression* is an inadequate term to describe Sade's writings. If we go back to Foucault's formulation, in his "Preface to Transgression," it becomes clearer why this term fails to account for the liminal character of Sade's work:

> Transgression does not seek to oppose one thing to another, nor does it achieve its purpose through mockery or by upsetting the solidity of foundations. . . . Transgression is neither violence in a divided world (in an ethical world) nor a victory over limits (in a dialectical or revolutionary world); and exactly for this reason its role is to measure the excessive distance that it opens at the heart of the limit and to trace the flashing line that causes the limit to arise.[34]

Foucault correctly underlines the fact that transgression must be dissociated from its negative ethical and dialectical associations, and thus from an oppositional logic. However, he situates the domain of transgression outside both parody and the question of philosophical foundations. His formulation is both a critique and an elaboration of Klossowski's and Bataille's philosophical recovery of transgression as an antitheology by affirming Nietzsche's and Blanchot's "'yes' of contestation."

By not considering the bitterly ironic and caricatural character of Sade's representations of transgression, however, the philosophical readings of Sade foreclose the interrogation of its literary character. Foucault's interpretation of transgression as a gesture beyond "mockery" or parody implies that transgression as a philosophical gesture may exceed the limits of literature while inevitably tracing out its impossible and excessive outline. The problem is that the encyclopedic aspects of Sadean discourse are bracketed in Sade's work by the foreclosure of classical representation, not merely by extending its limits (its transgressive function), but by actually short-circuiting its codes and discourses (its parodic function). Consequently, the excess produced in the order of representation through parody results in the abolition of difference and the inassimilable deferral within representation of the possibility of constituting a foundational order.

Sade's complicitous relation to nature and to his own position as writer-victim is made explicit in *Reflections on the Novel*. In one of the most recognized passages of this work, he elucidates the status of the writer in relation to nature, claiming that as the "son" and "lover of nature," the writer must become her incestuous lover:

> O you who wish to venture upon this difficult and thorny career, bear ever in mind that the novelist is the child of Nature, that she has created him to be her painter; if he does not become his mother's lover the moment she gives birth to him, let him never write, for we shall never read him. But if he feels that burning need to portray everything, if, with fear and trembling he probes into the bosom of Nature, in search of his art and for models to discover, if he possesses the fever of talent and the enthusiasm of genius, let him follow the hand that leads him; once having divined man, he will paint him.[35]

This comment allows us to bring together our reflections on both representation and nature. Briefly, Sade's description of the novelist as the true man of nature involves the fundamental task of representing nature. However, this relation of depiction *(peindre)* is interpreted by Sade according to the logic of parody as an incestuous relationship, a relation of crime and complicity. As nature's lover and son, Sade situates the novelistic project in the space of culture, where the imitation of nature is perverted through the deployment of a scandalous filiation, associated with incest. The task of the author, according to Sade, is not simply to replicate nature, but to imitate its sublime excesses. The act of writing is tied to the production of excess in the domain of representation, which because of its parodic nature disrupts irrevocably the conventional formulation of novelistic mimesis. The attempt to mimic nature, by being truly faithful to her designs, leads to the complicitous identification of the hand of nature with that of the author. While appearing to follow nature ("the hand that leads him"), the hand of the author incestuously traces out the criminal excesses of literature.

A similar incident appears at the end of *Philosophy in the Bedroom,* where Eugénie's apprenticeship culminates in the attempt to violate the maternal body by becoming the putative lover of nature. Eugénie's perverse education in *Philosophy in the Bedroom* results in her rewriting her natural origins through the violation of her mother's body. Her figurative incest with her mother, which is accompanied by the sewing up of her genitals with a red thread (a gesture doubled by Dolmancé's sewing up of her anus) enacts in a fantastic and violent sense Sade's definition of the novelist as the lover of nature.[36] The equation of the gesture of writing (as a stand-in for culture) reifies and displaces the maternal body (as a site for natural repro-duction). Eugénie's violent marking of her mother's body is already the rep-etition of the marks of flagellation administered by her libertine father. Eugénie's violent emergence into the symbolic order can be seen as the dou-bling of paternal violence and the inscription of its patriarchal legacy upon the maternal body. However, this equation of culture and violence also becomes the site for the reinscription of the opposition of nature and cul-ture, since by denaturing nature, Eugénie, like the Sadean author, redefines the project of writing as a criminal gesture whose violence disrupts the func-tion of nature as origin and generator of categories.

Eugénie's suture of the maternal body excludes it from the natural system of social reproduction and exchange that describes female sexuality. The mother's body is saturated by totality, generating an excess beyond totality. Thus the gesture of simulation produces an incalculable excess, that of the play of representation itself. The violence of this operation upon the mother, described in clinical terms, mimics the violence of the act of writing. As a simulacrum of nature, the maternal body becomes at the same time the site of transgression of the order of nature, which it ostensibly copies. Eugénie's sewing needle and red thread figure, through this process of disfiguration, the position of the writer in Sade, whose pen has become a sewing needle. Thus writing embodies through this violent patchwork the doubly gendered hand of a feminine nature and masculine culture.

The ending of *The Misfortunes of Virtue* presents yet another scenario of writing as a criminal activity. The arbitrary destruction of Justine, just as she begins to enjoy the fruits of virtue, once again functions as a sign of the perverse complicity of the novelist and nature. It is as if her sense of destiny as a victim invites and prescribes her final violation: her death by a lightning bolt at the hands of nature. Justine's grotesque destruction and erasure from the world of the novel etches upon her body the disfiguring material trace of nature, which she had always refused to acknowledge: "Lightning had entered by the right breast, it burned the chest, and came out through her mouth, disfiguring her face so much that her face inspired horror."[37] The final disfiguration of Justine by the lightning bolt, the mark of the arbitrary character of nature, summarizes Sade's effort to present historical being by equating it with natural contingency. Passing through the right breast and coming out through the mouth, writing emerges as a process of figuration that reproduces the body through disfiguration. Having functioned as a mere mouthpiece for values that did not come from the heart, Justine's caricatural existence is erased by the hand of the author, mimic and lover of nature. The perverse fidelity of the author, as the incestuous lover of nature, becomes transfigured in the act of writing presented undecidably as the hand of both nature and man. This undecidability reveals something fundamental about the function of representation in Sade: the refusal to found a stable principle for representation. Through the expenditure of mimesis, as an endless play of simulations, the Sadean text represents itself as a copy with no original, as pure parody. In *The Misfortunes of Virtue,* this undecidability is put to an end only when all representation stops: when the author puts down his pen and/or sewing needle.

In conclusion, we are left to ponder Sade's peculiar position in the history of literature. In so doing we turn to Sollers's provocative question regarding the paradoxical legacy of the Sadean text for modernity: "How is it that Sade is at once prohibited and accepted, prohibited as fiction (as writing) and accepted as reality; forbidden as general reading and accepted as psychological and physiological reference?"[38] Sollers's question summarizes in a radical fashion the objections that this study has raised to reading Sade as a transgressive author. Even if we regard the space of transgression as a positive space of contestation, the fact remains that such readings uphold sexuality as the ultimate referent of contestation with the real. By maintaining the distinction between fiction and reality, without understanding how Sade erodes their mutual boundaries through parody, the transgressive readings reinforce the paradox of the Sadean text that is banned as fiction while being upheld as the referent of our psychological and physiological reality.

Can Sade's literary representation of sexuality be banned while sexuality itself is given an "extraliterary" status? As this study has demonstrated, the Sadean project, as reflected in both his novelistic practice and philosophical reflections, can be better understood as a discourse of parody whose strategic imitation of previous literary and philosophical conventions upsets the very traditions that it simulates. The sexual referent in the Sadean text has no more privilege than the nature it ostensibly replicates. The sexual fortunes or misfortunes of the Sadean heroines are profoundly literary. The eroticism of the Sadean text is not defined by the choice of objects it chooses to represent, be it the body, perversity, or crime. Rather, eroticism is a reflection of Sade's interpretation of writing as a complicitous, perverse, and at times even criminal gesture. As Simone de Beauvoir has pertinently noted: "It was not murder that fulfilled Sade's erotic nature: it was literature."[39]

Writing in the shadow of a French Revolution that culminates in the Reign of Terror, Sade the libertine philosopher and writer radically challenges the Cartesian legacy by questioning both the preeminence of reason and the representational order it entails. Sade's emphasis on the body and sexuality as the primary vehicles for his interrogation of the limits of thought reflects his efforts to undermine the Cartesian ontological imprint, insofar as the notion of ontological difference also determines sexual difference. While relying on the materialist and mechanist account of the body, he subverts the rational order that underlies it by parodying and thus perverting the supposed laws of nature. The initial diremption from nature, implicit in the Cartesian mechanization of the body and later reinforced by materialist interpretations of man, is parodically magnified by Sade. He dehumanizes the notion of human nature by including within its purview activities that range from perversity to crime. And he denatures "nature" by subverting the logic of its universal laws to accommodate violence and evil. Nature is thus deregulated, and the principles that govern its organization are subsumed within an irrational order. Moreover, the exaggerated violence and terror that Sade unleashes upon the body, which reflect its initial philosophical objectification and subjection, are transposed to and legitimized by the social domain that enacts, through discipline and punishment, the submission of the body to institutional norms and rules. Thus the corporeality of the body emerges as a function of its social administration and disposition, in terms of techniques of power, rather than as the expression of its embodied character. As Michel Foucault observes: "In Sade, sex is without any norm or intrinsic rule that might be formulated from its own nature."[40] For the logic of the body is restricted to the regimes of power that govern its administration, thereby adumbrating its future legacy as subject of both violence and terror. Sade's literary and philosophical parodies foreshadow the historical destiny of the body, its subjection and victimization scripted by a culture of violence.

Conclusion

The genealogies of the modern body outlined in the pages of this volume present us with a paradoxical legacy. We find ourselves today turning back to early modern conceptions of the body in order to question and overcome the predominance of modern conceptions. It is precisely those aspects of the body that were foreclosed by the foundation of modern notions that enable us to challenge their conceptual framework and their ostensible factual authority and solidity. Rather than treating the body as a given, this study has sought to inquire into its cultural construction, its conceptual and representational modes of materialization or consolidation, in order to recover what had become unpresentable and thus postponed in the modern interpretations of the body. The emphasis on experience and embodiment evidenced in these early modern notions of the body, which are grounded in reflections on the nature of representation, open up the horizon of body toward postmodern forms of inquiry and thought. Insofar as they stage the question of the body in terms of communicability, understood as both in an intersubjective and intercorporeal modality, these works adumbrate conceptual developments central to postmodernity. It is this representational approach that is supplanted by the emergence of Cartesian and post-Cartesian paradigms that have informed and shaped decisively our modern understandings of the body. However, the consolidation of these modern conceptual models involves the derealization, even evacuation of the lived body, in favor of abstract analogues whose material logic is informed by the regime of the machine. The progressive virtualization of the body, its schematization, mechanization, and ultimate spectralization, coincides with the evisceration of corporeality and the contingencies of its multiple embodiments. The dematerialization of the body as lived entity implies its paradoxical return as a material thing, that is to say its "rematerialization" not as body but as material abstraction defined by epistemological constraints.

It is precisely the idealism inherent in this legacy to modernity, which bypasses corporeality by recourse to virtual entities and hypothetical worlds, that is taken to task by Nietzsche in *The Twilight of the Idols* (1889), which vehemently reclaims the primacy of the lived body as the locus of culture:

> It is decisive for the fortune of nations and of mankind that one should inaugurate culture in the *right place*—*not* in the "soul" (as has been the fateful superstition of priests and quasi-priests): the right place is the body, demeanor, diet, physiology: the rest follows.[1]

Reacting against Christian theological traditions that upheld the preeminence of the soul by devaluing and rejecting the body, through the elaboration of notions of transcendence that sought to escape human embodiment, Nietzsche insists on the centrality of the body and its modalities of embodiment as the site for locating and elaborating culture. Nietzsche's emphasis on the body radically challenges not only religious traditions that valorized the soul, but philosophical traditions as well. His attempts to "philosophize with a hammer" in order to "sound out idols" make violently audible his attack against the hollowness of religious and philosophical systems based on ideals that universalize and essentialize being by removing it from the purview of embodiment and its horizon of becoming: "There are more idols in the world than there are realities" (21). This proliferation of idealized concepts that are solidified into stone, endemic to the history of European philosophy since Plato, attests to the division of the world into a "real" and "apparent" world, a distinction which can only be sustained by ascribing the priority of conceptual abstractions that override the logic of appearance that describes the world. Whether in the "manner of Christianity or Kant" (39), these religious and philosophical systems that uphold the "reality" of an ideal world in order to dismiss the actual world suffer from a lack of historical sense and the incapacity of engaging with notions of becoming. According to Nietzsche, this inability to engage becoming—rather than being understood as abstracted essence—relegates philosophers to handling mere "conceptual mummies," eviscerated from fabric of a living world: "All that philosophers have handled for millennia have been conceptual mummies; nothing actual has escaped from their hands alive" (35).

Nietzsche alludes to the hypothetical abstractions or virtual entities evoked throughout the history of philosophy whose validity is derived from either the negation or the voiding of notions of being grounded in the world. As Nietzsche observes: "The characteristics which have been assigned to 'real being' of things are characteristics of non-being, of *nothingness*—the 'real world' has been constructed out of the contradiction to the actual world" (39). This philosophical effort to dehistoricize the being of things, *sub specie aeterni,* ascribes to it features of nonbeing that pit the virtual "reality" of religious, axiomatic, or fictive constructions against the actual world. Relying on Heraclitus, the philosopher of becoming, and his contention that "being is an empty fiction," Nietzsche denounces the falsification and usurpation of the "apparent world" by the philosophical fiction of a "real" world emptied of multiplicity and contingency: "The 'apparent' world is the only one: the 'real' world has only been *lyingly added*" (36).

At the heart of the distinction between apparent and real, which eviscerates the world from the realm of appearances and the subject from its embodied condition, lies the philosophical preeminence accorded to reason. To religious mistrust and dismissal of the world in favor of an otherworldly reality is now added the deliberate condemnation of the body, no longer simply a sexual entity, but also a cognitive one. As Nietzsche observes, the evidence of the senses comes into doubt only by presuming the ascendancy of reason as the grounding condition: "'Reason' is the cause of our falsification of the evidence of the senses" (36). This misrepresentation that transforms the evidence of the senses into a lie eradicates the body from the purview of both cognition and embodiment. Consequently, this denunciation and ultimate dismissal of the senses implies the derealization of the body and the actual world in favor of a virtual being that derives its meaning from the failure to ground being in the actual world. Nietzsche's call for a return to a notion of culture grounded in the body and its historical modalities of becoming recovers precisely what philosophy, beginning with Plato and especially since Descartes, has removed from its purview by positing the priority of reason. His revalorization of sense perceptions, recovered from their prior associations with deception and doubt and redeployed as the insignia of appearance, reinscribes the logic of becoming as the constitutive condition of a reflection on the body in terms that take into account its historically contingent, contextual, and representational character. His emphasis on the body and the senses as the insignia of appearance also calls upon a reflection on language and its representational powers in order to interrogate the "basic presuppositions of the metaphysics of language" (38). Such a reflection on language and representation does not reflect simply a literary bias, but also a philosophical one. For it is within the framework of language and representation that the metaphysical foreclosure of the body has already taken place. Nietzsche does not merely urge a reengagement of the body and its sensorial realm, but also a radical reconsideration of its representational status in order to challenge its linguistic presuppositions. These engagements with the body as sensorial horizon, as representation, and, hence, as contingency emerge as the signatory features of modern philosophical efforts to think the body in terms of its embeddedness in the world.[2] This study has sought to answer Nietzsche call by retracing one of the crucial Western cultural moments in the definition of the body: the passage from notions of body and embodiment based on experience and grounded in representation to the Cartesian material and mechanical reduction of the body and its subsequent legacy to the development of French materialism in the eighteenth century. If Montaigne is pivotal to this study, this is because he was first to alert us of the dangers of an "inhuman wisdom" that would make us disdainful enemies of the "culture of the body." Montaigne's premonitory warning regarding the responsibility of defining knowledge in terms of its engagement with the body and its modes of cultivation attests to his efforts to ground thought within the purview of human experience and modes of representation. His denunciation of "transcendental humors" as an effigy of the efforts to transcend the human as an embodied condition anticipate the dangers entailed in the elaboration of transcendental subjectivity in Descartes, particularly as regards the elimination of the body as conduit for knowledge and its reduction to the inhuman implicit in its definition as a machine.

However, as this study demonstrated, Montaigne's emphasis on the experiential body, be it in the perceptual or the social realm, leads to its redefinition in the modality of a script, the provisional staging of the body as a scenario that attains its meaning through its position and transposition in various cultural contexts. Montaigne's philosophical and textual account of the body is shared by other baroque authors such as d'Urfé, who resist essentialist interpretations by presenting the body not as a given, but as a process of embodiment that necessarily references representational practices. It is this emphasis on the body as a site of communicability, as a process of embodiment operating within representation, that inscribes the baroque interpretations in the writings of Montaigne and d'Urfé within a postmodern horizon of reflection on representation and notions of becoming. These baroque works open up an understanding of the body as intersubjective and intercorporeal exchange functioning in the modality of an address whose philosophical, aesthetic, and ethical character derives from an engagement with the world.

Despite the archaic nature of these works, whose influence has been usurped by the emergence of the Cartesian mind-body dualism, their philosophical and discursive implications open up new conceptual possibilities for representing and understanding the body. Their emphasis on locating the logic of embodiment within the order of representation (understood as appearance and changing semblance) opens up the body and its identity to nonessentialist interpretations. Although they appear before the advent of the modern age, these works locate the question of the body and its culture within the horizon of language and communication, theoretically elaborated only in the latter part of the twentieth century in the late works of Merleau-Ponty and in structuralism and poststructuralism. Thus despite the identification of these works with the late Renaissance and baroque humanism, implicit in their emphasis on experience, their explorations of embodiment as a function of representation also suggest postmodernist and posthumanist inferences. Their understanding of embodiment as the materializing effect of representation decenters the embodied subject by inscribing it within a horizon that exceeds purely phenomenological determinations, insofar as the subjective presence of the body is scripted within the fabric of the world.[3]

As Nietzsche's comments suggest, and as this study has demonstrated, in Descartes's writings the experiential body suffers radical redefinition as a material and mechanical thing, its logic disengaged from the order of rational knowledge and the fabric of the world. The preeminence granted to rational consciousness and the subjection of the body as material thing sever the objective reality of the body from its subjective existence. As this study has shown, the emergence of a disembodied subject and the mind-body dualism will render embodiment moot, since issues of embodiment can no longer be considered from the purview of the lived body and are transposed to the institutional frameworks that attend to its administration as a mechanical object. Moreover, the absence of a temporal horizon that would ensure the duration of subjectivity in time preempts embodiment by annulling the possibility of becoming. This failure to temporalize subjectivity heralds the impossibility of ethics, since the subject's relation to the ethical, according to Emmanuel Levinas, is grounded in the recognition of the alterity of temporality not as virtual abstraction but as event.[4] The technological legacy of Descartes's works is most visible in his strategies of virtualization, that of dismissing the reality of the lived, experiential body by substituting for it mechanical analogues haunted by specters of the inhuman. These strategies entail the philosophical derealization and reduction of the world to deceptive appearances that can only be overcome by positing hypothetical worlds, whose virtual and axiomatic logic references notions of an idealized, rather than worldly, reality.

It is interesting to note that despite the impact that Descartes's analogy of the human organism to the machine has had on philosophical and technological developments from the eighteenth century into the early part of the twentieth century, mechanical models and analogies are being supplanted by the rise of new conceptual paradigms in information and biotechnologies.[5] As Descartes's mechanist account of the body and La Mettrie's description of man as a machine reveal their limitations and potential obsolescence, Montaigne's scriptorial account of the body opens up new possibilities. Montaigne's legacy lies not merely in his revalorization of experience, and thus the sensorial body, but more significantly in his programmatic understanding of experience that configures the body as a function of reiterative processes of encoding, decoding, and transcription. His interpretation of the body as discursive and communicative site opens the question of the body toward its consideration as an intersubjective and intercorporeal system for communication and exchange. Since the meaning of the body is derived from its representational character, the logic of the body is embedded within the material, signifying processes of representation. By foreclosing the body within the logic of the mechanism, Descartes's and La Mettrie's accounts postponed the advent of our current understanding of the body in the biology, biotechnology, and information-based sciences.[6] For the operative paradigms within these new disciplines are modeled on the vocabulary of linguistics and communication theory, that of the transmission of message or information, through processes of encoding, decoding, and transcription.[7]

Given the emphasis on the body in terms of embodiment, sexuality and sexual difference have proved central to this study. This volume has, on the one hand, provided accounts of sexuality that preceded Descartes's elaboration of ontological difference and his mechanization of the body; on the other hand, it has outlined the legacy of his philosophical positions on the development of French materialist thought and literature. In the baroque writings of Montaigne and d'Urfé the representation of sexuality is not defined in essentialist terms, by reference to sexual difference and thus established gender positions, male or female. The freedom of embodiment, of occupying different gender positions at the same time, or of taking on different sexual roles, attests to an understanding of sexual difference that is not foundational, since it is merely the effect of representation defined as a play of resemblances. By recognizing that the ostensibly deceptive or illusionistic effects of representation reflect the traces of contingency and becoming, these authors inscribe the mark of alterity not between the sexes, but within sexuality, thereby deferring its essentialist consolidation. In making these claims, I do not suggest that the late sixteenth or early seventeenth century was either more free socially or more enlightened than the modern period. Rather, the absence an epistemological foundation and rational framework enabled accounts of corporeality that are fluid insofar as embodiment necessarily involves assuming multiple positions within representation. Just as the self and its relations to others and the world are contextually bound, so does the body emerge not as a given but derive its specific meanings from its embeddedness in a variety of contexts. If sexual identity is open to multiple gender determinations, this is because corporeality is provisional upon its modes of materialization. By subsuming the logic of sexuality within an understanding of representation as shifting semblance, Montaigne and d'Urfé explore the meanings attached to representation in order to elaborate a notion of sexuality whose intersubjective character is marked by intersexual overtones. These gestures reposition sexuality in the intersubjective realm of communication and exchange, where the corporeal is redefined as the bearer of alterities that postpone its consolidation into a body. Rather than functioning as the dividing mark between the sexes, this notion of alterity opens up sexuality by inscribing it in an intersexual horizon of becoming.

While Descartes's disembodiment of the rational subject and his equation of the body to a machine at first sight appears to have erased sexuality from its purview, the relation between Descartes's elaboration of ontological difference and its impact on notions of sexual difference suggest otherwise. In this context, La Mettrie and Sade document both the implied consequences of the Cartesian materialization and objectification of the body, and the difficulty of challenging its metaphysical premises. While questioning mind-body dualism, by attempting to subsume reason within a materialist framework La Mettrie and Sade nonetheless preserve the Cartesian mechanist ideology and his technological legacy. For it is no longer just the body but the idea of man that becomes subject to technical manipulations in a variety of domains, including medicine and science and, in the case of Sade, social and political institutions. The materialist body that they reclaim has little in common with its baroque predecessors, since the materiality of the body is constituted not through its contingent encounters with the world, but its forceful submission and discipline to institutional and social codes. The physical body becomes reified through institutional and social practices that govern its administration, so that sexuality and sexual pleasure are redefined in terms of the violence entailed in the submission, control, and instrumentalization of the body. While Sade seems to challenge conventional notions of sexual difference by claiming sexuality as a form of expression equally available to men and women, his understanding of sexuality is founded on a model of social violence and sadism that only confirms the dispossession of the body by the social systems that govern the logic of its administration. The ethical deficiencies in Sade lie not in his affirmation of sexual perversion, but in his inability to move beyond the will to power and nihilism implicit in his redeployment of Cartesian subjectivity. Missing in Sade's writings is not merely an ethical dimension that would mediate the relation of the self to others, but more importantly, the recognition of contingency that the alterity of one's own body or the body of another could present to the self. It is precisely the enigma of inhabiting the world as a body and the ethics of encountering other bodies that the Sadean text tries to demystify, only to fall back into the philosophical traditions whose legacy it seeks so violently and desperately to overcome. The Cartesian account of subjectivity, which reduces the body to a material and mechanical thing devoid of experiential and historical reality, bequeaths to modernity a body that has ceased to be a "culture." It will take Nietzsche's violent injunctions to reclaim the body as the nodal point for inaugurating notions of culture, as crucial to philosophical investigation. Following Nietzsche, the philosophical reembodiment of subjectivity and the recovery of the body from its virtual and instrumental functions as mere backdrop and apparatus for the projection of subjectivity will find its most eloquent developments in the philosophy Maurice Merleau-Ponty. Concluding his discussion of the Cartesian cogito in *The Phenomenology of Perception,* Merleau-Ponty affirms that the elaboration of subjectivity must take as its necessary horizon the lived body as situated in the world. If, "when I reflect on the essence of subjectivity, I find it bound up with that of the body and that of the world, this is because my existence as subjectivity is merely one with my existence as a body and with the existence of the world, and because the subject that I am, when taken concretely, is inseparable from this body and this world."[8] As Merleau-Ponty points out, the meaning of subjectivity cannot be contained by the notion of rational consciousness nor imply the reduction of the body and the world to ideas. For the disclosure of the world necessarily entails embodiment, a condition whose alterity decenters subjectivity in the very process of fleshing it out.

Merleau-Ponty's efforts to address embodiment and overcome the Cartesian legacy of the subject-object dichotomy will span his later works and strain the bounds of philosophical language. In *The Visible and the Invisible* he invites us to think about the body in the world as a dialogue between the "flesh of the body" and the "flesh of the world."[9] This invitation to think the embeddedness of the body in the world as an intersubjective exchange that implies "intercorporeity" opens up new possibilities for understanding the body's embodiments, its modalities of becoming as fabric of the world. Already audible in the margins of Montaigne and d'Urfé writings, the whispered encounters between the flesh of the body and the flesh of the world resonate with new urgency as we seek to find new ways of understanding the meaning of embodiment as a culture that works through the past toward an already nascent future.

Notes

Introduction

1. Starting with Michel Foucault's *History of Sexuality* (1976–84), Elaine Scarry's *The Body in Pain* (1985), Catherine Gallagher and Thomas Laqueur, eds., *The Making of the Modern Body: Sexuality and Society in the Nineteenth Century* (1987), and Michel Feher, Ramona Hadoff, and Nadia Tazi, eds., *Fragments for a History of the Human Body* (1989), we see a renewed effort to inquire into the constitution of the body as physical, discursive, and social entity, followed by a proliferation of critical works in the 1990s. For a survey and discussion of the critical literature on the body, see Carolyn Bynum's "Why All the Fuss about the Body? A Medievalist's Perspective," in *Critical Inquiry* 22 (autumn 1995): 1–31.

2. Maurice Merleau-Ponty, "Everywhere and Nowhere," in *Signs*, trans. Richard C. Cleary (Evanston: Northwestern University Press, 1964), 154.

3. Michel de Montaigne, *The Complete Essays of Montaigne*, trans. Donald Frame (Stanford: Stanford University Press, 1985), III, 13: 849; book, chapter, and page number. All references to the original French text are to *Essais de Montaigne*, ed. Maurice Rat, vols. 1 and 2 (Paris: Garnier Frères, 1962).

4. The French word *culture* in the late sixteenth and early seventeenth century is translated into English as "culture," "tillage," or "husbandry," that is, implying agricultural cultivation. See Randle Cotgrave, *A Dictionarie of the French and English Tongues* (London: Adam Islip, 1611; rpt., Columbia: University of South Carolina Press, 1950), no page number. Given Montaigne's knowledge of and reliance on Latin traditions, his use of the word *culture* also reflects its Latin usage, which includes the cultivation of the body in the physical and moral sense, as well as tradition.

5. Montaigne's claims for the cultivation of the body are more than mere reiterations of Stoic and Epicurean principles involving techniques of the body, since they represent his emphasis on the formative character of experience, the personal character of which is framed by cultural determinations.

6. See Foucault's "History of Systems of Thought," in *Language, Counter-Memory, Practice*, ed. Donald F. Bouchard, trans. Donald F. Bouchard and Sherry Simon (Ithaca, N.Y.: Cornell University Press, 1977), 200.

7. For an analysis of Nietzsche's genealogical approach, see Michel Foucault, "Nietzsche, Genealogy, History," in *Language, Counter-Memory, Practice*, 148.

8. See Jean-François Lyotard, *The Postmodern Condition: A Report on Knowledge,* trans. Geoffrey Bennington and Brian Massumi (Minneapolis: University of Minnesota Press, 1984), 81.

9. These divisions are indebted to literary history and to Michel Foucault's periodization of the discourses of knowledge and representational systems of the early modern period in *Les Mots et les choses: Une archéologie des sciences humaines* (Paris: Gallimard, 1966), pt. 1, pp. 19–224.

10. In his last, uncompleted work, *The Visible and the Invisible* (trans. Alphonso Lingis [Evanston: Northwestern University Press, 1968]), Merleau-Ponty's analysis focuses on vision and the viewing subject in order to argue that the chiasmatic interplay and enfoldedness of the visible and the invisible is no longer accessible to a humanist subject. See also "Eye and Mind," in *The Privacy of Perception,* ed. James M. Edie, trans. Carleton Dallery (Evanston: Northwestern University Press, 1964): 159–90.

11. For a discussion of this epistemological shift in Montaigne and Descartes, see my *Subjectivity and Representation in Descartes: The Origins of Modernity* (Cambridge: Cambridge University Press, 1988), 8–85, 187–95.

12. Martin Heidegger, *What Is a Thing?* trans. W. B. Barton and V. Deutsch (Chicago: Henry Regnery, 1967), 99.

13. Michel Foucault's emphasis on notions of discursive practice relocates the logic of the phenomenological body within the reiterative order of discursive practices. See *The History of Sexuality,* vol. 1, *An Introduction* (1976), trans. Robert Hurley (New York: Vintage Books, 1990), 5–13, 61–73, 92–102. Also see Judith Butler's *Bodies That Matter: On the Discursive Limits of "Sex"* (New York: Routledge, 1993), 1–23.

14. Foucault's and Butler's discussions of sexuality reference Foucault's earlier analysis of the subjection of the body to "power-knowledge relations," elaborated in *Discipline and Punish: The Birth of the Prison* (1975), trans. Alan Sheridan (New York: Vintage Books, 1995), 25–30.

15. Foucault suggests that the emergence of the discourse of sexuality in the seventeenth century is tied to the social institutionalization of confessional discourse that organizes and regulates its usage (*The History of Sexuality,* vol. 1). His claim enables a reading of earlier representations of sexuality in terms that are not reducible to the regulative norms at work in modern interpretations of sexuality.

Chapter 1

1. Nicolas Malebranche, *The Search after Truth,* trans. Thomas M. Lennon and Paul Olscamp (Columbus: Ohio State University Press, 1980), bk. 2, pt. 3, chap. 5, p. 184.

2. As Albert Thibaudet points out, what is lacking in Montaigne's style is lacking in the period as a whole: discipline and order. See *Montaigne* (Paris: Gallimard, 1963), 491.

3. Guez de Balzac, *Entretiens,* vol. 18, *De Montaigne et de ses écrits* (1657 ed.), 209.

4. Malebranche, *The Search after Truth,* 184–85.

5. As Merleau-Ponty points out, Montaigne's consciousness is not mind from the outset, nor does it involve the self-possession implied in the Cartesian understanding ("Reading Montaigne," in *Signs,* 199).

6. For an analysis of classical and baroque style, see Henry Peyre, *Qu-est ce que le classicisme? Essai de mise au point* (Paris: Droz, 1942); R. A. Sayce, "Renaissance, Mannerism and Baroque," in *The Essays of Montaigne: A Critical Exploration* (Evanston: Northwestern University Press, 1972), 313–26; and Morris W. Croll, *"Attic" and Baroque Prose Style: The Anti-Ciceronian Movement,* ed. J. Max Patrick, Robert O. Evans, and John M. Wallace (Princeton: Princeton University Press, 1969).

7. For general studies on Montaigne's style, see Thibaudet, *Montaigne;* Floyd Gray, *Le Style de Montaigne* (Paris: Nizet, 1958); Sayce, *The Essays of Montaigne,* 280–312; Gisèle Mathieu-Castellani, *Montaigne: L'écriture de l'essai* (Paris: Presses Universitaires de France, 1988), 115–32. On Montaigne and rhetoric, see Frank Lestringant, ed., *Rhétorique de Montaigne* (Paris: Honoré Champion, 1985).

8. The question of Montaigne's style is inseparable from broader epistemological concerns that mark the distinction between the baroque and classical worldviews. See Walter Benjamin's comments on allegory in *The Origin of German Tragic Drama,* trans. John Osborne (London: NLB, 1977), 159–82; and Foucault, *Les Mots et les choses,* 32–59.

9. Jules Brody, *Lectures de Montaigne* (Lexington, Ky.: French Forum, 1982), 55–92, and *Nouvelles Lectures de Montaigne* (Paris: Honoré Champion, 1994), 105–78; Terence Cave, "Montaigne," in *The Cornucopian Text: Problems of Writing in the French Renaissance* (Oxford: Clarendon Press, 1979), 271–321; Robert D. Cottrell, *Sexuality/Textuality: A Study of the Fabric of Montaigne's Essays* (Columbus: Ohio State University Press, 1981); Lawrence D. Kritzman, *The Rhetoric of Sexuality and the Literature of the French Renaissance* (New York: Columbia University Press, 1993), 57–73, 73–92, 133–47; Mathieu-Castellani, *Montaigne,* 135–253; Jean Starobinski, *Montaigne in Motion,* trans. Arthur Goldhammer (Chicago: University of Chicago Press, 1985), 138–213.

10. On this much-discussed essay see the following related works: Barbara C. Bowen, "Montaigne's Anti-*Phaedrus:* 'Sur des vers de Virgile' (Essais, III, V)," *Journal of Medieval and Renaissance Studies* 5 (1975): 107–21; Erica Harth, " 'Sur des vers de Virgile': Antinomy and Totality in Montaigne," *French Forum* 2 (1977): 3–21; Cave, "Montaigne," 271–321; Jean Starobinski, "Speaking Love," in *Montaigne in Motion,* 185–213; Lawrence D. Kritzman, "My Body, My Text: Montaigne and the Rhetoric of Self-Portraiture," in *Rhetoric of Sexuality,* 133–47; Floyd Gray, "Eros et écriture: 'Sur des vers de Virgil,'" in *Les Parcours des "Essais": Montaigne 1588–1988,* ed. Marcel Tetel and G. Mallary Masters (Paris: Aux Amateurs du Livre, 1989), 263–72; Géralde Nakam, "Eros et les Muses dans 'Sur des vers de Virgile,'" in *Montaigne: La manière et la matière* (Paris: Klincksieck, 1992),

133–44; Patricia Parker, "Gender Ideology, Gender Change: The Case of Marie Germain," *Critical Inquiry* 19 (winter 1993): 337–64.

11. Robert D. Cottrell interprets Montaigne's allusion to Aristotle's *Metaphysics* as an effort to emphasize the role of desire ("Representation and the Desiring Subject in Montaigne's 'De l'expérience," in Tetel and Masters, *Les Parcours des "Essais,"* 97–98). For a comprehensive account of Montaigne's borrowings from Aristotle, see Edilia Traverso, *Montaigne e Aristotele* (Florence: Felice Le Monnier, 1974).

12. For an analysis of the prevalence of the term *forme* in this essay, see Brody, *Nouvelles Lectures de Montaigne,* 112–17.

13. Commenting implicitly on Montaigne, Michel Foucault recognizes only the analogical aspects of reason based on resemblance, not on difference (*Les Mots et les choses,* 63–67). While it is true that difference is not posited in Montaigne as a foundational term constitutive of the ontology of being, difference nonetheless functions as one of the constitutive paradigms of the operations of reason.

14. Cottrell understands this anecdote as an allegory of desire, as the effort to seek and possess the object of desire ("Representation and Desiring Subject," 101–3, 105–6).

15. For a general account of law in Montaigne, see Carol Clark, "Montaigne and Law," in *Montaigne and His Age,* ed. Keith Cameron (Exeter: University of Exeter Press, 1981), 49–68.

16. For a general analysis of medicine in Montaigne, see Margaret Brunyate, "Montaigne and Medicine," in Cameron, *Montaigne and His Age,* 27–38; for a broader account of Renaissance medicine, see Vivian Nutton, "Medicine in the Age of Montaigne," in *Montaigne and His Age,* 15–25.

17. As Géralde Nakam points out, illness in Montaigne can be as much the effect of physical developments as of the imagination, and it may be treated in kind ("Corps physique, corps social: La maladie et la santé," chap. 4 in *Montaigne,* 61–65).

18. Examining Montaigne's earlier pronouncements on medicine in "Of the Resemblance of Children to Their Fathers," Starobinski claims that Montaigne criticizes traditional empiricism without proposing anything to take its place. He interprets the essay "Of Experience" as a gloss on this earlier essay (*Montaigne in Motion,* 150–56).

19. For Montaigne's earlier exploration of the notion of custom, see "Of Custom, and Not Easily Changing an Accepted Law" (I, 23). Also see Tzvetan Todorov's discussion of custom and natural law, "L'Etre et l'autre: Montaigne," in "Montaigne: Essays in Reading," an issue of *Yale French Studies* 64 (1983): 113–21.

20. While noting that personal customs or habits may be subject to change, Ullrich Langer focuses on the relation of custom to the law. See "Montaigne's Customs," *Montaigne Studies: An Interdisciplinary Forum* 4, nos. 1–2 (1992): 82, 83–95.

21. For an analysis of the role of the imagination in Montaigne, see Dora Pol-

lachek, "Montaigne and Imagination: The Dynamics of Power and Control," in Tetel and Masters, *Les Parcours des "Essais,"* 135–45.

22. See Etienne Gilson's discussion of Thomas Aquinas in *Etudes sur le rôle de la pensée médievale dans la formation du système cartésien,* 5th ed. (Paris: J. Vrin, 1984).

23. This is not surprising, since as Merleau-Ponty observes, self-understanding implies a dialogue with the self ("Reading Montaigne," 199).

24. My reading differs with Merleau-Ponty's claim, "Death is the act of one person alone" ("Reading Montaigne," 201), since death also implies subjection to forms of both necessity and contingency that cannot be resumed under the aegisis of agency.

25. Starobinski, *Montaigne in Motion,* 183.

26. For Kritzman, Montaigne's gesture leads to the transformation of the text into a surrogate object of pleasure, so that sexuality as the lost object may be recaptured through writing (*Rhetoric of Sexuality,* 134–35).

27. For an analysis of this statement as a dialectical movement, see Harth, "Sur des vers de Virgile," 4–5.

28. This mark of engraving, this incision that marks the beginning of the text, is playfully echoed by the reiterative quality of the letter *V,* which shows up in the alliterative structure of the title and as the Roman numeral of the essay.

29. The onerous corporeality of thought corresponds to the sexualization of the common soul, represented as being too often erect *(âme bandée)* (III, 5: 638). As Montaigne suggests, it is now the turn of the body to guide the spirit toward reformation (III, 5: 638). Bowen understands Montaigne's emphasis on the body as a reaction against the Neoplatonist emphasis on the soul ("Montaigne's Anti-*Phaedrus,*" 114).

30. As Starobinski reminds us, Montaigne's recourse to citations is ambiguous: "It is not only an *ostentatious* display of knowledge, but also a display of *borrowed* knowledge and hence of one's own inadequacy" (*Montaigne in Motion,* 208). For a comprehensive study, see Mary B. McKinley, *Words in a Corner: Studies in Montaigne's Latin Quotations* (Lexington, Ky.: French Forum, 1981).

31. Cave, "Montaigne," 284.

32. For the psychoanalytic implications of this event, see Lawrence Kritzman, "Pedagogical Graffiti and the Rhetoric of Conceit," in *Rhetoric of Sexuality,* 61–67.

33. Mary McKinley understands Montaigne's appeal to literature to represent sexual experience as an appeal to an indirect language of self-exposure that expresses sexuality through periphrasis (*Words in a Corner,* 83).

34. Kritzman suggests that Montaigne's privileging of reproduction to create the illusion of giving life to an inanimate object reflects his own inscription of the intellectual act (*Rhetoric of Sexuality,* 88).

35. McKinley observes that the central role of these Latin quotations is to help define the structure of the essay, thus participating in Montaigne's rhetorical strategy (*Words in a Corner,* 79). See also Gray's comment that the essay owes its formal schema to these organizing citations (*Le Style de Montaigne,* 203).

36. According to McKinley, these portraits of Venus by the Latin authors depict Venus as a metaphor of sexual passion as experienced by the male (*Words in a Corner*, 87). The question is whether the choice of these passages by Montaigne is motivated by the fact that they describe sexual pleasure as a kind of dialogue or interval between speech and silence.

37. Gray notes Montaigne's systematic mixing of Virgil's and Lucretius's language ("Eros et écriture," 272). Mathieu-Castellani comments on the implications of Montaigne's gesture, observing that "words make love" and "have a sex" (*Montaigne*, 129–30).

38. As McKinley points out, even before their existence in the *Essays*, the Virgil and Lucretius passages were closely linked, signaling Montaigne's recognition of Virgil's borrowing from Lucretius (*Words in a Corner*, 90–91). For an analysis of Virgil's borrowing from Lucretius, see Michael C. J. Putnam, *The Poetry of the Aeneid: Four Studies in Imaginative Unity* (Cambridge: Harvard University Press, 1965), 137.

39. Starobinski interprets Montaigne's act of borrowing as a gesture of both dependence and rivalry, one that mediates Montaigne's own self-possession (*Montaigne in Motion*, 112–14).

40. For a philosophical and psychoanalytic analysis of performativity as citationality, see Butler, *Bodies That Matter*, 12–16.

41. Kritzman interprets this symbolic image of an "idealized masculine language" as an inverse image of the essayist, in *Rhetoric of Sexuality*, 67.

42. Kritzman notes the indeterminacy of the interplay between rhetoric and sexuality: "The text sets up an indeterminate play between rhetoric and sexuality at the same time that it expresses the wish for a rhetorical potency that would capture and authentically represent the energies figured in the self-portrait" (*Rhetoric of Sexuality*, 137).

43. Parker interprets Montaigne's pronouncements on the virile style as the continuation of a long-standing Latin tradition that opposes "manly style" to feminized laxness. However, she also notes that when Montaigne actually deploys these terms in their sexual sense in his essay, they are associated not with the affirmation of virility, but with its failure ("Gender Ideology, Gender Change," 252–54). Carol Clark observes that this opposition is not consistently sustained in Montaigne's writings, since feminized laxness and softness are also treated in an approbatory fashion. See *The Web of Metaphor: Studies in the Imagery of Montaigne's "Essais"* (Lexington, Ky.: French Forum, 1978), 91–96, 161–62.

44. Kritzman notes Montaigne's tendency to "bitextuality," to the traces of the feminine in a masculine mode, as a sign of ambivalence within the textual subject (*Rhetoric of Sexuality*, 68–71).

45. For Montaigne's comments on impotence, see *Essays*, I, 2; I, 21; I, 54; and III, 5. See also Lee R. Entin-Bates, "Montaigne's Remarks on Impotence," *Modern Language Notes* 91 (May 1976): 640–54; and Lawrence D. Kritzman, "Montaigne's Fantastic Monsters and the Construction of Gender," in *Writing the Renaissance: Essays on Sixteenth-Century French Literature in Honor of Floyd Gray*, ed. Ray-

mond C. La Charité (Lexington, Ky.: French Forum, 1992), 191–94; cf. Parker's discussion in "Gender Ideology, Gender Change," 345–46, 348–53.

46. According to Hugo Friedrich, the insufficiency of French compared to Latin reflects a common humanist bias against the so-called vulgar languages. However, this supposed imperfection of the French language is but an invitation for Montaigne to use it (Hugo Friedrich, *Montaigne,* trans. Robert Rovini [Paris: Gallimard, 1968], 377).

47. Montaigne's conclusion is hard to reconcile with Bowen's claim that he is antifeminist ("Montaigne's Anti-*Phaedrus,*" 107).

48. For Cave's comment regarding Montaigne's revalorization of language, see *Cornucopian Text,* 288.

49. Parker comments that Montaigne's sometime reliance on the Aristotelian orthodoxy of women's greater passivity is undermined by an overwhelming number of anecdotes documenting activity ("Gender Ideology, Gender Change," 351–52, 354–56).

50. Cf. Marc E. Blanchard's discussion of the representation of female sexuality in *Trois portraits de Montaigne: Essai sur la représentation à la Renaissance* (Paris: Nizet, 1990), 209–11.

51. Although the number six appears to be arbitrary, it is in excess of the roman numeral V of the essay "On Some Verses of Virgil" (III, 5). At the inception of this essay, Montaigne puns exhaustively on the coincidence of the letter *V,* in verses and Virgil, etc., and the roman numeral V.

52. Montaigne adds that sexual pleasure becomes vicious either by immoderation or by indiscretion (III, 5: 668). Kritzman interprets Montaigne's description of pleasure in a Freudian sense, as a lowering of tension through a process of emptying out (*Rhetoric of Sexuality,* 146).

53. For a general analysis of "mutual obligations" as they pertain to both marriage and love, see Starobinski, *Montaigne in Motion,* 198–207. While Starobinski distinguishes between the contractual nature of marriage and the love "bargain," which he defines as an exchange in desire (202), my own analysis focuses on sexual pleasure in both contexts as a transactional and transitive category.

54. McKinley observes that "the subject of text focuses the problem of quotation" as a productive principle, both enabling and restraining (*Words in a Corner,* 102).

55. See Richard Regosin, *The Matter of My Book: Montaigne's "Essais" as the Book of the Self* (Berkeley: University of California Press, 1977), 199. However, in this passage he privileges exclusively the self-reflexive aspects of language as the essential entity and medium of incarnation of the essay.

56. John O'Neill notes Montaigne's reliance on Stoic criteria, particularly in his preference for a "palpable" or energetic style. See *Essaying Montaigne: A Study of the Renaissance Institution of Writing and Reading* (London: Routledge and Kegan Paul, 1982), 93–95.

57. Cf. Starobinski, *Montaigne in Motion,* 208.

58. As Starobinski comments: "Doubling does not secure replication of identity

but introduces difference, inaugurating the whole infinite series of the countable" (*Montaigne in Motion*, 20).

59. François Rigolot powerfully argues for the fluidity and metamorphic character of Montaigne's self-presentation. See *Les Métamorphoses de Montaigne* (Paris: Presses Universitaires de France, 1988), 227–29.

60. Regosin, *Matter of My Book*, 203.

61. For the dynamism of the text as a generative, living body, see Lawrence D. Kritzman, *Destruction/découverte: Le fonctionnement de la rhétorique dans les "Essais" de Montaigne* (Lexington, Ky.: French Forum, 1980), 102–5, 107. Rigolot suggests that Montaigne's theory of textual generation is based on Ovid's *Metamorphoses* (*Les Métamorphoses de Montaigne*, 126).

62. For an analysis of the body forged in the text as a transcription of the movement of desire, see Kritzman, "Montaigne's Family Romance," in *Rhetoric of Sexuality*, 77.

63. Cave suggests that Montaigne is a fold in his own text (*Cornucopian Text*, 282).

64. For an analysis of Montaigne's name both as a proper name and as a geographical location, see François Rigolot, "Sémiotique et onomastique: Le nom propre de Montaigne," in Tetel and Masters, *Les Parcours des "Essais,"* 147–49.

Chapter 2

1. *Astrea* was published in five parts, the first part in 1607, the second in 1610, the third in 1619, and an incomplete fourth part (comprising the first four books) in 1625. After d'Urfé's death in 1625, his secretary, Balthazar Baro, to whom the book had originally been dictated, completed the fourth part and published this version in 1627, followed by a fifth part that he claimed was based on the author's notes, also in 1627. This chapter is an expanded and revised version of "Emblematic Legacies: Hieroglyphs of Desire in *L'Astrée*," in *EMF: Studies in Early Modern France*, ed. David L. Rubin (Charlottesville, Va.: Rockwood Press, 1995), 31–54.

2. *The Princess of Clèves* is considered to formally inaugurate the birth of the novel in the French tradition, though the early part of the century is replete with several other novelistic traditions, such as the pastoral, the precious, and the comic novels. It is important to note that this genealogy of the origins of the French novel conveniently overlooks Charles Sorel's parody of *Astrea* entitled *The Extravagant Shepherd*, which was republished in the 1633 edition with the subtitle *The Anti-Novel*. Thus it would seem that the emergence of the antinovel in France precedes the emergence of the novel.

3. The insistence on normative and idealist aesthetic criteria such as verisimilitude *(vraisemblance)* and plausibility *(bienséance)* and the concomitant effort to censure and purify both theatrical and novelistic discourse relegated previous novelistic efforts to obsolescence. Such developments also suggest the potential impact of the classical rule of the three unities elaborated in the dramatic context of the novel,

insofar as the construction of subjectivity, setting, and multiple narratives becomes more restrictive and tightly structured.

4. For a brief history and analysis of this analogy, see Wendy Steiner, *The Colors of Rhetoric: Problems in the Relation between Modern Literature and Painting* (Chicago: Chicago University Press, 1982), 1–18.

5. Heinrich Wölfflin, *Renaissance and Baroque*, trans. Kathrin Simon (Ithaca, N.Y.: Cornell University Press, 1967), and *Principles of Art History: The Problem of the Development of Style in Later Art*, trans. M. D. Hottinger (New York: Dover, 1950).

6. Wölfflin, *Principles of Art History*, 14, 27.

7. Wölfflin, *Principles of Art History*, 27.

8. For an analysis of perspective as a symbolic form in the Renaissance, see Erwin Panofski, *La Perspective comme forme symbolique*, trans. Guy Ballangé (Paris: Minuit, 1975); for an analysis of anamorphosis as artistic and optical experimentation in the baroque period, see Jurgis Baltrusaitis, *Anamorphic Art*, trans. W. J. Strachan (New York: Harry J. Abrams, 1977).

9. See Foucault, *Les Mots et les choses*; and José Antonio Maravall, *The Culture of the Baroque: Analysis of a Historical Structure*, trans. Terry Cochran (Minneapolis: University of Minnesota Press, 1986). The significance of both of these studies is the effort to designate the baroque as a historical concept. In the case of Foucault, the baroque implies a particular epistemological formation, a ternary concept of the sign, as well as a theory of representation based on interpretation. Although Maravall's attention focuses on how the baroque reflects the specific social, political, and economic conditions of the Spanish context, his analysis suggests that his periodization (1605–50) may also apply to other European countries (4).

10. In *Barocco* (Paris: Seuil, 1975), Severo Sarduy explores the Keplerian basis of baroque cosmology based on a decentered notion of ellipsis, while in *La Doublure* (Paris: Seuil, 1981) he elaborates the aesthetic implications of this position. Christina Buci-Glucksmann's *La Raison baroque: De Baudelaire à Benjamin* (Paris: Galilée, 1984) and her *La Folie du voir: De l'esthétique baroque* (Paris: Galilée, 1986) explore the visual and rhetorical categories of baroque aesthetics, as a concept that is both historical and transhistorical. The most nuanced philosophical exploration of the baroque is to be found in Gilles Deleuze, *The Fold: Leibniz and the Baroque*, trans. Tom Conley (Minneapolis: University of Minnesota Press, 1993).

11. In Sarduy's and Buci-Glucksmann's later work we see renewed emphasis on the plastic character of vision, as well as the effort, by Buci-Glucksmann (basing herself on Benjamin, *German Tragic Drama*), to explore vision itself as an allegorical concept.

12. Carl Horst, *Barock-probleme* (Munich: E. Rentsch, 1912), 39–40; cited by Benjamin, *German Tragic Drama*, 177.

13. Benjamin, *German Tragic Drama*, 177.

14. Benjamin, *German Tragic Drama*, 162. Deleuze underlines the originality of Benjamin's contribution in interpreting allegory neither as failed symbol nor as

abstract personification, but as a figurative device that "uncovers nature and history according to the order of time" (*The Fold,* 12).

15. See Albrecht Schöne, *Emblematik und Drama im Zeitalter des Barock* (Munich: Beck, 1964); Dietrich Jons, *Das "Sinnen-bild": Studien zur allegorischen Bildlichkeit bei Andreas Gryphius* (Stuttgart: Metzder, 1966); and Peter M. Daly's discussion of their contribution in *Emblematic Theory: Recent German Contributions to the Characterization of the Emblem Genre* (Nendeln: KTO Press, 1979), 21–77. For an analysis of emblems and their impact on literature see Daly's *Literature in Light of the Emblem* (Toronto: University of Toronto Press, 1979); and Daniel S. Russell's groundbreaking *The Emblem and Device in France* (Lexington, Ky.: French Forum, 1985).

16. In order to get a better idea of the scope and variety of emblem books, see Mario Praz's bibliography of over six hundred authors in *Studies in Seventeenth-Century Imagery* (London: Warburg Institute, 1939–47), vols. 1–2. See in particular his discussion of Andrea Alciati, *Emblematum liber,* considered the seminal source of the emblematic genre, particularly as regards his reliance on the Greek epigrammatic tradition (1:22–31).

17. See Daniel S. Russell's persuasive argument in "Du Bellay's Emblematic Vision of Rome," *Yale French Studies* 47 (1972): 100.

18. Schöne, *Emblematik und Drama,* 21; also quoted in Daly, *Literature in Light,* 38.

19. See Angus Fletcher, *Allegory: The Theory of a Symbolic Mode* (Ithaca, N.Y.: Cornell University Press, 1964), 3.

20. This statement, attributed by Plutarch to Simonedes of Ceos, has a major resurgence during the Renaissance and baroque periods, as demonstrated by the writings of Pompeo Garigliano, Marino and others. See Giulio Marzot, *L'ingegno e il genio del Seicento* (Florence: La Nuova Italia, 1944).

21. Except as noted, translations are based on *Astrea: A Romance,* 3 vols. (London: Printed by W. W. for H. Moseley, T. Dring, and H. Herringman, 1657–58), as emended by Leonard Hinds and the author to reflect more closely the text's literal and figurative language and to update spelling. Quotations of the original French are from *L'Astrée,* ed. Hugues Vaganay, 5 vols. (Lyon: Pierre Masson, 1925). Both French and English versions are cited by volume and page, the translation listed first, then the original French.

22. Gérard Genette, "Le Serpent dans la Bergerie," introduction to *L'Astrée,* ed. Gérard Genette (Paris: Union générale d'Editions, 1964), 10. For Louise Horowitz, on the contrary, in *Honoré d'Urfé* (Boston: Twayne Publishers, 1984), 16, *L'Astrée* is geographically accurate to the extent that it represents an idealized Forez.

23. I am referring here to such details as the yellow and fly-spotted wallpaper in Balzac's *Eugénie Grandet,* where the most minute details in the environment reflect the psychological and social instincts of the characters, as well as to Zola's novels, where environmental influences are translated into congenital disorders.

24. For an analysis of the significance of the river, see M. Gerhardt, "Un Person-

nage principal de *L'Astrée:* Le Lignon," in *Colloque commémoratif du quatrième centenaire de la naissance d'Honoré d'Urfé* (Montbrison: La Diana, 1970), 47–56.

25. Jean Rousset, *La Littérature de l'âge baroque en France: Circé et le paon* (Paris: Corti, 1960), describes the baroque obsession with flowing water as an "orgie hydraulique," 144; cf. Wölfflin, *Renaissance and Baroque,* 154.

26. As Alexandru Ciorenescu points out in regard to Montemayor and Cervantes (*Astrée*'s pastoral models), there is little curiosity for nature in its own right. See *Barocul sau descoperirea dramei,* trans. G. Tureacu (Cluj: Editura Dacia, 1980), 57–67.

27. But what appears to be an initial personalization of the river results in the opposite effect: nature is personalized "not as to be made more inward, but, on the contrary—so as to be deprived of soul" (Benjamin, *German Tragic Drama,* 187 n. 69, quoting Cysarz).

28. Horowitz, *Honoré d'Urfé,* 21. This study will demonstrate that the novel presents a critique, rather than an affirmation, of Platonic and Neoplatonic doctrine.

29. See Honoré d'Urfé's *Epitres Morales* (1595–1608), where he expounds his philosophy based on the sixteenth-century Italian treatises on love by Bembo, Castiglione, and Léon Hébreu, as discussed by Antoine Adam, "La Théorie mystique de l'amour dans *L'Astrée* et ses sources italiennes," *Revue d'Histoire de la Philosophie* (1937).

30. Benjamin, *German Tragic Drama,* 164–65 n. 13, quoting Creuzer.

31. Unlike Jacques Lacan's mirror stage, where the constitution of the self as an image involves both self-reflection and the alienation or division of the self, this mirror reflects less the question of individual identity (the imaginary) than that of its social constitution (the symbolic). See "Le Stade du miroir," in *Écrits* (Paris: Seuil, 1966).

32. In "An Impossible Response: The Disaster of Narcissus," in *Literature and the Ethical Question,* a special issue of *Yale French Studies* 79 (1991): 127–34, Claire Nouvet proposes a new reading of Ovid's myth, one in which the reflective powers of the water stage the figurative aspects of the subject in the process of self-representation, as a "disastrous scene of writing."

33. Charles Anton, *Classical Dictionary* (New York: Harper and Brothers, 1873), s.v. "Narcissus," 871.

34. Edward Baron Turk notes that the anagram-configurations suggested by the syllabic makeup of the proper names indicate its significance as a structuring device in the baroque novel: "the dispersal of discrete syllables in protean contexts reinforces the sense of motility and instability, whereas the recurrence of the same syllables forming networks of concatenated segments reinforces the sense of inter-relatedness and fused integrity." *Baroque Fiction-Making: A Study of Gomberville's "Polexandre"* (Chapel Hill: University of North Carolina Department of Romance Languages, 1978), 51.

35. Translated from the original. The French is provided here since certain wordplay is impossible to translate exactly.

Nymphe, qui sens dedans ces roches creuses
Quel est le mal des peines amoureuses,
N'auray-je donc jamais allegements?   *Je ments.*
Comment, Echo, n'est-ce point un blaspheme
De t'accuser et dire que tu ments?
Ce que j'entens est-ce bien ta voix mesme?   *Ayme.*

(II, 10)

36. This is exactly the pleasure that Narcissus is unable to enjoy, since he is unable to recognize the echoes of his own speech (Nouvet, "An Impossible Response," 122–23).

37. For an analysis of how subjective effects are arbitrarily generated through the use of the first person, see Emile Benveniste, "De la subjectivité dans le language," in *Problèmes de linguistique générale* (Paris: Gallimard, 1966).

38. For a preliminary analysis of this passage in relation to the graphic and stylistic dimension of the text, see my "The Graphic Text: The Nude in *L'Astrée*," *Papers in French Seventeenth Century Literature* 15, no. 29 (1988): 532–33.

39. It is only with Descartes and the advent of classicism that the mind-body distinction will become firmly established.

40. The philosophical implications of this incident are elaborated in the context of Descartes's hyperbolic doubt argument in my *Subjectivity and Representation in Descartes,* 22–23, 155–59.

41. See the definition of hyperbole in *The Winston Dictionary: Encyclopedic Edition* (Philadelphia: John C. Winston Co., 1957), 475.

42. In his reading of *L'Astrée,* Gerard Genette emphasizes the transgressive dimension of the novel, the fact that the code of love only exists to engender fraud. His interpretation reflects a dialectical conception of desire, where desire is defined in terms of its own negation ("Le Serpent dans la Bergerie," 19–21).

43. Despite its structuralist character, Jacques Ehrmann's analysis is heavily indebted to Sartre, to a dialectical and humanist essentialism. See *Un Paradis désespéré: L'amour et l'illusion dans "L'Astrée"* (New Haven: Yale University Press, 1963), 4.

44. Horowitz, *Honoré d'Urfé,* 111–12.

45. Horowitz perceptively examines the thematic dimensions of disguise, without inquiring, however, into how they express the status of representation in the novel (*Honoré d'Urfé,* 96–125).

46. As Horowitz suggests, "Céladon becomes a woman, through our reading of a female name" (*Honoré d'Urfé,* 114).

47. Horowitz, *Honoré d'Urfé,* 98.

48. Jean-Louis Schefer, "On the Object of Figuration," trans. T. Corrigan and D. Judovitz, *Sub-Stance* 39 (1983): 30.

49. As the narrator tells us from the beginning, love involves the appropriate loss of oneself: "The truth is, if one must acquire some happiness in the loss of oneself, (Celadon) could consider himself lost so well unto the purpose" (1:1) [Il est vray que

si en la perte de soy mesme on peut faire quelque acquisition, dont on se doive contenter, il se peut dire heureux de s'estre perdu si à propos] (1:10).

50. It is interesting to note that the English translation has Alexis pressing Astrea's body against her bosom, while the original version uses the word *estomach*, which loosely refers not to the stomach, but the middle of the body, considered at the time as the true repository of affection.

51. For Sigmund Freud, the fetish is substitute for the maternal phallus; see "Fetishism" (1927), in *Sexuality and the Psychology of Love,* ed. Philip Rieff (New York: Collier Books, 1974), 215.

52. For instance, Celadon's hat is not just a hat, to the extent that within the folds of its lining are hidden the couple's letters. This item of clothing is tossed back and forth with the couple's correspondence.

53. In the closing moments of d'Urfé's novel, Astrea competes with Alexis, claiming to be Astrea, in order to save Alexis's life. Her argument to Polemas regarding the truth of her identity is based on an appeal to her clothes: "consult these clothes which I wear" (3:185) [demandez-le à ces habits que je porte] (4:752). Clothes in this context function in the manner of speech: they provide the visual response to a query regarding the competing claims of two individuals for the same name. However, Polemas is not persuaded, and he sentences them both to death: "Since you are both the daughters of that villain, I order that you both be treated accordingly" (3:185) [Puis donc, que vous estes toutes deux filles de ce meschant homme, j'ordonne que vous soyez toutes deux traitées comme telles] (4:752). Unable to tolerate resemblance, Polemas settles the danger posed by these competing doubles by suppressing both of the terms.

54. As if to verify the perfection of this new disguise, we are told that the sight of Astrea, alias Celadon/Alexis, invites the amorous advances of Hylas.

55. Deleuze also notes in reference to baroque sculpture that folds are not simply decorative effects, but convey the "intensity of a spiritual force exerted on the body" (*The Fold*, 122).

Chapter 3

1. This difference cannot be accounted for simply by invoking generic distinctions, by assigning Montaigne's *Essays* to literature and Descartes's *Discourse on Method* to philosophy, for the distinctions between these domains are not yet firmly established in France in the late sixteenth and early seventeenth centuries. These works mix philosophical and literary concerns and conceits as they elaborate on subjectivity and its relation to knowledge and self-knowledge. This chapter expands ideas first presented in "Descartes' Virtual Bodies: Anatomy, Technology, and the Inhuman," in *Writing the Body,* spec. issue of *Paroles Gelées* 16, no. 1 (1998): 21–41.

2. In postulating this rupture, I am relying on Michel Foucault's notion of epistemic rupture, that is, of a historical discontinuity between the world of the late Renaissance and the baroque and the world of the Cartesian and classical, based on

entirely different codes and discursive practices in knowledge, language, representation, and subjectivity. See Foucault's discussion in *Les Mots et les choses*, 13–15, 32–91.

3. For a general analysis of Galen's humoral theories, see Rudolph E. Siegel, *Galen's System of Physiology and Medicine* (Basel: S. Karger, 1968), 205–24.

4. For an analysis of the role of signatures in the late Renaissance and early baroque European culture, see Foucault, *Les Mots et les choses*, 40–45.

5. Michel Foucault examines the relations of blood to power and understands this transition as a passage from a *symbolics of blood* to an *analytics of sexuality* (*History of Sexuality*, 1:147–48).

6. For a general account of Descartes's debt and reaction to Harvey, see Etienne Gilson, *Etudes sur le rôle de la pensée médiévale dans la formation du système cartésien*, 5th ed. (Paris, J. Vrin, 1984), 51–101. See also Marjorie Grene, "The Heart and Blood: Descartes, Plemp, and Harvey," in *Essays in the Philosophy of Science of René Descartes,* ed. Stephen Voss (New York: Oxford University Press, 1993), 324–35.

7. Georges Canguilhem's comment in *A Vital Rationalist: Selected Writings from Georges Canguilhem,* ed. François Delaporte, trans. Arthur Goldhammer (New York: Zone Books, 1994), 130–31.

8. For a detailed analysis of Harvey's work, see Walter Pagel, *William Harvey's Biological Ideas: Selected Aspects and Historical Background* (New York: Hafner, 1967), 51–59.

9. These analogies are visible in Harvey's dedication to Charles I, which equates the sun, the king, and the heart. See Owsei Temkin, "Metaphors of Human Biology," in *The Double Face of Janus and Other Essays in the History of Medicine* (Baltimore: Johns Hopkins University Press, 1977), 281–82.

10. Harvey's interpretation of the pulse as a mechanical impulse, conferred on blood by the movement of contraction and relaxation of the heart, replaces the Galenic interpretation of pulse as "force" generated by the arterial wall (Pagel, *William Harvey's Biological Ideas,* 51–54).

11. See Pagel's comments regarding these mechanical analogies and their subservience to Aristotelian vitalism (*William Harvey's Biological Ideas,* 80–81).

12. See Descartes's letter to Plempius, February 15, 1638, in *The Philosophical Writings of Descartes,* ed. John Cottingham, Robert Stoothoff, and Dugald Murdoch, trans. John Cottingham, 3 vols. (Cambridge: Cambridge University Press, 1985), 3:79–80 (hereafter cited as *PWD*) and his comments in *Description of the Human Body* (1664; *PWD,* 1:318–19). Also see Anne Bitbol-Hespériès's discussion in *Le Principe de la vie chez Descartes* (Paris: J. Vrin, 1990), 55–102. Descartes's preference for a model based on heat might be explained by his efforts to account for both the motion of blood and its distillation into the minute corpuscles of the animal spirits.

13. This distinction between Harvey's use of mechanist analogies and Descartes's definition of the body as a machine adds nuance to Jonathan Sawday's

assimilation of their positions. See *The Body Emblazoned: Dissection and the Human Body in Renaissance Culture* (London: Routledge, 1995), 23–32.

14. See *The Philosophical Works of Descartes,* trans. E. S. Haldane and G. R. T. Ross (Cambridge: Cambridge University Press, 1969), 1:101 (hereafter cited as *HR*).

15. Canguilhem also notes the dependence of Descartes's theory of the animal machine on the cogito (*A Vital Rationalist,* 227).

16. George Louis Leclerc, Comte de Buffon critiques the interpretation of the circulation of blood in mechanical terms. In *Histoire naturelle des animaux* (1748), he comments: "It is obvious that neither the circulation of blood nor the movement of the muscles nor the animal functions can be explained in terms of impulse or any of the laws of ordinary mechanics" (chap. 10, as quoted by Canguilhem, *A Vital Rationalist,* 165). For a general account of Descartes's mechanical interpretation of nature, see E. J. Dijksterhuis, *The Mechanization of the World Picture* (Oxford: Clarendon Press, 1961), 403–18.

17. Marie-Christine Pouchelle, *Corps et chirurgie à l'apogée du Moyen Age* (Paris: Flammarion, 1983), 170–73. Mondeville privileges the architect, who is defined by the capacity to design a plan of action. This privilege, accorded to architects as a guiding paradigm for surgeons, also occurs in Descartes's analogies in part 2 of the *Discourse,* which compares the philosopher with the architect who operates according to an overall blueprint.

18. For these analogies, see Pouchelle, *Corps et chirurgie,* 176–83. Aristotle also makes an analogy between animal movements and automatic mechanical movements like those in war machines such as the catapult. See Alfred Espinas, "L'Organisation ou la machine vivante en Grèce au IVe siècle avant J.-C.," *Revue de Métaphysique et de Morale* (1903): 702–17.

19. Pouchelle elaborates this cohesion between anatomical and social categories in Mondeville in *Corps et chirurgie,* 189–92.

20. See Aquinas's *Summa Theologiae* (I, II, 13, 2) and Antoniana-Margarita Gomez-Pereira, *Opus nempe physicis medicis ac thelogicis non minus utile quam necessarium* (Medina del Campo, 1555–58). In his letter to Mersenne, June 23, 1641, Descartes denies knowledge of Gomez's work and dismisses it offhand, but the similarity of their positions is striking. See G. A. Lindebom's discussion in *Descartes and Medicine* (Amsterdam: Rodopi, 1979), 61–62.

21. A possible literary source may include Jean Froissart's "L'Horloge amoureus" (ca. 1368), in which an analogy is elaborated between the mechanisms of a clock and those of love. I want to thank Patrick Wheeler for bringing this text to my attention.

22. For an analysis of the meaning of this term as presented in late-seventeenth-century dictionaries, see Claude Reichler, "Machine et machinations: La ruse des signes," *Revue des Sciences Humaines* 58, nos. 186–87 (1982): 33–39. Also see Gérard Simon's analysis of this term in "Les Machines au XVIIe siècle: Usage, typologie, résonances symboliques," in *Revue des Sciences Humaines* 58, nos. 186–87 (1982): 10–13.

23. See Georges Canguilhem's comments in *A Vital Rationalist,* 206–7; see also

his general discussion of the relation of the Cartesian machine to the notion of the organism, in "Machine and Organism," in "Incorporations," ed. Jonathan Crary and Sanford Kwinter, special issue of *Zone* 6 (winter 1992): 45–69.

24. John Cottingham notes that Descartes is referring here to "fictional men," introduced in an earlier and (lost) part of the *Treatise on Man*, analogously to his use of the "new world" in the *World* (*PWD*, 1:99). For a detailed analysis of the role of the fictional and the axiomatic in the *World*, see my *Subjectivity and Representation in Descartes*, 87–97.

25. Canguilhem, "Machine and Organism," 53–54.

26. For an analysis of the mathematical and epistemological underpinnings of Descartes's philosophy, see my *Subjectivity and Representation in Descartes*, 39–85.

27. In his letter to Reneri for Pollot, Descartes argues that the statement "I am breathing, therefore I exist," is insufficient as an argument for existence, since the thought of breathing implies existence in the mode of "I am thinking, therefore I exist" (April or May 1638; *PWD*, 3:98).

28. Canguilhem, *A Vital Rationalist*, 207.

29. Carolyn Merchant, *The Death of Nature: Women, Ecology, and the Scientific Revolution* (San Francisco: Harper and Row, 1980), 194–205.

30. Descartes's descriptions of gardens and hydraulic statues are possibly based on the royal gardens of Saint-Germain-en-Laye. See Ferdinand Alquié's annotation in René Descartes, *Oeuvres Philosophiques de Descartes,* 3 vols., ed Ferdinand Alquié (Paris: Garnier, 1973), 1:390. A possible scholarly source for the analysis of the mechanical forces at stake may include Salomon de Caus, *Les Raisons des forces mouvantes avec diverses machines tant utiles que plaisantes auxquelles sont jointes plusieurs desseings de grottes et de fontaines* (Frankfurt, 1615).

31. Descartes's description of gardens echoes Montaigne's own astonishment before the hydraulic marvels of his own time, in *Journal de voyage en Italie par la Suisse et l'Allemagne en 1550–1581* (Paris: Club Français du Livre, 1954), 109. For a general analysis of French seventeenth-century gardens and their relations to cartesian metaphysics, see Allen S. Weiss, *Mirrors of Infinity: The French Formal Garden and 17th-Century Metaphysics* (New York: Princeton Architectural Press, 1995).

32. In the medieval and renaissance traditions, the animal spirits are invoked to mediate the relation of body and soul. See David P. Walker's discussion in "Medical Spirits in Philosophy and Theology from Ficino to Newton," in *Arts du spectacles et histoire des idées: Recueil offert en hommage à Jean Jacquot* (Tours: Centre d'études supérieures de la Renaissance, 1984), 287–300.

33. Descartes's dramatic representation of the human body through the unfolding scenography of garden displays recalls the staging devices of dissection in the anatomy theater. See Sawday's analysis of the theatricality of dissection in *The Body Emblazoned,* 146–58.

34. For an analysis of dissection as a spectacle of display that renders visible the scientific gaze and the perspective of natural philosophy, see Francis Barker, *The Tremulous Private Body: Essays on Subjection* (Ann Arbor: University of Michigan Press, 1995), 65–76.

35. Jean-Claude Beaune, *L'Automate et ses mobiles* (Paris: Flammarion, 1980), 173, (my translation).

36. For an analysis of the clock as the prototype for automatic machines and the key machine of the modern industrial age, see Lewis Mumford, *Technics and Civilization* (New York: Harcourt Brace, 1963), 14–18.

37. According to Gary Hatfield, the vegetative soul controls growth, nutrition, and reproductive generation, while the sensitive soul governs sense perception, appetites, and animal motion. Descartes grants the vegetative and sensitive souls to animals alone. See "Descartes' Physiology and Its Relation to His Psychology," in *The Cambridge Companion to Descartes,* ed. John Cottingham (Cambridge: Cambridge University Press, 1992), 344.

38. Stephen Gaukroger, *Descartes: An Intellectual Biography* (Oxford: Oxford University Press, 1995), 278.

39. Descartes, *Oeuvres Philosophiques,* 1:480.

40. See Leonora Cohen Rosenfeld's discussion of these Neoplatonic and mystical traditions in the works of Henry Cornelius Agrippa and of Marcilio Ficino in *From Beast-Machine to Man-Machine: Animal Soul in French Letters from Descartes to La Mettrie* (New York: Octagon Books, 1968), xxiii–xxiv.

41. According to Descartes, the vegetative and sensitive souls should not be called souls since they belong to an entirely different genus from the rational soul (letter to Regius, *PWD,* 3:182).

42. In his letter to More, February 5, 1649, Descartes notes that animals possess neither thought nor the ability to use speech (*PWD,* 3:366). In his letter to the marquess of Newcastle, November 23, 1646, he explains that he differs with Montaigne, who attributes thought to animals (*PWD,* 3:302).

43. See Descartes's letter to Plempius for Fromondus, October 3, 1637 *(PWD,* 3:62). For an analysis of La Mettrie's materialism, see Frederick Albert Lange's *History of Materialism,* trans. Ernest Chester Thomas (New York: Harcourt, Brace, 1925), 49–91. For an analysis of Sade's materialism, see my discussion in chapter 5.

44. Gilbert Ryle, *The Concept of Mind* (New York: Hutchinson, 1969), chap. 1.

45. Jean-Pierre Séris, *Languages et machines à l'âge classique* (Paris: Hachette, 1995), 24 (my translation).

46. Séris refers to Descartes's letter to Henri More, February 5, 1649, which states that "speech is the only certain sign of a thought hidden in a body" (*PWD,* 3:366). Hiram Caton, however, in *The Origin of Subjectivity: An Essay on Descartes* (New Haven: Yale University Press, 1973), 99, argues that Descartes should have posited thought, rather than speech, as the true distinction between men and animals.

47. Descartes's use of "organs" in this context underlines the overlap between the logic of the machine and that of the organism, be it human or animal.

48. See Descartes's comments in the Sixth Meditation and his Reply to the Sixth Objection. See also his correspondence with Princess Elizabeth of Sweden, especially letters of May 21 and June 28, 1643; by 1645 the question of the union of the mind and the body becomes an inquiry into the passions. This discussion of the interaction

of the mind and the body attains its fullest elaboration in *The Passions of the Soul* (completed 1645–46 and published in 1649).

49. My reading differs with Keith Gunderson's efforts to distinguish these two tests as (1) the language test and (2) the action test. See his *Mentality and Machines*, 2d ed. (Minneapolis: University of Minnesota Press, 1985), 8–17.

50. Cf. Barker, *The Tremulous Private Body*, 93–94.

Chapter 4

1. Harry Frankfurt has drawn our attention to the figures of demons, madmen, and dreamers and their crucial function in Descartes's justification of reason, without focusing specifically on the question of the body. See *Demons, Madmen, and Dreamers: The Defense of Reason in Descartes's Meditations* (Indianapolis: Bobbs-Merrill, 1970).

2. Gary Hatfield argues that Descartes relies not only on Loyola's exercises, which define the attainment of spirituality through sensory materials constructed by the imagination, but also on the Augustinian tradition that relies on a skeptical approach and the contemplation of thought. See "The Senses and the Fleshless Eye: The *Meditations* as Cognitive Exercises," in *Essays on Descartes's Meditations*, ed. Amélie Oksenberg Rorty (Berkeley: University of California Press, 1986), 48–54.

3. As I have suggested in an earlier study (*Subjectivity and Representation in Descartes*, 173–81) that the theological arguments for the existence of God serve to buttress Descartes's ontological arguments, in terms that concede the finitude of human understanding only to emphasize the infinite perfectibility of human will as a counterpart of the divine.

4. Drawing upon the writings Edmund Husserl and Maurice Merleau-Ponty, Drew Leder has noted the role of the body as epistemological obstruction. See *The Absent Body* (Chicago: University of Chicago Press, 1990), 128–34.

5. These arguments and the critical debates that accompany them are elaborated in detail in my analysis of the *Meditations* in *Subjectivity and Representation in Descartes*, 137–83.

6. In his reply to the Seventh Objection, Descartes uses the metaphor of a basket from which he removes all apples in order to determine which ones are rotten (*HR*, 2:282); cf. Anthony Kenny, *Descartes: A Study of His Philosophy* (New York: Random House, 1968), 18–19. The problem with this analogy is less the fact of calling into question our beliefs (as Kenny suggests) than that in attempting to escape deception engendered by the senses the Cartesian subject is willing to dispose of its own embodied nature and give up its natural condition as a body.

7. Descartes's decisions not to publish *The World* and to publish the *Discourse on Method* anonymously reflect his reaction to Galileo's condemnation by the church for his expressed support of the Copernican hypothesis. At the beginning of his *Optics*, Descartes discusses the discovery of lenses and their impact on the expansion of our knowledge of nature (*PWD*, 1:152).

8. See Descartes's example in the *Meditations* of our two different ideas of the

sun. The first, derived through the senses (adventitious ideas) presents the sun as extremely small, whereas the second, based on astronomical reasoning and instrumentation, presents the sun as several times larger than the earth (*HR,* 1:161).

9. For Michel Foucault, madness is inadmissible for the doubting subject, since its exclusion and internment founds the advent of rational discourse (*Folie et déraison: Histoire de la folie à l'âge classique* [Paris: Gallimard, 1972], 56–59).

10. These claims in the *Discourse* are far more radical, since they do away with the body altogether rather than attempt to consider and enumerate the various forms of deception entailed in madness and dreams.

11. Michel Foucault, in "My Body, This Paper, This Fire," *Oxford Literary Review* 4, no. 1 (1979): 16, returns to this passage in his response to Derrida to emphasize the centrality of madness for the Cartesian project.

12. The immediacy in question here is not merely that of sensory evidence, but of the simulation of sensation, the illusion of immediacy staged by the performative aspects of the text.

13. Descartes's examples of madness preponderantly involve instances of bodily misperception or denial, suggesting that the issue is less madness per se (as Foucault contends) than the body as its privileged object. For a critique of Foucault's position in his debate with Derrida, see my "Derrida and Descartes: Economizing Thought," in *Derrida and Deconstruction II,* ed. Hugh J. Silverman (New York: Routledge and Kegan Paul, 1989), 40–58.

14. It is in this context that the radicality of dreams, as opposed to madness, comes into view. Based on Martial Guéroult's position, Derrida will argue that it is in the case of sleep and not that of madness that the absolute totality of ideas of sensory origin becomes suspect. See his "Cogito and the History of Madness," in *Writing and Difference,* trans. Allan Bass (Chicago: University of Chicago Press, 1978), 51.

15. For Norman Malcolm the question of whether one is awake or dreaming is quite senseless to the extent that it would imply making judgments during dreams. See *Dreaming* (London: Routledge, 1959), 109.

16. Descartes's search for simples, as opposed to composites, here echoes the principles of the method announced in the *Discourse.* His discussion is patterned on his positing of color as the universal substrate of both dreams and painted representations. Cf. Caton, *The Origin of Subjectivity,* 115.

17. For a discussion of the passage from a deceptive God to the evil genius, see Caton, *The Origin of Subjectivity,* 118–21.

18. Martial Guéroult observes that hyperbolic doubt differs from skeptical doubt insofar as it proceeds not from the reality of things, but from the resolution to doubt everything. See *Descartes' Philosophy Interpreted According to the Order of Reasons,* trans. Roger Ariew, 2 vols. (Minneapolis: University of Minnesota Press, 1984–85), 1:20–21.

19. According to Guéroult, this metaphysical doubt attacks not merely natural doubt, but also the intrinsic objective validity of clear and distinct ideas, and as such is even contrary to the "nature of our mind" (*Descartes' Philosophy,* 1:21).

20. Cf. Derrida's analysis in "Cogito and Madness," 53.

21. Descartes's claims regarding the weakness of memory echo his earlier comments in the *Rules* (*HR*, 1:13–14, 33–34).

22. The inferential logic of the cogito as elaborated in the *Discourse* is no longer at issue, since thought does not function here as a founding premise. For a discussion of the inferential and performative aspects of the cogito, see Jaakko Hintikka, "*Cogito, Ergo Sum:* Inference or Performance?" in *Descartes: A Collection of Critical Essays,* ed. Willis Doney (Notre Dame: University of Notre Dame Press, 1968), 108–39.

23. Frankfurt claims that a premise entailing *sum* is necessarily when the reasonableness of asserting *sum* becomes a question *(Demons, Madmen, and Dreamers,* 111–12).

24. The statement "I am, I exist" does not elucidate the character of the meditating subject; it merely affirms the capacity of any subject to constitute itself through its locutionary position within language (Judovitz, *Subjectivity and Representation in Descartes,* 162–67).

25. In the Cartesian dialogue in *The Search after Truth,* Eudoxus labels Aristotle's definition of man as a rational animal a "metaphysical maze," since the absence of knowledge regarding the prior meaning of these terms leads to interminable inquiry and may even lapse into tautology (*HR,* 1:317).

26. For a discussion of thought in the context of the *sum* argument, see Kenny's *Descartes,* 65–70. See also Norman Malcolm, "Descartes's Proof That His Essence Is Thinking," in Doney, *Descartes,* 312–37.

27. Frankfurt underlines the fact that the cogito, or any such equivalent statement, does not appear anywhere in the *Meditations* (*Demons, Dreamers and Madmen,* 92). See also L. J. Beck's comments in *The Metaphysics of Descartes: A Study of the Meditations* (Oxford: Oxford University Press, 1965), 77–92.

28. It is interesting to note that Descartes will provide two different versions regarding the content of his definition that he is a thinking thing (*sum res cogitans*).

29. Caton points out that Descartes's first definition of the *sum res cogitans* argument excludes both imagination and sensation (*The Origin of Subjectivity,* 144–47).

30. Kenny draws attention to Descartes's *Replies* to underline the fact that in the Second Meditation Descartes does not claim that there is nothing corporeal in the soul, but simply that nothing corporeal is known to exist in it (*Descartes,* 88).

31. Gaukroger, *Descartes,* 349–50.

32. Guéroult, *Descartes' Philosophy,* 44–47. Caton interprets Descartes's position as a methodological answer to the ontological question of what the mind is, "which construes the being of mind in terms of its respective cognitive relations towards the world (its modes of thought)" (*The Origin of Subjectivity,* 150).

33. Daniel Garber considers the wax argument to be a foretaste of Descartes's full doctrine of the body, especially as regards the idea of bodies as extended things (*Descartes' Metaphysical Physics,* [Chicago: University of Chicago Press, 1992], 78).

34. It is important to note that the wax shows up earlier in Descartes's writings, specifically in the *Rules,* where the wax-and-seal analogy is a metaphor for the passive and receptive character of the senses (*HR,* 1:38).

35. In his reply to Hobbes, Descartes explains that he does not consider the perceptual qualities of the wax to belong to the formal nature of the wax itself (*HR,* 2:63).

36. This becomes the abiding sameness or essence of the wax that is independent of its experiential qualities. Caton observes that this argument will lead to the conclusion that both the body and the mind can only be known "supersensibly" (*The Origin of Subjectivity,* 153–55).

37. Descartes's critique of the reliability of the senses and the imagination was the focus of my earlier essay, "Vision, Representation, and Technology in Descartes," in *Modernity and the Hegemony of Vision,* ed. David Michael Levin (Berkeley: University of California Press, 1993), 74–80.

38. For a comprehensive historical and analytical account of vision and its elaboration in Descartes, see Martin Jay, "The Noblest of the Senses: Vision from Plato to Descartes," in *Downcast Eyes: The Denigration of Vision in Twentieth-Century French Thought* (Berkeley: University of California Press, 1993), 21–82. For a philosophical critique of Cartesian vision, see Maurice Merleau-Ponty, "Eye and Mind," in *The Primacy of Perception,* ed. James M. Edie, trans. Carleton Dallery (Evanston: Northwestern University Press, 1964), 159–90.

39. For a detailed analysis of Descartes's critique of vision and the transposition of its properties to the mental domain, see my "Vision, Representation, and Technology in Descartes," 63–84.

40. Alain Vizier mentions this digressive passage as an instance of Descartes's dismissal of the exterior and exteriority as a form of sensorial knowledge. See "Descartes et les automates," *Modern Language Notes* 3 (1996): 693–94.

41. Gassendi observes, in his Reply to the Fourth Objection, that to strip a substance of those attributes by which we apprehend it is to destroy our knowledge of it (*HR,* 2:98–99). Descartes acknowledges Gassendi's objection in his letter to Clerselier (*HR,* 2:134).

42. See Augustine's comments on Ambrose's introspective reading of the Bible (book 6) and on memory and the mind (book 10), in *Confessions,* trans. R. S. Coffin (London: Penguin, 1961).

43. See Montaigne's essay "Of Experience" and the analysis of it in chapter 1.

44. Merleau-Ponty, *Visible and Invisible,* 234.

45. Cf. Maurice Merleau-Ponty, "The Body as Expression and Speech," in *The Phenomenology of Perception,* trans. Colin Smith (London: Routledge and Kegan Paul, 1995), 174–99; see also Leder's discussion of language, thought, and the body in *The Absent Body,* 121–25.

46. For an eloquent critique of this position, see Jean-François Lyotard, "Can Thought Go On without a Body?" in *The Inhuman: Reflections on Time,* trans. Geoffrey Bennington and Rachel Bowlby (Stanford: Stanford University Press, 1991), 8–23.

47. Garber notes that in the Sixth Meditation, the commonsense, sensual bodies that appear earlier in the *Meditations* have been replaced by the lean, spare objects of geometry (*Descartes's Metaphysical Physics*, 75–76).

48. In reference to the Fifth Meditation, Garber observes that Descartes's focus on the geometrical features of the body is the capacity to perform proofs about them (*Descartes's Metaphysical Physics*, 81).

49. For a general examination of the role of imagination in Descartes's works, see Jean H. Roy, *L'Imagination selon Descartes* (Paris: Gallimard, 1944).

50. Given that the first example of a body provided by Descartes is that of a chiliagon, a mathematical object, there is a question as to the precise meaning of "body." Caton also notes that the "body" to which imagination turns remains a mystery (*The Origin of Subjectivity*, 162).

51. Commenting on the Sixth Meditation, Gassendi reproaches Descartes for attempting to distinguish imagination from intellection, because for him these two are the actions of one and the same faculty, rather than types of internal cognition (*HR*, 2:190–91). Descartes replies by reaffirming their distinctness as "wholly diverse modes of operation," for in thinking the mind employs itself alone, whereas in imagining it contemplates a corporeal form (*HR*, 2:229).

52. It is important to note that Descartes deliberately chose not an ordinary object, but a virtual one, in order to demonstrate the capacity of the mind to hypothesize in the context of mathematical schematism, as a way of underlining the imagination's figurative failure to attain such schematization.

53. Caton presents the imagination and the understanding as equal modes of applying the same power of knowledge or mind (*The Origin of Subjectivity*, 161–62). However, this modal interpretation overlooks Descartes's explicit privileging of the understanding over the imagination, which is necessary in order to maintain the virtual nature of Cartesian rationality.

54. Dennis L. Sepper examines the relation between the imagination and *ingenium* in order to argue for the centrality of the imagination in Descartes's early writings and its subsequent abandonment. See "*Ingenium,* Memory Art, and the Unity of Imaginative Knowing," in *Essays on the Philosophy and Science of René Descartes*, ed. Stephen Voss (New York: Oxford University Press, 1993), 142–57.

55. We must keep in mind Gassendi's query to Descartes, regarding the fact that the mind may be unable to turn toward itself or toward any idea, without turning toward something corporeal or represented by corporeal ideas (*HR,* 2:192).

56. In the Fifth Objection Gassendi recognizes that the senses may lead sometimes to error, but he wonders whether such error is sufficient to renounce all sensory perception (*HR,* 2:193). Also compare Leder's analysis of the body as a site of error and dysfunction (*The Absent Body,* 131–32).

57. Merleau-Ponty argues that perceptual "synthesis" has to be incomplete, since it cannot present a "reality" other than by running the risk of error (*The Phenomenology of Perception,* 377).

58. For Montaigne, it is precisely the diversity and multiplicity of experience that constitute its universality ("Of Experience," *Essays,* III, 13: 815).

59. Leder considers Cartesian epistemology to be a *motivated misreading*, insofar as its conclusions are motivated by lived experience, albeit misread into a reified ontology (*The Absent Body*, 132).

60. John W. Yolton presents Descartes's critique of perception in the context of his larger critique of resemblance (the lack of similarity between felt experience and physical causes) and his elaboration of perception in the mode of signs. See *Perceptual Acquaintance from Descartes to Reid* (Minneapolis: University of Minnesota Press, 1984), 22–25.

61. Gassendi objects to Descartes's example, since he claims that in individuals who have suffered no bodily loss, pain indubitably references the body (*HR*, 2:193).

62. Cf. Merleau-Ponty's discussion in *The Phenomenology of Perception*, 85–86.

63. This conclusion is reiterated in Descartes's last work, *The Passions of the Soul* (pt. 1, art. 30), where he observes that although the soul is joined to the whole body, "it is of a nature that has no relation to extension, nor dimensions, nor other properties of matter of which the body is composed" (*HR*, 1:345).

64. In his "Synopsis" of the *Meditations*, Descartes restates the difference between the mind and the body: whereas the human mind is pure substance unaffected by accidents, the body is defined by accidents and may lose its identity as a result of change in the sum of its parts. He concludes that this difference in nature may explain why the body perishes, as opposed to the immortality of the mind (*HR*, 2:141).

65. According to John Cottingham, Descartes's incorporeality thesis may reflect the religious dictates of the time, which required the immortality of the soul. See "Cartesian Dualism: Theology, Metaphysics, and Science," in *Cambridge Companion to Descartes*, 237–41.

66. According to Beck, Descartes's dualistic thesis regarding the radical separation of the mind and the body and the effort to subsequently explain their interaction has left an insoluble problem to his successors, as witnessed by the occasional causes of Malebranche, the parallelism of Spinoza, and the preestablished harmony of Leibniz (*The Metaphysics of Descartes*, 269–76).

67. Descartes will reiterate this argument for substantial union in his letter to Arnauld (July 29, 1648), as well as later in the *Principles of Philosophy*, pt. 1, art. 48 (*HR*, 2:238) and pt. 2, art. 3 (*HR*, 1:255). For a general discussion of this question, see Beck, *The Metaphysics of Descartes*, 262–80.

68. Despite Descartes's explicit attempt to refute this Platonic doctrine, insofar as his argument maintains that nothing corporeal belongs to the essence of man and hence is defined entirely as spirit, it follows, Arnauld contends, that man is a spirit who makes use of the body (*HR*, 2:84).

69. We should keep in mind Descartes's clarification in the *Principles* regarding the mistaken belief that pain is located in various parts of the body (pt. 1, art. 67; *HR*, 1:247). As Ruth Mattern points out, both in the *Meditations* and the *Principles* Descartes is committed to a physiological account of the mind as located in the brain and not diffused throughout the body. See "Descartes's Correspondence with Eliza-

beth: Conceiving Both the Union and Distinction of the Mind and Body," in *Descartes: Critical and Interpretative Essays,* ed. Michael Hooker (Baltimore: Johns Hopkins University Press, 1978), 217–19.

70. In his reply to the Fifth Objection, Descartes affirms the union, but not the coextensive nature, of the mind with the body: "though the mind is united with the whole body, it does not follow that it itself is extended throughout the body" (*HR,* 2:232).

71. As Descartes himself admits in his letter to Elizabeth (June 28, 1643), it is difficult for the human mind to conceive at the same time the distinction between the mind and the body and their union (*PWD,* 3:227).

72. In the Fourth Objection, Arnauld observes that Descartes's distinction and separation of the mind and the body is so radical as to make it difficult to rejoin them (*HR,* 2:84–85). Rather than addressing directly Arnauld's objection, Descartes replies by noting that his proof for substantial union does not preclude having a clear and distinct idea of the mind on its own (*HR,* 2:102–3).

73. Cf. Geneviève Rodis-Lewis's critique, "Limitations of the Mechanical Model in the Cartesian Conception of the Organism," in Hooker, *Descartes,* 152–65; reprinted and revised in *L'Anthropologie cartésienne* (Paris: Presses Universitaires de France, 1990), 149–67.

74. Descartes's invocation of memory is all the more surprising given his earlier critiques in his correspondence, the *Rules,* and the *Discourse,* critiques of both the tradition of the arts of memory, and memory as a faculty (Judovitz, *Subjectivity and Representation in Descartes,* 26–32, 59–60, 68–73).

75. For a critique of Descartes's notion of temporality and its instantaneous character, see Jean Wahl, *Du rôle de l'idée de l'instant dans la philosophie de Descartes* (Paris: Alcan, 1920).

76. Martin Heidegger noted Descartes's exclusion of temporality, other than that defined by the present of the presence-at-hand, in *Being and Time,* trans. John Macquarrie and Edward Robinson (New York: Harper and Row, 1962), 129.

77. Tom Conley notes that Gilles Deleuze's interpretation of Leibnizian monadology suggests that Leibniz resolves Cartesian mind-body dualism through physical means grasped as foldings, without recourse to occasionalism or parallelism. See his remarks introductory to *The Fold,* xii. For Deleuze's detailed analysis, see 5–26, 85–99, 126–37.

Chapter 5

1. A preliminary version of some of the ideas elaborated in this chapter was presented as a paper to the North American Association for Seventeenth Century French Literature Conference, at Wake Forest University, March 1987, and published as "Royal Power or The Social Body in Corneille," in *Actes de Wake Forest,* ed. Milorad R. Margitic and Byron R. Wells, Coll. Biblio 17, no. 37 (Tübingen: Papers on Seventeenth Century Literature, 1987), 59–73.

2. These comments were published anonymously in a pamphlet entitled *Le Jugement du Cid, Composé par un Bourgeois de Paris, Marguiller de sa Paroisse,* but are attributed to Charles Sorel, one of France's earliest literary critics. See Armand Gasté's reprint in *La Querelle du Cid* (Paris: H. Welter, 1899), 230–40, and his discussion of his attribution to Sorel in his introduction, 51–55.

3. For the prevalence of blood, in particular, as a significant metaphor in French seventeenth-century literature, see Clifton Cherpack, *The Call of Blood in French Classical Tragedy* (Baltimore: Johns Hopkins University Press, 1958).

4. See Scudéry's *Obsérvations sur le Cid,* 71–111; and also Chapelain's *Les Sentiments de l'Academie Françoise sur la Tragi-Comedie du Cid,* 355–417, both reprinted in the Gasté edition, *La Querelle du Cid.* The extensive debates surrounding the performance and publication of the play present a unique occasion to assess the reception of Corneillian figurative language by his contemporaries.

5. All translations of *Le Cid* are from Pierre Corneille, *The Cid, Cinna, The Theatrical Illusion,* trans. John Cairncross (New York: Penguin Books, 1975). Quotations of the French text are from the 1660 edition of *Le Cid,* in *Théatre choisi de Corneille,* ed. Maurice Rat (Paris: Garnier Frères, 1961). Unlike John Cairncross who hispanicizes Chimène's and Rodrigue's names in his translation, I have kept to the French original.

6. See Gasté's reprint of Sorel's pamphlet, trans. Patrick Wheeler, in *La Querelle du Cid,* 238.

7. For an analysis of class structures and political conflicts in the seventeenth century, see Robert Mandrou, *Introduction à la France moderne, 1500–1640: Essai de psychologie historique* (Paris: Albin Michel, 1974), 142–91.

8. Jacques Ehrmann, "Structures of Exchange in *Cinna,*" *Yale French Studies* 36/37 (1965): 169–99.

9. Serge Doubrovsky, *Corneille ou la dialectique du héros* (Paris: Gallimard, 1963), 92–97.

10. Cf. Leonard Barkin's discussion of the anthropomorphic vision of the commonwealth in *Nature's Work of Art: The Human Body as Image of the World* (New Haven: Yale University Press, 1975), 61–115. Barkin's analysis, however, does not explicitly deal with the transformation of the body as a function of different systems of social exchange, feudal or mercantile.

11. This analysis draws on Ernst Kantorowicz's groundbreaking work *The King's Two Bodies: A Study in Medieval Political Theology* (Princeton: Princeton University Press, 1957), 119–50.

12. For an analysis of the aristocratic ethos of *The Cid,* see Milorad R. Margitic, *Essai sur la mythologie du Cid,* Romance Monographs (Oxford: University of Mississippi, 1976), 25–52.

13. See Sorel's comments in the Gasté edition, *La Querelle du Cid,* 237.

14. Jean Starobinski, *L'Oeil vivant* (Paris: Gallimard, 1961), 65, emphasis added; trans. Patrick Wheeler.

15. See Kantorowicz's definition of the king as a "twinned person" (*The King's Two Bodies,* 141).

16. Mitchell Greenberg examines the role of genealogy in Corneille insofar as it functions to create man as a transhistorical essence: "It imposes a metaphorical essence (masculinity) on a metonymical (biological) displacement. It is this shift from metonymy to metaphor in genealogy that allows Patriarchy to exist as history and yet to transcend the historical moment." See "Stage Whispers: Corneille's Absolutism," in *Les Contes de Perrault: La contestation et ses limites; Furetière, Actes de Banff*, ed. M. Bareau, J. Barchillon, D. Stanton, and J. Alter (Paris: Biblio 17/30, 1987), 170.

17. See Anne Ubersfeld's analysis of the decline of royalty and the concomitant erasure of the female body, "Corneille: Du roi au tyran, un itinéraire," in Margitic and Wells, *Actes de Wake Forest,* 13–39.

18. Ubersfeld, "Corneille," 22–23.

19. This appeal to the state reflects the increasing centralization of nobiliary power under the auspices of kingship in the early seventeenth century in France.

20. Greenberg interprets Chimène's claims to justice as the expression of a suppressed maternal register ("Stage Whispers," 174–77).

21. For an analysis of the paradoxes of kingship in the French seventeenth-century context, see Jean-Marie Apostolidès, *Le Prince sacrifié: Théatre et politique au temps de Louis XIV* (Paris: Minuit, 1985), 11–53, 60–63.

22. Greenberg suggests that marriage is the real conundrum of the play ("Stage Whispers," 171).

23. Cf. Jean-Claude Joye, *Amour, pouvoir et transcendance chez Pierre Corneille* (Berne: Peter Lang, 1986), particularly chap. 1, "A propos du *Cid*: Réflections sur certains aspects de la condition féminine et de l'image de la femme," 13–35.

24. The English translation of this passage does not fully communicate the preponderance of juridical terms that are used by Corneille in this passage.

25. Pierre Corneille, *Examen de 1660,* trans. Patrick Wheeler, reprinted in Gasté, *La Querelle du Cid,* 139.

26. Barker, *The Tremulous Private Body,* 103.

27. It is interesting to note that later classical dramatists such as Jean Racine, who seek to affirm desire as a form of individual expression, do so only at the price of the mortification and sacrifice of the physical body. In *Phèdre* (1677), desire plays a redemptive role reclaiming, through the sacrificial death of the body, the rights of subjective expression before the law.

28. Thomas Hobbes, *Leviathan,* ed. Michael Oakeshott (Oxford: Basil Blackwell, 1960); also cited and discussed by Barkin, *Nature's Work of Art,* 114.

Chapter 6

1. See my discussion in chapter 4.

2. Aram Vartanian, *Diderot and Descartes: A Study of Scientific Naturalism in the Enlightenment* (Princeton: Princeton University Press, 1953), 10.

3. François Poullain de la Barre, *De l'égalité de deux sexes: Discours physique et moral* (Paris, 1673), 59.

4. For an analysis of the post-Enlightenment legacy of this neutrality and the neuter as it references the notion of being in Martin Heidegger's elaboration of *dasein,* see Jacques Derrida's discussion in "Geschlecht: Différence sexuelle, différence ontologique," in *Psyché: Inventions de l'autre* (Paris: Galilée, 1987), 395–407.

5. According to Thomas Laqueur, "An anatomy and physiology of incommensurability replaced a metaphysics of hierarchy in the representation of women to men." See "Orgasm, Generation, and the Politics of Reproductive Biology," in *The Making of the Modern Body: Sexuality and Society in the Nineteenth Century,* ed. Catherine Gallagher and Thomas Laqueur (Berkeley: University of California Press, 1987), 3.

6. For a historical and philosophical account of materialism in France in the seventeenth and eighteenth centuries, see Lange's groundbreaking study *The History of Materialism,* bk. 1, 12–32; 49–123; 253–69.

7. Vartanian convincingly argues that Descartes's natural philosophy and the conception of science it entailed made possible the genesis and development of scientific naturalism (*Diderot and Descartes,* 3–8).

8. My analysis differs from Kathleen Wellman's claims regarding La Mettrie's ironic use of Descartes and his putative success in overcoming Cartesian dualism. See *La Mettrie: Medicine, Philosophy, and the Enlightenment* (Durham, N.C.: Duke University Press, 1992), 181–84.

9. La Mettrie, *Man a Machine and Man a Plant,* trans. Richard A. Watson and Maya Rybalka, intro. Justin Leiber (Indianapolis: Hackett, 1994) (henceforth abbreviated *MM*), 63. Please note that the numeration here does not indicate page numbers, but refers to the section numbers on the sides of the text that designate the pages in the original Berlin edition of 1751.

10. While recognizing the power of embodiment associated with the faculty of the imagination, Montaigne does not equate it with the soul.

11. This insistence on the imagination as a constitutive element for the development of intellectual genius can also be seen in a variety of nineteenth-century works: in Villiers de l'Isle Adam's *L'Eve Future,* Friedrich Schiller's *Aesthetic Education of Man,* or the writings of Samuel Coleridge, particularly in the *Biographia Literaria,* to name but a few.

12. For an analysis of issues of gender difference in medical illustrations of the eighteenth century, see Londa Schiebinger, "Skeletons in the Closet: Illustrations of the Female Skeleton in Eighteenth Century Anatomy," in Gallagher and Laqueur, *Making of Modern Body,* 42–82.

13. As Laqueur points out, by the end of the eighteenth century medical science ceases to regard female orgasm as relevant to generation ("Orgasm, Generation," 1).

14. La Mettrie's account contradicts the ancient Galenic-Hippocratic two-seed model of conception linked to both male and female orgasm (Laqueur, "Orgasm, Generation," 5–8).

15. Karl Stern, *The Flight from Woman* (New York: Farrar, Straus and Giroux, 1965), 104; and Susan Bordo, "The Cartesian Masculinization of Thought and the

Seventeenth-Century Flight from the Feminine," in *The Flight to Objectivity: Essays on Cartesianism and Culture* (Albany: State University of New York Press, 1987), 97–118.

16. Stern, *The Flight from Woman*, 104.

17. Bordo, *The Flight to Objectivity*, 99.

18. Merchant, *The Death of Nature*, 4–16. Bordo interprets this flight from the feminine and the "Cartesian masculinization of thought" in terms of both his mechanist reconstruction of the world and the objectivist reconstruction of knowledge (*The Flight to Objectivity*, 101).

19. Vartanian, *Diderot and Descartes*, 205.

20. While eighteenth-century thinkers such as La Mettrie and Diderot will challenge the metaphysical principles of Descartes's thought, their materialist and empiricist orientation will leave intact his scientific method.

21. Wellman stresses La Mettrie's emphasis on empirical demonstration, on the authority of the physician over the metaphysician and theologian (*La Mettrie*, 185).

Chapter 7

1. Charles Baudelaire, "Projets et notes diverses," in *Oeuvres complètes* (Paris: Seuil, 1968), 705.

2. For Georges Bataille's writings on Sade, see "L'Homme souverain de Sade" and "Sade et l'homme normal," in *L'Érotisme* (Paris: Minuit, 1957), and "Sade," in *La Littérature et le mal* (Paris: Gallimard, 1957); also see Pierre Klossowski, *Sade mon prochain* (Paris: Seuil, 1967); and Maurice Blanchot, *Lautréamont et Sade* (Paris: Union générale d'Editions, 1967). For a general account of these three major contributors, see Jane Gallop, *Intersections: A Reading of Sade with Bataille, Blanchot, and Klossowski* (Lincoln: University of Nebraska Press, 1981).

3. Michel Foucault, "A Preface to Transgression," in *Language, Counter-Memory, Practice*, 31.

4. See Foucault's comments on representation in *Les Mots et les choses*, 60–91.

5. Marquis de Sade, "Reflections on the Novel," in *The Marquis de Sade: The 120 Days of Sodom and Other Writings*, compiled and trans. Austryn Wainhouse and Richard Seaver (New York: Grove Press, 1966), 97.

6. Aristotle observes, "Fear and pity can be caused by the spectacle or by the plot structure itself" ("The Poetics," in *On Poetry and Style*, trans. G. M. A. Grube [New York: Bobbs-Merrill, 1979], 26). Aristotle's partiality for plot as the favored vehicle for eliciting emotion is parodied by Sade's exaggerated plots.

7. Sade, "Reflections on the Novel," 115–16.

8. Villeterque's review of *Les Crimes de l'Amour* first appeared in *Le Journal des Arts, des Sciences, et de la littérature*, October 22, 1800, 281–84, reprinted as "Villeterque's Review of *Les Crimes de l'amour*," in Sade, *Marquis de Sade*, 117–19; Sade's response appears in the same volume, "The Author of *Les Crimes de l'amour* to Villeterque, Hack Writer," 121–29.

9. Sade, "Villeterque, Hack Writer," 128.

10. Sade, "Villeterque, Hack Writer," 129.

11. Maurice Blanchot, "Sade," a reprint of a section of *Lautréamont et Sade,* in Sade, *The Complete Justine, Philosophy in the Bedroom, and Other Writings,* trans. Richard Seaver and Austryn Wainhouse (New York: Grove Press, 1965), 57.

12. Marquis de Sade, *Les Infortunes de la vertu* (Paris: Garnier-Flammarion, 1969), 75.

13. Marcel Hénaff, *Sade: L'invention du corps libertin* (Paris: Presses Universitaires de France, 1978), 205. Instead of an industrial model, I have chosen to use here a mercantile model, which describes more adequately concepts of social exchange and production.

14. Sade, *Les Infortunes de la vertu,* 123.

15. "Language to Infinity," in *Language, Counter-Memory, Practice,* 62.

16. For a general analysis of the writings and trends of thought of the Enlightenment, see Daniel Mornet, *La Pensée française au XVIIIe siècle* (Paris: Colin, 1965).

17. Philippe Sollers, "Sade dans le texte," *Tel Quel* 28 (1967): 44.

18. Michel Tort, "L'Effet Sade," *Tel Quel* 28 (1967): 78.

19. Marquis de Sade, "Philosophy in the Bedroom" (henceforth abbreviated *PB*), in *Complete Justine,* 203.

20. For a comprehensive analysis of the role of vision in the eighteenth century, see Jay, *Downcast Eyes,* 83–113.

21. For a distinction between the *lyrical body* and Sade's *corps à la lettre,* see Hénaff, *Sade,* 23–26.

22. Sade's critique of the notion of foundational difference anticipates Martin Heidegger's definition of "ontological difference," understood as the "differentiation of beings and Being," in *Nietzsche,* vol. 4, *Nihilism,* ed. David F. Krell, trans. Frank A. Capuzzi (San Francisco: Harper and Row, 1982), 153–55.

23. Jean Fabre suggests that Sade's concept of nature founds a new tradition that must be distinguished from the classical interpretations of nature. See *Idées sur le roman: De Madame de Lafayette à Marquis de Sade* (Paris: Klincksieck, 1979), 187.

24. For an interpretation of Sade's writing as escape from physical detention, see Béatrice Didier, *Sade: Une écriture du désir* (Paris: Denoël-Gonthier, 1976).

25. Sade, *Eugénie de Franval,* in *Complete Justine,* 119.

26. For an analysis of incest and its relation to poetic practice in Sade's works, see Josué V. Harari, *Scenarios of the Imaginary* (Ithaca, N.Y.: Cornell University Press, 1987), 172–87.

27. Marquis de Sade, *Oeuvres complètes* (Paris: Pauvert, 1956–70), 9:569.

28. Hénaff, *Sade,* 44–48.

29. Cf. Barthes's comment that the crime of incest involves a transgression of semantic rules, by creating homonymy: it makes "one signified receive simultaneously several signifiers that are traditionally distinct." This leads him to conclude that transgression is merely a linguistic ploy, one of naming outside lexical divisions: the "act *contra-naturum* is exhausted in an utterance of counter-language." See *Sade, Fourier, Loyola* (Paris: Seuil, 1971), 137–38.

30. For a discussion of Sade's interpretation of nature in relation to d'Holbach

and Hélvetius, see Pierre Naville, "Sade et la philosophie," in *Oeuvres complètes du Marquis de Sade,* ed. Gilbert Lely, vol. 11 (Paris: Au Cercle du Livre précieux, 1962–64).

31. Blanchot suggests that Sade's struggle with nature represents a more advanced dialectical stage than his struggle with God, since by showing that the notion of nothingness or nonbeing belongs to the world, "one cannot conceive of the world's nonbeing except from within a totality, which is still the world" (in Sade, *Complete Justine,* 63).

32. Cited by Pierre Klossowski, "Nature as a Destructive Principle," in Sade, *Marquis de Sade,* 72–73.

33. Barthes distinguishes the conventions of the social and realistic novel from the conventions of the Sadean novel, which is the "repeated production of a practice (and not of an historical 'picture')" (*Sade, Fourier, Loyola,* 131).

34. Foucault, "A Preface to Transgression," 35.

35. Sade, "Reflections on the Novel," 110–11.

36. Barthes describes this gesture of sewing in Sade as follows: "To sew is finally to remake a world without sewing, to return to the divinely cut-up body—whose cut-up state is the source of all Sadean pleasure—to the abjection of the smooth body, the total body" (*Sade, Fourier, Loyola,* 169).

37. Sade, *Les Infortunes de la vertu,* 184.

38. Sollers, "Sade dans le texte," 38.

39. Simone de Beauvoir, "Must We Burn Sade?" in Sade, *Marquis de Sade,* 33.

40. Foucault, *The History of Sexuality,* 1:149.

Conclusion

1. Friedrich Nietzsche, *Twilight of the Idols,* trans. R. J. Hollingdale (Baltimore: Penguin Books, 1968), 101.

2. It is important to note in this context that Nietzsche's interpretation of the body also involves notions of force, both active and reactive. See Gilles Deleuze's comments in *Nietzsche and Philosophy,* trans. Hugh Tomlinson (New York: Columbia University Press, 1983), 39–44.

3. The scriptorial model elaborated in chapters 1 and 2 suggests that the presentation of the lived, perceiving body is framed by linguistic and representational concerns that decenter through their impersonal character a humanist interpretation of the subject. It is precisely this shift between humanism and posthumanism that marks Merleau-Ponty's late thought as he engages with linguistics and psychoanalysis in order to move beyond a phenomenological understanding of the body, by considering its embodiment and embeddedness in the world. See his *Prose of the World,* ed. Claude Lefort, trans. John O'Neill (Evanston: Northwestern University Press, 1973).

4. Emmanuel Levinas, "Time and the Other," in *The Levinas Reader,* ed. and intro. Seán Hand (Oxford: Basil Blackwell, 1989), 38–58.

5. Although Bruce Mazlish convincingly argues for the coevolution of humans and machines, it is clear that these mechanical analogies are challenged by new developments that involve an understanding of living organisms based on information models, or the use of actual biological organisms as sophisticated computational devices. See *The Fourth Dimension: The Co-Evolution of Humans and Machines* (New Haven: Yale University Press, 1993).

6. Canguilhem notes that developments in contemporary biology understand biological heredity as the communication of information. This implies dropping the vocabulary and conceptual principles of classical mechanics for new models based on linguistics and communication theory (*A Vital Rationalist*, 316–17).

7. However, by devising the test of the human and the machine in terms of language and representation, Descartes foreshadows the possibility of a linguistic model whose logic would supersede mechanics, redefining the machine itself as an informational device.

8. Merleau-Ponty, *The Phenomenology of Perception*, 408.

9. In his note "Flesh of the World—Flesh of the Body—Being" (May 1960), Merleau-Ponty explains that while the "flesh" of the body is self-sensing, the flesh of the world is "sensible and not sentient." He emphasizes that it is by the flesh of the world that one can understand the lived body (*Visible and Invisible*, 248–50).

Bibliography

Adam, Antoine. "La Théorie Mystique de l'Amour dans *L'Astrée* et ses sources Italiennes." *Revue d'Histoire de la Philosophie* (1937).

Anton, Charles. *Classical Dictionary.* New York: Harper and Brothers, 1873.

Apostolidès, Jean-Marie. *Le Prince sacrifié: Théatre et politique au temps de Louis XIV.* Paris: Minuit, 1985.

Aquinas, Saint Thomas. *Summa Theologica.* London: Eyre and Spottiswoode, 1964.

Aristotle. "The Poetics." *On Poetry and Style.* Trans. G. M. A. Grube. New York: Bobbs-Merrill, 1979.

Augustine, Saint, Bishop of Hippo. *Confessions.* Trans. R. S. Coffin. London: Penguin, 1961.

Baltrusaitis, Jurgis. *Anamorphic Art.* Trans. W. J. Strachan. New York: Harry J. Abrams, 1977.

Balzac, Guez de. *Entretiens.* Vol. 18, *De Montaigne et de ses écrits.* Paris, 1657.

Barker, Francis. *The Tremulous Private Body: Essays on Subjection.* Ann Arbor: University of Michigan Press, 1995.

Barkin, Leonard. *Nature's Work of Art: The Human Body as Image of the World.* New Haven: Yale University Press, 1975.

Barthes, Roland. *Sade, Fourier, Loyola.* Paris: Seuil, 1971.

Bataille, Georges. *L'Érotisme.* Paris: Minuit, 1957.

———. *La Littérature et le mal.* Paris: Gallimard, 1957.

Baudelaire, Charles. "Projets et notes diverses." *Oeuvres Complètes.* Paris: Seuil, 1968.

Beaune, Jean-Claude. *L'Automate et ses mobiles.* Paris: Flammarion, 1980.

Beauvoir, Simone de. "Must We Burn Sade?" *The Marquis de Sade: The 120 Days of Sodom, and Other Writings.* Compiled and trans. Austryn Wainhouse and Richard Seaver. New York: Grove Press, 1966.

Beck, L. J. *The Metaphysics of Descartes: A Study of the Meditations.* Oxford: Oxford University Press, 1965.

Benjamin, Walter. *The Origin of German Tragic Drama.* Trans. John Osborne. London: NLB, 1977.

Benveniste, Emile. "De la subjectivité dans le language." *Problèmes de linguistique générale.* Paris: Gallimard, 1966.

Bitbol-Hespériès, Anne. *Le Principe de la vie chez Descartes.* Paris: J. Vrin, 1990.

Blanchard, Marc E. *Trois portraits de Montaigne: Essai sur la représentation à la Renaissance.* Paris: Nizet, 1990.

Blanchot, Maurice. *Lautréamont et Sade.* Paris: Union générale d'Editions, 1967.

———. "Sade." *The Complete Justine, Philosophy in the Bedroom and Other Writings.* By Marquis de Sade. Compiled and Trans. Richard Seaver and Austryn Wainhouse. Intro. Jean Paulhan and Maurice Blanchot. New York: Grove Press, 1966.

Bordo, Susan. *The Flight to Objectivity: Essays on Cartesianism and Culture.* Albany: State University of New York Press, 1987.

Bowen, Barbara C. "Montaigne's Anti-*Phaedrus*: 'Sur des vers de Virgile' (Essais, III, V)." *Journal of Medieval and Renaissance Studies* 5 (1975): 107–21.

Brody, Jules. *Lectures de Montaigne.* Lexington, Ky.: French Forum, 1982.

———. *Nouvelles Lectures de Montaigne.* Paris: Honoré Champion, 1994.

Brunschvicg, Léon. *Descartes et Pascal, lecteurs de Montaigne.* Paris: Brentano, 1944.

Brunyate, Margaret. "Montaigne and Medicine." *Montaigne and His Age.* Ed. Keith Cameron. Exeter: University of Exeter, 1981.

Buci-Glucksmann, Christina. *La Raison baroque: De Baudelaire à Benjamin.* Paris: Galilée, 1984.

———. *La Folie du voir: De l'esthétique baroque.* Paris: Galilée, 1986.

Butler, Judith. *Bodies That Matter: On the Discursive Limits of "Sex."* New York: Routledge, 1993.

Bynum, Carolyn. "Why All the Fuss about the Body? A Medievalist's Perspective." *Critical Inquiry* 22 (autumn 1995): 1–31.

Canguilhem, Georges. "Machine and Organism." *Incorporations.* Ed. Jonathan Crary and Sanford Kwinter. Spec. issue of *Zone* 6 (winter 1992): 45–69.

———. *A Vital Rationalist: Selected Writings from Georges Canguilhem.* Ed. François Delaporte. Trans. Arthur Goldhammer. New York: Zone Books, 1994.

Caton, Hiram. *The Origin of Subjectivity: An Essay on Descartes.* New Haven: Yale University Press, 1973.

Caus, Salomon de. *Les Raisons des forces mouvantes avec diverses machines tant utiles que plaisantes auxquelles sont jointes plusieurs desseings de grottes et de fontaines.* Frankfurt, 1615.

Cave, Terence. *The Cornucopian Text: Problems of Writing in the French Renaissance.* Oxford: Clarendon Press, 1979.

Chapelain, André. "Les Sentiments de l'Academie Françoise sur la Tragi-Comedie du Cid." *La Querelle du Cid.* By Armand Gasté. Paris: H. Welter, 1899.

Cherpack, Clifton. *The Call of Blood in French Classical Tragedy.* Baltimore: Johns Hopkins University Press, 1958.

Ciorenescu, Alexandru. *Barocul sau descoperirea dramei.* Trans. G. Tureacu. Cluj: Editura Dacia, 1980.

Clark, Carol. "Montaigne and Law." *Montaigne and His Age.* Ed. Keith Cameron. Exeter: University of Exeter, 1981.

————. *The Web of Metaphor: Studies in the Imagery of Montaigne's "Essais."* Lexington, Ky.: French Forum, 1978.

Compagnon, Antoine. *Nous, Michel de Montaigne.* Paris: Seuil, 1980.

Conley, Tom. Foreword. *The Fold: Leibniz and the Baroque.* By Gilles Deleuze. Trans. and intro. Tom Conley. Minneapolis: University of Minnesota Press, 1993.

Corneille, Pierre. *The Cid, Cinna, The Theatrical Illusion.* Trans. John Cairncross. New York: Penguin Books, 1975.

————. *Théatre choisi de Corneille.* Ed. Maurice Rat. Paris: Garnier Frères, 1961.

Cotgrave, Randle. *A Dictionarie of the French and English Tongues.* London: Adam Islip, 1611. Rpt., Columbia: University of South Carolina Press, 1950.

Cottingham, John. "Cartesian Dualism: Theology, Metaphysics, and Science." *The Cambridge Companion to Descartes.* Ed. John Cottingham. Cambridge: Cambridge University Press, 1995.

Cottrell, Robert D. *Sexuality/Textuality: A Study of the Fabric of Montaigne's Essays.* Columbus: Ohio State University Press, 1981.

————. "Representation and the Desiring Subject in Montaigne's 'De l'expérience'." *Les Parcours des "Essais": Montaigne 1588–1988.* Ed. Marcel Tetel and G. Mallary Masters. Paris: Aux Amateurs du Livre, 1989.

Croll, Morris W. *"Attic" and Baroque Prose Style: The Anti-Ciceronian Movement.* Ed. J. Max Patrick, Robert O. Evans, and John M. Wallace. Princeton: Princeton University Press, 1969.

Daly, Peter M. *Emblematic Theory: Recent German Contributions to the Characterization of the Emblem Genre.* Nendeln: KTO Press, 1979.

————. *Literature in Light of the Emblem.* Toronto: University of Toronto Press, 1979.

Deleuze, Gilles. *The Fold: Leibniz and the Baroque.* Trans. Tom Conley. Minneapolis: University of Minnesota Press, 1993.

————. *Nietzsche and Philosophy.* Trans. Hugh Tomlinson. New York: Columbia University Press, 1983.

Derrida, Jacques. "Cogito and the History of Madness." *Writing and Difference.* Trans. Allan Bass. Chicago: University of Chicago Press, 1978.

————. "Geschlecht: Différence sexuelle, différence ontologique." *Psyché: Inventions de l'autre.* Paris: Galilée, 1987.

Descartes, René. *Oeuvres de Descartes.* 13 vols. Ed. Charles Adam and Paul Tannery. Paris: Léopold Cerf, 1913.

————. *Oeuvres Philosophiques de Descartes.* 3 vols. Ed. Ferdinand Alquié. Paris: Garnier, 1973.

————. *The Philosophical Writings of Descartes.* 3 vols. Ed. John Cottingham, Robert Stoothoff, and Dugald Murdoch. Trans. John Cottingham. Cambridge: Cambridge University Press, 1985.

————. *The Philosophical Works of Descartes.* 2 vols. Trans. E. S. Haldane and G. R. T. Ross. Cambridge: Cambridge University Press, 1969.

Didier, Béatrice. *Sade: Une écriture du désir.* Paris: Denoél-Gonthier, 1976.

Dijksterhuis, E. J. *The Mechanization of the World Picture.* Oxford: Clarendon Press, 1961.

Doubrovsky, Serge. *Corneille ou la dialectique du héros.* Paris: Gallimard, 1963.

Ehrmann, Jacques. *Un Paradis désespéré: L'amour et l'illusion dans "L'Astrée."* New Haven: Yale University Press, 1963.

———. "Structures of Exchange in *Cinna.*" *Yale French Studies* 36/37 (1965): 169–99.

Entin-Bates, Lee R. "Montaigne's Remarks on Impotence." *Modern Language Notes* 91 (May 1976): 640–54.

Espinas, Alfred. "L'Organisation ou la machine vivante en Grèce au IVe siècle avant J.-C." *Revue de Métaphysique et de Morale* (1903): 702–17.

Fabre, Jean. *Idées sur le roman: De Madame de Lafayette au Marquis de Sade.* Paris: Klincksieck, 1979.

Feher, Michel, Ramona Haddoff, and Nadia Tazi, eds. *Fragments for a History of the Human Body.* 3 vols. New York: Zone Books, 1989.

Fletcher, Angus. *Allegory: The Theory of a Symbolic Mode.* Ithaca, N.Y.: Cornell University Press, 1964.

Foucault, Michel. *Discipline and Punish: The Birth of the Prison.* Trans. Alan Sheridan. New York: Vintage Books, 1995.

———. *Folie et déraison: Histoire de la folie à l'âge classique.* Paris: Gallimard, 1972.

———. *The History of Sexuality.* Vol. 1, *An Introduction.* Trans. Robert Hurley. New York: Vintage Books, 1990.

———. *The History of Sexuality.* Vol. 2, *The Use of Pleasure.* Trans. Robert Hurley. New York: Vintage Books, 1990.

———. *The History of Sexuality.* Vol. 3, *The Care of the Self.* Trans. Robert Hurley. New York: Vintage Books, 1988.

———. "History of Systems of Thought." *Language, Counter-Memory, Practice.* Ed. and intro. Donald F. Bouchard. Trans. Donald F. Bouchard and Sherry Simon. Ithaca, N.Y.: Cornell University Press, 1977.

———. *Madness and Civilization: A History of Insanity in the Age of Reason.* Trans. Richard Howard. New York: Vintage Books, 1973.

———. *Les Mots et les choses: Une archéologie des sciences humaines.* Part 1. Paris: Gallimard, 1966.

———. "My Body, This Paper, This Fire." Trans. Geoffrey P. Bennington. *Oxford Literary Review* 4, no. 1 (1979): 9–28.

———. "Nietzsche, Genealogy, History." *Language, Counter-Memory, Practice.*

———. *The Order of Things: An Archaeology of the Human Sciences.* Trans. Alan Sheridan. New York: Vintage Books, 1973.

———. "A Preface to Transgression." *Language, Counter-Memory, Practice.*

Frankfurt, Harry. *Demons, Madmen, and Dreamers: The Defense of Reason in Descartes's Meditations.* Indianapolis: Bobbs-Merrill, 1970.

Freud, Sigmund. "Fetishism." 1927. *Sexuality and the Psychology of Love.* Ed. Philip Rieff. New York: Collier Books, 1974.

Friedrich, Hugo. *Montaigne.* Trans. Robert Rovini. Paris: Gallimard, 1968.

Gallagher, Catherine, and Thomas Laqueur, eds. *The Making of the Modern Body: Sexuality and Society in the Nineteenth Century.* Berkeley: University of California Press, 1987.

Gallop, Jane. *Intersections: A Reading of Sade with Bataille, Blanchot, and Klossowski.* Lincoln: University of Nebraska Press, 1981.

Garber, Daniel. *Descartes's Metaphysical Physics.* Chicago: University of Chicago Press, 1992.

Gasté, Armand. *La Querelle du Cid.* Paris: H. Welter, 1899.

Gaukroger, Stephen. *Descartes: An Intellectual Biography.* Oxford: Oxford University Press, 1995.

Genette, Gérard. "Le Serpent dans la Bergerie." Introduction to *L'Astrée.* By Honoré d'Urfé. Ed. Gérard Genette. Paris: Union générale d'Editions, 1964.

Gerhardt, M. "Un Personnage principal de *L'Astrée:* Le Lignon." *Colloque commémoratif du quatrième centenaire de la naissance d'Honoré d'Urfé,* 47–56. Montbrison: La Diana, 1970.

Gilson, Etienne. *Etudes sur le rôle de la pensée médiévale dans la formation du système cartésien.* 5th ed. Paris: J. Vrin, 1984.

Gomez-Pereira, Antoniana-Margarita. *Opus nempe physicis medicis ac thelogicis non minus utile quam necessarium.* Medina del Campo, 1555–58.

Gray, Floyd. *Le Style de Montaigne.* Paris: Nizet, 1958.

———. "Eros et écriture: 'Sur des vers de Virgil.'" *Les Parcours des "Essais": Montaigne 1588–1988.* Ed. Marcel Tetel and G. Mallary Masters. Paris: Aux Amateurs du Livre, 1989.

Greenberg, Mitchell. "Stage Whispers: Corneille's Absolutism." *Les Contes de Perrault: La contestation et ses limites; Furetière, Actes de Banff.* Ed. M. Bareau, J. Barchillon, D. Stanton, and J. Alter. Paris: Biblio 17/30, 1987.

Grene, Marjorie. "The Heart and Blood: Descartes, Plemp, and Harvey." *Essays in the Philosophy of Science of René Descartes.* Ed. Stephen Voss. New York: Oxford University Press, 1993.

Guéroult, Martial. *Descartes' Philosophy Interpreted According to the Order of Reasons.* 2 vols. Trans. Roger Ariew. Minneapolis: University of Minnesota Press, 1984–85.

Gunderson, Keith. *Mentality and Machines.* 2d ed. Minneapolis: University of Minnesota Press, 1985.

Harari, Josué V. *Scenarios of the Imaginary.* Ithaca, N.Y.: Cornell University Press, 1987.

Harth, Erica. "'Sur des vers de Virgile': Antinomy and Totality in Montaigne." *French Forum* 2 (1977): 3–21.

Hatfield, Gary. "Descartes' Physiology and Its Relation to His Psychology." *The Cambridge Companion to Descartes.* Ed. John Cottingham. Cambridge: Cambridge University Press, 1992.

———. "The Senses and the Fleshless Eye: The *Meditations* as Cognitive Exercises." *Essays on Descartes's Meditations.* Ed. Amélie Oksenberg Rorty. Berkeley: University of California Press, 1986.

Heidegger, Martin. *Being and Time*. Trans. John Macquarrie and Edward Robinson. New York: Harper and Row, 1962.

———. *Nietzsche*. Vol. 4, *Nihilism*. Ed. David F. Krell. Trans. Frank A. Capuzzi. San Francisco: Harper and Row, 1982.

———. *What Is a Thing?* Trans. W. B. Barton and V. Deutsch. Chicago: Henry Regnery, 1967.

Hénaff, Marcel. *Sade: L'invention du corps libertin*. Paris: Presses Universitaires de France, 1978.

Hintikka, Jaakko. "*Cogito, Ergo Sum:* Inference or Performance?" *Descartes: A Collection of Critical Essays*. Ed. Willis Doney. Notre Dame: University of Notre Dame Press, 1968.

Hobbes, Thomas. *Leviathan*. Ed. Michael Oakeshott. Oxford: Basil Blackwell, 1960.

Horowitz, Louise. *Honoré d'Urfé*. Boston: Twayne Publishers, 1984.

Horst, Carl. *Barock-probleme*. Munich: E. Rentsch, 1912.

Jay, Martin. *Downcast Eyes: The Denigration of Vision in Twentieth-Century French Thought*. Berkeley: University of California Press, 1993.

Jons, Dietrich. *Das "Sinnen-bild": Studien zur allegorischen Bildlichkeit bei Andreas Gryphius*. Stuttgart: Metzler, 1966.

Joye, Jean-Claude. *Amour, pouvoir et transcendance chez Pierre Corneille*. Berne: Peter Lang, 1986.

Judovitz, Dalia. "Descartes' Virtual Bodies: Anatomy, Technology, and the Inhuman." *Writing the Body*. Spec. Issue of *Paroles Gelées* 16, no. 1 (1998): 21–41.

———. "Emblematic Legacies: Hieroglyphs of Desire in L'Astrée." *EMF: Studies in Early Modern France*. Ed. David L. Rubin, 31–54. Charlottesville: Rockwood Press, 1995.

———. "Derrida and Descartes: Economizing Thought." *Derrida and Deconstruction II*. Ed. Hugh J. Silverman. New York: Routledge and Kegan Paul, 1989.

———. "The Graphic Text: The Nude in L'Astrée." *Papers in French Seventeenth Century Literature* 15, no. 29 (1988): 532–33.

———. "Royal Power or The Social Body in Corneille." *Actes de Wake Forest*. Ed. Milorad R. Margitic and Byron R. Wells. Coll. Biblio. 17, no. 37. Tübingen: Papers on Seventeenth Century French Literature, 1987.

———. *Subjectivity and Representation in Descartes: The Origins of Modernity*. Cambridge: Cambridge University Press, 1988.

———. "Vision, Representation, and Technology in Descartes." *Modernity and the Hegemony of Vision*. Ed. David Michael Levin. Berkeley: University of California Press, 1993.

Kantorowicz, Ernst. *The King's Two Bodies: A Study in Medieval Political Theology*. Princeton: Princeton University Press, 1957.

Kenny, Anthony. *Descartes: A Study of His Philosophy*. New York: Random House, 1968.

Klossowski, Pierre. *Sade mon prochain*. Paris: Seuil, 1967.

Kritzman, Lawrence D. *The Rhetoric of Sexuality and the Literature of the French Renaissance*. New York: Columbia University Press, 1993.

———. "Montaigne's Fantastic Monsters and the Construction of Gender." *Writing the Renaissance: Essays on Sixteenth-Century French Literature in Honor of Floyd Gray*. Ed. Raymond C. La Charité, 191–94. Lexington, Ky.: French Forum, 1992.

———. *Destruction/découverte: Le fonctionnement de la rhétorique dans les "Essais" de Montaigne*. Lexington, Ky.: French Forum, 1980.

Lacan, Jacques. "Le Stade du miroir." *Ecrits*. Paris: Seuil, 1966.

Lafayette, Marie-Madeleine de. *La Princesse de Clèves*. Paris: Garnier-Flammarion, 1966.

———. *The Princesse of Clèves*. Ed. and trans. John d. Lyons. New York: W. W. Norton, 1994.

La Mettrie, Julien Offray de. *L'Homme machine. Oeuvres philosophiques de M. de La Mettrie*. Berlin, 1774.

———. *Man a Machine and Man a Plant*. Trans. Richard A. Watson and Maya Rybalka. Intro. Justin Leiber. Indianapolis: Hackett, 1994.

Lange, Frederick Albert. *The History of Materialism*. Trans. Ernest Chester Thomas. New York: Harcourt, Brace, 1925.

Langer, Ullrich. "Montaigne's Customs." *Montaigne Studies: An Interdisciplinary Forum* 4, nos. 1–2 (1992): 83–95.

Laqueur, Thomas. "Orgasm, Generation, and the Politics of Reproductive Biology." *The Making of the Modern Body: Sexuality and Society in the Nineteenth Century*. Ed. Catherine Gallagher and Thomas Laqueur. Berkeley: University of California Press, 1987.

Leder, Drew. *The Absent Body*. Chicago: University of Chicago Press, 1990.

Lestringant, Frank, ed. *Rhétorique de Montaigne*. Paris: Honoré Champion, 1985.

Levinas, Emmanuel. "Time and the Other." *The Levinas Reader*. Ed. and Intro. Seán Hand. Oxford: Basil Blackwell, 1989.

Lindebom, G. A. *Descartes and Medicine*. Amsterdam: Rodopi, 1979.

Lyotard, Jean-François. "Can Thought Go On without a Body?" *The Inhuman: Reflections on Time*. Trans. Geoffrey Bennington and Rachel Bowlby. Stanford: Stanford University Press, 1991.

———. *The Postmodern Condition: A Report on Knowledge*. Intro. Frederic Jameson. Trans. Geoffrey Bennington and Brian Massoumi. Minneapolis: University of Minnesota Press, 1984.

Malcolm, Norman. *Dreaming*. London: Routledge, 1959.

———. "Descartes's Proof That His Essence is Thinking." *Descartes: A Collection of Critical Essays*. Ed. Willis Doney. Notre Dame: Notre Dame University Press, 1968.

Malebranche, Nicolas. *The Search after Truth*. Trans. Thomas M. Lennon and Paul Olscamp. Columbus: Ohio State University Press, 1980.

Mandrou, Robert. *Introduction à la France moderne, 1500–1640: Essai de psychologie historique*. Paris: Albin Michel, 1974.

Maravall, José Antonio. *The Culture of the Baroque: Analysis of a Historical Structure*. Trans. Terry Cochran. Minneapolis: University of Minnesota Press, 1986.

Margitic, Milorad R. *Essai sur la mythologie du Cid*. Romance Monographs. Oxford: University of Mississippi, 1976.

Marzot, Giulio. *L'ingegno e il genio del Seicento*. Florence: La Nouva Italia, 1944.

Mathieu-Castellani, Gisèle. *Montaigne: L'écriture de l'essai*. Paris: Presses Universitaires de France, 1988.

Mattern, Ruth. "Descartes's Correspondence with Elizabeth: Conceiving Both the Union and Distinction of the Mind and Body." *Descartes: Critical and Interpretative Essays*. Ed. Michael Hooker. Baltimore: Johns Hopkins University Press, 1978.

Mazlish, Bruce. *The Fourth Dimension: The Co-Evolution of Humans and Machines*. New Haven: Yale University Press, 1993.

McKinley, Mary B. *Words in a Corner: Studies in Montaigne's Latin Quotations*. Lexington, Ky.: French Forum, 1981.

Merchant, Carolyn. *The Death of Nature: Women, Ecology and the Scientific Revolution*. San Francisco: Harper and Row, 1980.

Merleau-Ponty, Maurice. "The Body as Expression and Speech." *The Phenomenology of Perception*. Trans. Colin Smith. London: Routledge and Kegan Paul, 1995.

———. "Eye and Mind." *The Primacy of Perception*. Ed. James M. Edie. Trans. Carleton Dallery. Evanston: Northwestern University Press, 1964.

———. "Everywhere and Nowhere." *Signs*. Trans. Richard C. Cleary. Evanston: Northwestern University Press, 1964.

———. *The Prose of the World*. Ed. Claude Lefort. Trans. John O'Neill. Evanston: Northwestern University Press, 1973.

———. "Reading Montaigne." *Signs*. Trans. Richard C. Cleary. Evanston: Northwestern University Press, 1964.

———. *The Visible and the Invisible*. Trans. Alphonso Lingis. Evanston: Northwestern University Press, 1968.

Montaigne, Michel de. *The Complete Essays of Montaigne*. Trans. Donald Frame. Stanford: Stanford University Press, 1985.

———. *Essais de Montaigne*. Ed. Maurice Rat. 2 vols. Paris: Garnier Frères, 1962.

———. *Journal de voyage en Italie par la Suisse et l'Allemagne en 1550–1581*. Paris: Club Français du Livre, 1954.

Mornet, Daniel. *La Pensée française au XVIIIe siècle*. Paris: Colin, 1965.

Mumford, Lewis. *Technics and Civilization*. New York: Harcourt Brace, 1963.

Nakam, Géralde. "Eros et les Muses dans 'Sur des vers de Virgil.'" *Montaigne: La Manière et la matière*. Paris: Klincksieck, 1992.

———. "Corps physique, corps social: La maladie et la santé." *Montaigne: La Manière et la matière*.

Naville, Pierre. "Sade et la philosophie." *Oeuvres complètes du Marquis de Sade*. Ed. Gilbert Lely. Vol. 11. Paris: Au Cercle du Livre Précieux, 1962–64.

Nietzsche, Friedrich. *Twilight of the Idols.* Trans. R. J. Hollingdale. Baltimore: Penguin Books, 1968.

Nouvet, Claire. "An Impossible Response: The Disaster of Narcissus." *Literature and the Ethical Question.* Ed. Claire Nouvet. Spec. issue of *Yale French Studies* 79 (1991): 103–34.

Nutton, Vivian. "Medicine in the Age of Montaigne." *Montaigne and His Age.* Ed. Keith Cameron. Exeter: University of Exeter, 1981.

O'Neill, John. *Essaying Montaigne: A Study of the Renaissance Institution of Writing and Reading.* London: Routledge and Kegan Paul, 1982.

Pagel, Walter. *William Harvey's Biological Ideas: Selected Aspects and Historical Background.* New York: Hafner, 1967.

Panofski, Erwin. *La Perspective comme forme symbolique.* Trans. Guy Ballangé. Paris: Minuit, 1975.

Parker, Patricia. "Gender Ideology, Gender Change: The Case of Marie Germain." *Critical Inquiry* 19 (winter 1993): 337–64.

Peyre, Henry. *Qu'est-ce que le classicisme? Essai de mise au point.* Paris: Droz, 1942.

Pollachek, Dora. "Montaigne and Imagination: The Dynamics of Power and Control." *Les Parcours des "Essais": Montaigne 1588–1988.* Ed. Marcel Tetel and G. Mallary Masters. Paris: Aux Amateurs du Livre, 1989.

Pouchelle, Marie-Christine. *Corps et chirurgie à l'apogée du Moyen Age.* Paris: Flammarion, 1983.

Poullain de la Barre, François. *De l'égalité de deux sexes: Discours physique et moral.* Paris, 1673.

Praz, Mario. *Studies in Seventeenth-Century Imagery.* 2 vols. London: Warburg Institute, 1939–47.

Putnam, Michael C. J. *The Poetry of the Aeneid: Four Studies in Imaginative Unity.* Cambridge: Harvard University Press, 1965.

Regosin, Richard L. *The Matter of My Book: Montaigne's "Essais" as the Book of the Self.* Berkeley: University of California Press, 1977.

Reichler, Claude. "Machine et machinations: La ruse des signes." *Revue des Sciences Humaines* 58, nos. 186–87 (1982): 33–39.

Rigolot, François. *Les Métamorphoses de Montaigne.* Paris: Presses Universitaires de France, 1988.

———. "Sémiotique et onomastique: Le nom propre de Montaigne." *Les Parcours des "Essais": Montaigne 1588–1988.* Ed. Marcel Tetel and G. Mallary Masters. Paris: Aux Amateurs du Livre, 1989.

Rodis-Lewis, Geneviève. *L'Anthropologie cartésienne.* Paris: Presses Universitaires de France, 1990.

———. "Limitations of the Mechanical Model in the Cartesian Conception of the Organism." *Descartes: Critical and Interpretative Essays.* Ed. Michael Hooker. Baltimore: Johns Hopkins University Press, 1978.

Rosenfeld, Leonora Cohen. *From Beast-Machine to Man-Machine: Animal Soul in French Letters from Descartes to La Mettrie.* New York: Octagon Books, 1968.

Rousset, Jean. *La Littérature de l'âge baroque en France: Circé et le paon.* Paris: Corti, 1960.

Roy, Jean H. *L'Imagination selon Descartes.* Paris: Gallimard, 1944.

Russell, Daniel S. *The Emblem and Device in France.* Lexington, Ky.: French Forum, 1985.

———. "Du Bellay's Emblematic Vision of Rome." *Image and Symbol in the Renaissance.* Spec. issue of *Yale French Studies* 47 (1972): 98–109.

Ryle, Gilbert. *The Concept of Mind.* London: Hutchinson, 1969.

Sade, Marquis de. "The Author of *Les Crimes de l'Amour* to Villeterque, Hack Writer." *The Marquis de Sade: The 120 Days of Sodom and Other Writings.* Compiled and trans. Austryn Wainhouse and Richard Seaver. New York: Grove Press, 1966.

———. "Eugénie de Franval." *The Complete Justine, Philosophy in the Bedroom and Other Writings.* Trans. Richard Seaver and Austryn Wainhouse. New York: Grove Press, 1965.

———. *Les Infortunes de la vertu.* Paris: Garnier-Flammarion, 1969.

———. *Oeuvres complètes.* Ed. Gilbert Lely. Paris: Au Cercle du Livre Précieux, 1962–64.

———. "Philosophy in the Bedroom." *The Complete Justine, Philosophy in the Bedroom and Other Writings.* Trans. Richard Seaver and Austryn Wainhouse. New York: Grove Press, 1965.

———. "Reflections on the Novel." *The Marquis de Sade: The 120 Days of Sodom and Other Writings.* Compiled and trans. Austryn Wainhouse and Richard Seaver. New York: Grove Press, 1966.

Sarduy, Severo. *Barocco.* Paris: Seuil, 1975.

———. *La Doublure.* Paris: Seuil, 1981.

Sawday, Jonathan. *The Body Emblazoned: Dissection and the Human Body in Renaissance Culture.* London: Routledge, 1995.

Sayce, R. A. *The Essays of Montaigne: A Critical Exploration.* Evanston: Northwestern University Press, 1972.

Scarry, Elaine. *The Body in Pain.* New York: Oxford University Press, 1985.

Schefer, Jean-Louis. "On the Object of Figuration." Trans. T. Corrigan and D. Judovitz. *Sub-Stance,* no. 39 (1983): 26–31.

Schiebinger, Londa. "Skeletons in the Closet: Illustrations of the Female Skeleton in Eighteenth Century Anatomy." *The Making of the Modern Body: Sexuality and Society in the Nineteenth Century.* Ed. Catherine Gallagher and Thomas Laqueur. Berkeley: University of California Press, 1987.

Schöne, Albrecht. *Emblematik und Drama im Zeitalter des Barock.* Munich: Beck, 1964.

Scudéry, Georges. "Obsérvations sur Le Cid." *La Querelle du Cid.* By Armand Gasté. Paris: H. Welter, 1899.

Sepper, Dennis L. "*Ingenium,* Memory Art, and the Unity of Imaginative Knowing." *Essays on the Philosophy and Science of René Descartes.* Ed. Stephen Voss. New York: Oxford University Press, 1993.

Séris, Jean-Pierre. *Languages et machines à l'âge classique*. Paris: Hachette, 1995.

Siegel, Rudolph E. *Galen's System of Physiology and Medicine*. Basel: S. Karger, 1968.

Simon, Gérard. "Les Machines au XVIIe siècle: Usage, typologie, résonances symboliques." *Revue des Sciences Humaines* 58, nos. 186–87 (1982): 10–13.

Sollers, Philippe. "Sade dans le lexte." *Tel Quel* 28 (1967): 38–50.

Sorel, Charles. *Le Berger extravagant*. Intro. Hervé de Bechade. Genève: Slatkine, 1972.

Starobinski, Jean. *Montaigne in Motion*. Trans. Arthur Goldhammer. Chicago: University of Chicago Press, 1985.

———. *L'Oeil vivant*. Paris: Gallimard, 1961.

Steiner, Wendy. *The Colors of Rhetoric: Problems in the Relation between Modern Literature and Painting*. Chicago: Chicago University Press, 1982.

Stern, Karl. *The Flight from Woman*. New York: Farrar, Straus and Giroux, 1965.

Temkin, Owsei. "Metaphors of Human Biology." *The Double Face of Janus and Other Essays in the History of Medicine*. Baltimore: Johns Hopkins University Press, 1977.

Thibaudet, Albert. *Montaigne*. Paris: Gallimard, 1963.

Todorov, Tzvetan. "L'Etre et l'autre: Montaigne." *Montaigne: Essays in Reading*. Spec. issue of *Yale French Studies* 64 (1983): 113–21.

Tort, Michel. "L'Effet Sade." *Tel Quel* 28 (1967): 66–83.

Traverso, Edilia. *Montaigne e Aristotele*. Florence: Felice Le Monnier, 1974.

Turk, Edward Baron. *Baroque Fiction-Making: A Study of Gomberville's "Polexandre."* Chapel Hill: University of North Carolina Department of Romance Languages, 1978.

Übersfeld, Anne. "Corneille: Du roi au Tyran, un itinéraire." *Actes de Wake Forest*. Ed. Milorad R. Margitic and Byron R. Wells. Coll. Biblio 17, no 37. Tübingen: Papers on Seventeenth Century Literature, 1987.

Urfé, Honoré d'. *Astrea: A Romance*. 3 vols. London: Printed by W. W. for H. Moseley, T. Dring, and H. Herringman, 1657–58.

———. *L'Astrée*. 5 vols. Ed. M. Hugues Vaganay. Lyon: Pierre Masson, 1925.

Vartanian, Aram. *Diderot and Descartes: A Study of Scientific Naturalism in the Enlightenment*. Princeton: Princeton University Press, 1953.

Villeterque. "Villeterque's Review of *Les Crimes de l'amour*." *The Marquis de Sade: The 120 Days of Sodom and Other Writings*. Compiled and Trans. Austryn Wainhouse and Richard Seaver. New York: Grove Press, 1966.

Vizier, Alain. "Descartes et les automates." *Modern Language Notes* 3 (1996): 693–94.

Wahl, Jean. *Du rôle de l'idée de l'instant dans la philosophie de Descartes*. Paris: Alcan, 1920.

Walker, David P. "Medical Spirits in Philosophy and Theology from Ficino to Newton." *Arts du spectacles et histoire des idées: Recueil offert en hommage à Jean Jacquot*. Tours: Centre d'études supérieures de la Renaissance, 1984.

Weiss, Allen S. *Mirrors of Infinity: The French Formal Garden and 17th-Century Metaphysics.* New York: Princeton Architectural Press, 1995.

Wellman, Kathleen. *La Mettrie: Medicine, Philosophy, and the Enlightenment.* Durham, N.C.: Duke University Press, 1992.

Wölfflin, Heinrich. *Renaissance and Baroque.* Trans. Kathrin Simon. Ithaca, N.Y.: Cornell University Press, 1967.

———. *Principles of Art History: The Problem of the Development of Style in Later Art.* Trans. M. D. Hottinger. New York: Dover, 1950.

Yolton, John W. *Perceptual Acquaintance from Descartes to Reid.* Minneapolis: University of Minnesota Press, 1984.

Index